REAL ESTATE FINANCE

Everything You Need To Know About The Dollars & Sense Of Financing Real Estate

A.G-Yohannes

PROBUS PUBLISHING COMPANY
Chicago, Illinois

To Abeba, Elizabeth, Mebrat, and Wubet

This publication is designed to provide accurate and authoritative information in regard to the subject matter covered. It is sold with the understanding that the publisher is not engaged in rendering legal, accounting or other professional service. If legal advice or other expert assistance is required, the service of a competent professional person should be sought.

FROM A DECLARATION OF PRINCIPLES JOINTLY ADOPTED BY A COMMITTEE OF THE AMERICAN BAR ASSOCIATION AND A COMMITTEE OF PUBLISHERS.

Library of Congress Cataloging-in-Publication Data Available

ISBN 1-55738-124-0

Printed in the United States of America
1 2 3 4 5 6 7 8 9 0

Contents

CHAPTER 1 INTRODUCTION

There are several good books on real estate finance. These books describe the nonquantitative aspects of real estate finance quite well. However, many of them do not stress the quantitative aspects, presumably because the authors do not wish to burden readers with formulas and other mathematical presentations. As a result, the reader who wishes to learn about and use the various formulas and quantitative procedures used in real estate finance is left without a clear guide that he or she can turn to.

The purpose of this book is to integrate the quantitative and descriptive aspects of real estate finance in a way that can be clearly understood and used. It covers the primary and secondary mortgage markets and the financing of residential and commercial properties.

The book has six major parts. In the first part, the sources of mortgage funds are discussed. These sources include primary and secondary lenders. For each institution covered there is a brief description, and an explanation of the sources and uses of funds.

The second part deals with the instruments and techniques used to finance residential and commercial properties. Secondary mortgage market instruments (mortgage-backed securities) are also discussed here.

For convenience, the instruments and techniques are grouped into conventional programs, government programs, other primary residential programs, secondary mortgage market programs, and programs for financing commercial properties. The different groups are not meant to be mutually exclusive. The third part presents procedures for performing comparative evaluations of specific mortgages. The procedures that are explained and illustrated in this part would be useful to loan officers, brokers, and financial advisors in recommending specific types of mortgages. Borrowers often ask which mortgage would be better for them: 15-year or 30-year; a loan with an interest rate of 10 percent and 2 points or a loan with an interest rate of 10.25 percent and 1 point; biweekly or monthly payment; refinanced or not refinanced.

The fourth part deals with items that are related directly or indirectly to the security of a loan. The topics covered in this part include how to qualify an applicant, appraising the property, mortgages and deeds of trust, private mortgage insurance, title insurance, hazard insurance, foreclosures, and loan closing.

The fifth part deals with interest rates and the use of financial futures to reduce exposure to interest rate risks.

The sixth part contains appendixes of computer programs and sample runs, reviews of compounding and discounting concepts, the Newton-Raphson method, financial leverage, and samples of real estate finance forms.

The book presents various formulas and procedures explicitly and illustrates their application in a manner that is meaningful and useful to the reader. For a presentation and application of many of the commonly used formulas, the reader should go to Chapter 6, "Fixed-Rate Mortgages." Many of the calculations in the other chapters are based on the formulas presented in that chapter.

Obviously, many of the calculations shown in the book would be time-consuming to do by hand. Fortunately, they do not have to be done manually. The book includes easy-to-use computer programs that can perform many of the calculations presented in the text. The programs are written in BASIC and they run on the IBM PC and compatibles. The listings of the programs and sample runs are included. For those who do not have the time to type in the programs themselves, program diskettes can be obtained directly from the author for $59.00. The address is: CFS, P.O. Box 2832, Farmington Hills, MI 48333.

Readers can also write their own programs. One reason for the explicit presentations of formulas is to show readers which formulas are used for each purpose. Once readers know the correct formula for a particular calculation and see its application, they can write their own programs or hire others to write the programs for them.

There are also commercial real estate finance programs that can be bought. Some of them are modestly priced. Here is a list of some of the programs, arranged by alphabetical order.

Name of Program	*Publisher*
AMORT	Computx, 14 Pierce Oak Ridge, NJ 07438 201-697-3141
Buyer Qualification +	P.C. Enterprises P.O. Box 1269 Annandale, VA 22003 703-941-4006
Creative Financing Decisions	Randle, Coray & Assoc., Inc. P.O. Box 1228 Logan, UT 84322 801-753-5681
MI-AMOR	Budget Computer, Inc. 160 S. 2nd St. Milwaukee, WI 53204 414-332-1222
Mortgage Analysis	Realty Micro Systems, Inc. P.O. Box 532 Lewiston, NY 14092 416-935-3032
Real Estate Models for the 80's	Commercial Software Systems, Inc. 7689 W. Frost Dr. Littleton, CO 80123 303-973-1325
Real Estate Tools I	Ansonn Software, Inc. 2801 N. Surrey Carrollton, TX 75006 214-446-4340

There are also programs that can handle loan processing, closing and tracking. Examples of such programs, again listed by alphabetical order, are:

Name of Program	*Publisher*
Loan Handler/Tracker	Contour Software 4960 Hamilton Ave., Suite #215 San Jose, CA 95130 408-370-1700
Loan Origination/ Tracking Program	Glenn Computer Corporation 24315 Northwestern Hwy. Southfield, MI 48075 313-352-1560 (1-800-482-0901)

Loan Track III	Professional Information Mgmt. 225 S. Troy St. Royal Oak, MI 48067 313-543-3404
Mortracs	Fannie Mae 3139 Campus Dr. Narcross, GA 20071 800-241-8291 (404-446-2533)

Although there are portable personal computers, it is not convenient to carry most computers around. Financial calculators can be used to do many of the calculations in the text. Some of them cannot calculate the interest rate corresponding to a graduated payment mortgage or the monthly payments unless the initial interest rate is given. It is also difficult to do comparative analyses of the type discussed in the third part of the book with calculators. For most calculations, however, the financial calculators would be useful. Some of them are modestly priced (under $30 in mid-1987).

Here is a list of some financial calculators, arranged alphabetically.

Cannon Financial Manager

Financial I
Calculated Industries, Inc.,
2010 N. Tustin Ave.
Suite B
Orange, CA 92665
1-800-854-8075

Hewlett-Packard Business Consultant

Hewlett-Packard 12 C

P*ROM 835A Hand-Held System
P*ROM Software, Inc.
60 Austin Dr.
Burlington, VT 05401
802-862-7500

Sharp Business/Financial Calculator

Texas Instruments Business Analyst II

This book can be useful to professionals in different fields, such as lenders, brokers, accountants, attorneys, financial planners, developers, engineers, architects, and investors.

I Sources of Mortgage Funds in the Primary and Secondary Mortgage Markets

CHAPTER

2 SOURCES OF MORTGAGE FUNDS: Depository Institutions

Depository institutions are financial institutions that accept demand, savings, and time deposits from the public and then use these deposits to make loans and investments. There are four groups of depository institutions: savings and loan associations, commercial banks, mutual savings banks, and credit unions.

SAVINGS AND LOAN ASSOCIATIONS

Savings and loan associations are the largest group of primary lenders in the mortgage market. Historically, their lending activities were primarily limited to mortgage loans. Recently, their activities have been expanded, but mortgage loans continue to be their main assets.

Description

Savings and loan associations are organized as mutual or stock companies and they are chartered either by the federal government or the states. Mutual savings and loans are owned by the depositors, and stock savings and loans are corporations-owned by the stockholders who purchase their shares. Some mutuals have been converting into the stock form of organization, mainly to raise more money by selling stocks.

Federally chartered savings and loan associations are supervised by the Federal Home Loan Bank System, and their deposits are insured by the Federal Savings and Loan Insurance Corporation (FSLIC) up to $100,000. Although insurance is optional for state-chartered savings and loan associations, the latter insures deposits at most of the state savings and loans associations. Savings and loans can also get loans from the Federal Home Loan Banks.

The Federal Home Loan Bank System consists of 12 regional Federal Home Loan Banks whose activities are coordinated by the Federal Home Loan Bank Board in Washington. The Federal Home Loan Banks are owned by the Federal savings and loan associations in their districts.

Sources of Funds

Savings and loan associations are depository institutions. They accept demand deposits (checking accounts) savings and time deposits. The time deposits include a variety of small and large ($100,000 or more) certificates of deposit (CDs). The demand deposits include regular checking accounts, negotiable order of withdrawal (NOW) accounts, and super-NOW accounts. The deposits are their main source of funds. Other sources include federal funds and repurchase agreements, and loans from the Federal Home Loan Bank. Federal funds are short-term funds borrowed from banks. Repurchase agreements (or repos) are securities (like Treasury bills) sold by savings and loans with the understanding that they will repurchase them at a later time. They provide temporary funds for the savings and loans.

The savings and time deposits were, until recently, subject to interest rate ceilings. As a result, when interest rates on money market securities like Treasury bills and commercial paper increased to levels higher than the deposit rates, depositors withdrew their funds from depository institutions and invested them in money market securities. This phenomenon is called *financial disintermediation,* and it reduced the amount of funds available to depository institutions.

The ceilings on deposit rates were gradually removed in the 1980s. While the removal of ceilings on deposit rates improved the competitive position of S&Ls in attracting new deposits, the combination of high deposit rates and low-yield, long-term fixed-rate mortgages put many S&Ls in a financial squeeze.

Their situation improved due to four factors: the introduction of adjustable-rate mortgages (explained in a subsequent chapter), their relatively new authority to make commercial and consumer loans (with shorter maturities than fixed-rate mortgage loans), the increased sales of mortgage loans in the secondary mortgage market, and the shortening of mortgage loan maturities. Now many S&Ls offer not only 30-year fixed- rate mortgages but also 15-year fixed-rate mortgages.

Uses of Funds

The most important use of the funds of savings and loan associations continues to be mortgage loans. The mortgage loans are mainly conventional, residential loans, but they also include loans insured by the Federal Housing Administration (FHA), loans guaranteed by the Veteran's Administration (VA), plus home improvement and construction loans.

In addition to mortgage loans, S&Ls make consumer loans and invest in U.S. government securities.

COMMERCIAL BANKS

Commercial banks are the largest group of financial institutions in the United States economy and—next to savings and loans—the largest primary lenders in the mortgage market.

Description

Like savings and loans, commercial banks are depository institutions. They accept deposits and make loans and investments. Some banks are chartered by the federal government and are called *national banks.* Others are chartered by the state governments; they are called *state banks.* National banks have to be members of the Federal Reserve System (the FED), and their deposits are insured by the Federal Deposit Insurance Corporation (FDIC) up to $100,000. For state banks, membership in the Federal Reserve System and obtaining deposit insurance are optional. Although most state banks are not members of the Federal Reserve System, very few are uninsured.

The federal bank regulatory agencies are the Federal Reserve System, the FDIC, and the comptroller of the currency. State banking commissions regulate state banks. To minimize duplication of effort, there is some sharing of regulatory responsibility among the federal regulatory agencies.

The Federal Reserve System consists of 12 regional Federal Reserve Banks whose activities are unified by the board of governors of the Federal Reserve System in Washington, D.C. The Federal Reserve Banks make loans to banks and hold their reserves. They are owned by the member banks.

Although there is a trend toward interstate banking, full-fledged interstate banks still do not exist. Furthermore, some states permit state-wide branching, while others allow very limited branching.

Sources of Funds

The most important sources of bank funds are deposits. The main types of deposits are savings deposits, small and large ($100,000 or more) time deposits, and checkable deposits or checking accounts. Checkable deposits include regular checking accounts, negotiable order of withdrawal (NOW) accounts, and super-NOW accounts. Time deposits include various small and large CDs. The deposits are the main sources of funds; other sources include federal funds, repurchase agreements, and stock sales, but they are relatively small.

Uses of Funds

The main uses of bank funds are commercial loans, mortgage loans, and consumer loans. Other uses include investment in Treasury securities, agency issues, and federal funds.

Like savings and loans, commercial banks make conventional residential loans, FHA-insured and VA-guaranteed loans, construction loans, and other real estate loans. However, real estate loans constitute less than 20 percent (as of 1985) of the total financial assets of commercial banks. This is a much smaller proportion than that of S&Ls.

MUTUAL SAVINGS BANKS

Mutual savings banks are thrift institutions. They were first introduced to meet the needs of the small saver. They are found mainly in the northeastern part of the United States.

Description

Although mutual savings banks may be chartered by the federal government, they are essentially state chartered depository institutions. They are owned by the depositors and their deposits may be insured by the Federal Deposit Insurance Corporation (FDIC), the Federal Savings and Loan Insurance Corporation (FSLIC), or by state insurance plans.

Sources of Funds

The primary sources of funds are deposits: demand deposits, savings deposits, and time deposits (including CDs). The mutual savings banks were the first institutions to offer NOW accounts. They started offering NOW accounts in the early 1970s.

Uses of Funds

Mutual savings banks are important sources of real estate loans. A large proportion of their funds is used for financing real estate. However, the proportion is smaller than that of savings and loans. Other uses of funds include investments in U.S. government securities, consumer credit, and corporate and foreign bonds.

CREDIT UNIONS

A third kind of thrift institution is a credit union. In recent years, credit unions have experienced rapid growth. However, they are still the smallest group of the thrifts.

Description

A credit union is an association of a group of people who enjoy a common bond. The members of the credit union may be employees of the same organization, share a particular profession in a given area, belong to the same church, or have some other common link.

The credit union may be chartered by a state or by the federal government. Federally chartered credit unions are supervised by the National Credit Union Administration (NCUA). NCUA also insures deposits at credit unions up to $100,000. State credit unions are supervised by state banking or financial institution commissions.

Sources of Funds

The main source of funds for credit unions is member share savings. Members may have share drafts (checkable deposits), savings accounts, and time deposits (including CDs).

Uses of Funds

Credit union funds are used primarily to finance consumer loans—personal loans and automobile loans. Real estate loans are limited (less than 10 percent of financial assets) and most of the real estate loans consist of home improvement loans. However, with time credit unions may use a greater proportion of their assets to finance real estate.

CHAPTER

3 Sources of Mortgage Funds: Nondepository Institutions

The institutions covered in this chapter do not accept deposits, but they use funds from one source or another for making loans or investing in mortgages. They are life insurance companies, mortgage companies, property and casualty insurance companies, pension funds, real estate investment trusts, and finance companies.

LIFE INSURANCE COMPANIES

In terms of total financial assets, life insurance companies were the third largest group of financial institutions in 1985. They were also the third largest source of real estate loans, next to savings and loans and commercial banks.

Description

Life insurance companies sell a variety of life insurance policies, annuities, and health and disability income policies. They sell term, whole life, universal life, and variable life policies and endowments. *Term insurance* is pure insurance, providing only protection against death. The other policies provide not only protection against death but also savings. They accumulate cash values. The annuities can be purchased with lump-sum payments or installments. Incomes from annuities can begin immediately (*immediate annuity*) or they can be deferred (*deferred annuity*) and the periodic incomes could be for life (*straight life annuity*) or the annuitant can receive a lump sum (*refund annuity*).

Life insurance companies are regulated by state governments and they are organized mostly as corporations, although some are mutuals. The corporations are owned by stockholders and the mutuals are owned by the policyholders.

Sources of Funds

The main sources of funds for life insurance companies are premiums for life, health, and disability income policies and annuities. Other sources of funds are investment incomes, that is, incomes on assets that the companies own.

Uses of Funds

Because the potential claims of the policy holders are fairly predictable, life insurance companies invest large amounts of their funds in long-term financial assets. Corporate bonds constitute the largest investments of life insurance companies, followed by residential and commercial mortgages. They also invest in U.S. government securities and a relatively small amount of stocks. Finally, they make policy loans to their policyholders.

Typically, life insurance companies invest in mortgages originated by other institutions. Furthermore, the institutions that originated the mortgage loans continue to service the loans.

MORTGAGE COMPANIES

Mortgage companies originate, close, and service billions of dollars of mortgage loans. The largest mortgage companies may use some of their own funds, but most of them use funds from other institutions to fund their loans.

Description

Mortgage companies are state chartered corporations. They are engaged primarily in financing real estate, but some of them may also provide other real estate-related services, such as appraising, property insurance and real estate sales. They finance residential as well as commercial real estate.

Some loans that mortgage companies originate are sold to investors or secondary market institutions such as the Federal National Mortgage Association (discussed in Chapter 5) but in most cases, they continue to service the loans. That is, they collect the periodic payments, administer escrow accounts for property taxes and insurance, send interest and tax statements to borrowers annually, pay taxes on behalf of the property owners, and handle foreclosures in case of defaults.

The mortgage companies are paid fees for mortgage servicing. This fee is a major source of income. Other sources of income are loan origination fees and possibly gains from the sales of mortgages.

The mortgages are sold mainly to savings and loan associations, mutual savings banks, life insurance companies, and the Federal National Mortgage Association (Fannie Mae). These institutions can invest in mortgages originated in different parts of the country without establishing offices there and gaining intimate knowledge of these areas. Mortgage companies serve as loan correspondents to many life insurance companies that are interested in investing in mortgages.

Sources of Funds

Major mortgage companies raise some funds by selling *commercial paper*, an unsecured short-term promissory note that matures in 30 to 270 days. They also get short-term mortgage warehouse loans from commercial banks to fund loans at closing. The mortgage warehouse loans are backed by the closed mortgage loans.

In a typical situation, a mortgage company secures commitment, for a fee, from an investor to purchase a group of mortgage loans with specified characteristics (face value, interest rate, maturity, and type of property) within a given period of time. The mortgage company funds the loans with short-term warehouse loans and places them in a warehouse until the required number of mortgages are assembled. What happens after the required package is prepared depends on the type of commitment obtained by the mortgage company. If the commitment is a firm or mandatory commitment, the mortgage company is required to deliver the mortgages to the investor. If the commitment is a standby or optional commitment, the mortgage company does not have to deliver the mortgages. The standby commitment allows the mortgage company to look for another buyer who might be able to offer the company a higher price. If another buyer with a better price is not found, the mortgage company can use the standby commitment.

The money from the sale of the mortgages is used to pay off the short-term loans. If there is a favorable spread between the interest rate on the mortgages and the yield required by the investor, the mortgage company would make money on the sale, in addition to the loan origination fees it received. So, the profit from the sale of the mortgage, the loan origination fee, and the mortgage servicing fee explained previously are important sources of income for the mortgage company.

Uses of Funds

Mortgage companies make single-family and multifamily residential loans, nonresidential loans, and construction loans. They also make relatively smaller numbers of land development loans. Of these loans, the single-family residential loans are the largest. Mortgage companies are major originators of Federal Housing Authority insured and Veterans Administration guaranteed loans.

PROPERTY AND CASUALTY INSURANCE COMPANIES

Property and casualty insurance companies are not major sources of real estate loans. They are covered here because they own a relatively small amount of real estate loans.

Description

Property and casualty insurance companies sell policies that cover individuals, businesses, or government units against a variety of perils or risks such as fire, wind, and collusion. Examples are automobile, homeowner's, marine, and liability insurance policies. These companies are mainly mutuals, but some are stock insurance companies.

Sources of Funds

The main sources of funds for property and casualty insurance companies are premiums and investment incomes. In this respect, they are like life insurance companies.

Uses of Funds

To minimize their tax liabilities, property and casualty insurance companies invest heavily in municipal (tax-exempt state and local government) bonds. The interest on municipal bonds is not subject to federal income taxes. To a smaller extent, they also invest in corporate stocks, U.S. government and agency securities and corporate and foreign bonds. Their investment in commercial mortgages is very limited.

PENSION FUNDS

In terms of total financial assets, private pension funds and state and local government employee retirement funds are second only to commercial banks. In 1985, their financial assets were larger than those of the other financial institutions surveyed in this chapter. Private pensions funds have more assets than the state and local government employee retirement funds, but they are smaller than savings and loans and life insurance companies.

Description

Pension funds are organized by private and government employers for the benefit of their employees. The funds accept contributions from employers and in some cases from employees. Funds may be administered by insurance companies (*insured funds*) or trustees (*uninsured funds*). In insured funds, the contributions are used to buy annuities for employees. The annuities pay periodic incomes for life or for a limited period of time. In uninsured funds, the contributions are managed by trustees, who may be trust departments of banks, the employers, employees, or other institutions for the benefit of employees. The pension plans may be *defined benefit plans,* in which future retirement benefits are based on service and future salaries of employees, or they may be *defined contribution plans,* in which employers (and possibly employees) contribute specific fractions of their wages and salaries every pay period.

If adequate funds are set aside to finance future retirement benefits, they are called *funded funds;* if no funds have been set aside, they are called *unfunded funds;* and finally, if some money has been set aside, they are called *partially funded funds.*

Sources of Funds

The periodic contributions by employers and in some cases by employees are the main sources of funds of funded pension funds. For funded pension funds, investment incomes are also important sources of funds.

Uses of Funds

Pension funds invest heavily in corporate equities and to a lesser extent in U.S. government and agency securities and corporate and foreign bonds. Pension funds also invest in mortgages, but their investment is very small, in relative terms.

REAL ESTATE INVESTMENT TRUSTS

Established under the Real Estate Investment Trust Act of 1960, real estate investment trusts (REITs) are relatively small and new financial institutions. Furthermore, REITs experienced major financial problems in the mid-1970s. However, in the mid- 1980s, they seem to be recovering.

Description

REITs invest in rental real properties (equity REITs), make short-term land development and construction loans (short-term REITs) or make long-term mortgage loans (long-term REITs). They are organized as corporations or trusts. In either case, their shares are traded in the securities markets and they offer liquidity to their investors. Furthermore, if they meet certain requirements pertaining to ownership, assets, incomes, and distributions, REITs are not subject to federal income taxes on distributions made to shareholders. The shareholders are liable for the taxes.

Sources of Funds

The major sources of funds are mortgage loans, sale of corporate bonds, and commercial paper (short-term promissory note) and bank loans. Equity REITs borrow money from mortgage lenders to buy rental real properties. Other REITs raise money for making mortgage loans by borrowing from banks or selling debt instruments (commercial paper and corporate bonds).

Uses of Funds

Equity REITs use their funds to acquire income properties, multifamily residential structures, and nonresidential structures. Other REITs use their funds to finance commercial properties and multifamily residential structures.

FINANCE COMPANIES

Finance companies are associated with consumer credit. They are covered here because they make substantial mortgage loans, as well.

Description

Finance companies make loans to consumers and businesses. Sales finance companies make loans for the purchase of automobiles, furniture and appliances. Personal finance companies make loans for a variety of personal activities, such as education and travel. Finally, business finance companies make inventory and accounts receivable loans to businesses. These are loans backed by business inventories or account receivables. Businesses may also sell or factor account receivables to finance companies.

Sources of Funds

Finance companies raise funds by borrowing from banks and by selling debt instruments—commercial paper and corporate bonds. The sale of commercial paper is the main source of funds followed by the sale of bonds.

Uses of Funds

As explained earlier, finance companies make business loans and consumer loans. They also invest in mortgage loans. In 1985, finance companies owned over $50 billion (or about 15 percent of their total financial assets) of mortgages.

CHAPTER

4 Sources of Mortgage Funds: Government Agencies

There are government agencies that make loans directly to home buyers or through participating financial institutions. They may also finance construction of buildings. In this chapter, the Farm Credit System, the Farmers Home Administration, and state housing finance agencies are discussed.

THE FARM CREDIT SYSTEM

The Farm Credit System provides credit and related services such as leasing to the agricultural sector. It is made up of Federal Land Banks, Federal Intermediate Credit Banks, and Banks for Cooperatives and other agencies.

Description

The Farm Credit System consists of 12 Farm Credit Districts, in which each district is served by a Federal Land Bank, a Federal Intermediate Credit Bank, and a Bank for Cooperatives. Federal Land Banks make long-term (5 to 40 years) loans for capital purchases through Federal Land Bank Associations. Federal Intermediate Credit Banks make short-term and intermediate term (1 season to 15 years) loans for operating expenses, livestock, and so on. The Banks for Cooperatives make seasonal and term loans to agricultural cooperatives.

The banks, associations, and cooperatives of the Farm Credit

System are owned by the borrowers. The borrowers elect the directors for boards of the banks' associations.

Items of interest to the whole system are handled by the *Farm Credit Corporation of America.* The Farm Credit System is regulated by a federal regulatory agency, the *Farm Credit Administration,* which, in turn, is guided by the *Federal Farm Credit Board.*

Sources of Funds

The Farm Credit System raises funds mainly by selling securities in the money and capital markets. The securities are bonds with 6-month, 9-month, and longer maturities and notes that mature in 5 to 365 days.

The *Federal Farm Credit Banks Funding Corporation* handles the sales of the securities.

Uses of Funds

The banks and cooperatives make seasonal and long-term loans to farmers and farm related businesses for a variety of purposes such as operating expenses, purchases of livestock, purchases of land, and building and improvements.

THE FARMERS HOME ADMINISTRATION

The Farmers Home Administration (FmHA) was established in 1935 to provide credit to families in rural areas. Its activities have expanded since then. Also it has operated under different names. Its current name (Farmers Home Administration) was given to it in 1946.

Description

FmHA is part of the U.S. Department of Agriculture. It is headquartered in Washington, D.C., but it has over 1900 county offices in all 50 states to implement its credit programs. FmHA makes loans to farmers and residents of rural areas. It also guarantees loans made by private lenders. The FmHA loans supplement private loans, because FmHA gives loans, primarily, to families who may not qualify for loans from private lenders.

Sources of Funds

The money for funding FmHA loans comes from repayments of existing loans and sales of government securities. In the case of guaranteed loans, the money comes from commercial lenders but FmHA guarantees the loans.

Uses of Funds

FmHA has a number of programs designed to promote rural development and increase the standard of living of farmers and other rural dwellers. The major programs are housing programs, farmer programs, community programs, and business and industrial programs. In its housing programs, FmHA makes loans to low- to moderate-income families with a maximum term of 33 years. The interest rate reflects the cost of the government borrowing, but interest credits may lower effective interest costs to borrowers.

The loans are available to families in rural communities with populations of less than 10,000 and to families in communities with populations between 10,000 and 20,000 if they are not part of a Metropolitan Statistical Area and the availability of credit to low or moderate income families in those communities is determined to be lacking.

Other housing programs include loans for rental housing for low- and moderate-income families, loans to families who wish to build their own homes, and home repair loans or grants to very low-income families.

The other programs of FmHA are not covered in this book.

STATE HOUSING FINANCE AGENCIES

State governments have established housing finance agencies (HFAs) to assist low- to moderate-income families to own homes. The interest rates on loans offered by HFAs have been lower than rates on conventional loans. For this reason, the demand for such loans has been much greater than the supply of loans.

Description

Housing finance agencies are usually established by state legislatures to meet the housing needs of the state's residents. Examples are the Michigan State Housing Development Authority, the Arkansas

Housing Development Agency, and the New York Housing Finance Agency.

Sources of Funds

State and local governments have issued tax-exempt bonds to fund mortgage loans. Since interest on the bonds (municipal bonds) is not subject to Federal income taxes, the interest rate on such bonds is relatively low. For this reason, state and local governments can offer loans at interest rates higher than the tax-exempt bond rates but lower than conventional loan rates.

Uses of Funds

The funds generated by the sale of tax-exempt bonds are used to finance purchases of single-family homes by low- to moderate-income families. The loans have to satisfy certain requirements. For example, the home should be used as the borrower's principal residence. The borrower should not have owned a home within the preceding three years, and the loan should be for new mortgages only. There may also be limits on the price of the home and the loan amount.

The loans are originated by participating financial institutions, and the HFAs may make a commitment to buy the mortgages or they may loan the funds to the financial institutions.

HFAs also finance the construction of multifamily and single-family homes.

Typically, the number of loan applicants is greater than the number that can be accommodated. For this reason, the loans are made either on a first-come, first-served basis or by using a lottery. Participating financial institutions accept and process loan applications and service the loans.

CHAPTER

5 SOURCES OF MORTGAGE FUNDS: Secondary Mortgage Market Agencies

The market where home buyers, developers, and others borrow money for financing real estate is called the *primary mortgage market,* and the institutions that make the loans in the primary mortgage market are called *primary lenders.* Examples of primary lenders are savings and loans, banks, and mortgage companies. The market where closed loans are sold is called the *secondary mortgage market.* The major secondary mortgage participants are the Federal National Mortgage Association, the Federal Home Loan Mortgage Corporation, and the Government National Mortgage Association.

THE FEDERAL NATIONAL MORTGAGE ASSOCIATION

The Federal National Mortgage Association (Fannie Mae) is the largest source of mortgage funds in the secondary mortgage market. It was established in 1938 as a federally sponsored corporation, but became a private corporation in 1968.

Description

Fannie Mae buys residential mortgages from primary mortgage lenders such as savings and loans, commercial banks, and mortgage companies. Initially, it was limited to buying FHA insured and VA guaranteed mortgages. In 1970, however, it was authorized to buy conventional mortgages, as well.

The purchases of mortgages by Fannie Mae provides liquidity to the primary lenders. The primary lenders do not have to keep their loans until maturity. Since Fannie Mae raises funds by issuing a variety of debt instruments, it is able to attract funds from the other capital markets and to channel them to the mortgage market.

Fannie Mae's home office is in Washington, D.C., but it has regional offices in different parts of the country.

Sources of Funds

Fannie Mae raises funds for its programs by issuing a variety of debt instruments. It sells notes, debentures, and mortgage-backed securities. The notes are short-term, promissory notes maturing in less than one year and debentures have maturities of up to 25 years. *Mortgage-backed securities* are securities backed by pools of mortgages. Some of these securities are sold in Europe and Japan. In 1985, Fannie sold its first debentures denominated in yens in the domestic market. The maturity structure of the debt issues depends on interest costs and the duration of its assets.

Uses of Funds

Fannie Mae issues mortgage-backed securities and buys government-backed and conventional mortgages, participation interests (50 percent to 95 percent) in pools of conventional mortgages, conventional second mortgages, and mortgages on multifamily dwellings. The first mortgages can be fully amortizing 15-year or 30-year fixed-rate mortgages, balloons, growing equity mortgages, and adjustable-rate mortgages.

Fannie Mae issues mandatory delivery and standby commitments to buy standard mortgages. In its mandatory delivery commitment, the primary lender is required to deliver a specified type of loan at a specified yield and within a specified period of time. In the standby commitment, Fannie Mae provides protection against interest rate increases for a limited period of time. A standby commitment may also be issued for a mortgage that has a limited or no market. There are commitment fees for both mandatory delivery and standby commitments, but in the latter case, delivery is optional.

A primary lender could get a commitment from Fannie Mae

before the loan is made to a borrower. This type of commitment is called a *forward commitment.* If the loan has already been made to a borrower, the primary lender or seller can seek an *immediate commitment* for immediate purchase.

THE FEDERAL HOME LOAN MORTGAGE CORPORATION

The Federal Home Loan Mortgage Corporation, nicknamed Freddie Mac, is another supplier of mortgage funds to primary lenders. It purchases conventional mortgages from primary lenders, assembles the mortgages into pools, and issues securities backed by the mortgages. The securities are sold to investors.

Description

Freddie Mac was established in 1970 under the Emergency Home Finance Act of 1970. It is owned by the Federal Home Loan Banks. These banks are part of the Federal Home Loan Bank System, the authority that supervises federal savings and loans. Its main office is in Washington, D.C., but it has regional offices in different parts of the country.

Sources of Funds

Freddie Mac raises funds by selling notes and debentures, issuing mortgage participation certificates, guaranteed mortgage certificates, and collateralized mortgage obligations (CMOs). The notes are unsecured discount notes maturing in one year or less. The debentures are unsecured long-term promissory notes of the corporation. The mortgage participation certificates (PCs) and the guaranteed mortgage certificates (GMCs) are similar in that they represent undivided interests in pools of mortgages. They are sold to investors or primary lenders. However, PC holders receive monthly interest and principal, while the holders of GMCs receive interest semiannually and principal annually.

The CMO was designed and introduced by Freddie Mac in 1983. It is a debt instrument or security secured by a pool of conventional mortgages that Freddie Mac owns. The principal and interest payments from the underlying mortgages are allocated to different classes of CMO series, serially.

Uses of Funds

Freddie Mac's funds are used to purchase mortgages from approved sellers or seller/servicers. They include fixed-rate mortgages, adjustable-rate mortgages, graduated-payment mortgages, and junior mortgages. These mortgage products have to meet specific loan eligibility requirements.

Commitments to purchase are issued for mandatory deliveries or optional deliveries. There are no commitment fees for mandatory deliveries, but Freddie Mac charges commitment fees for optional commitments. The commitments may be for different periods.

For cash sales, Freddie Mac specifies the required net yields on loans. These yield quotes can be obtained by calling daily. The required net yield is the rate of return that Freddie Mac would like to earn on the loan purchases. It does not include mortgage servicing fees. The seller of the mortgage adds an amount large enough to cover the servicing fee to the required net yield to determine the rate that the borrower should pay on the loan.

THE GOVERNMENT NATIONAL MORTGAGE ASSOCIATION

The Government National Mortgage Association (GNMA), also called Ginnie Mae, is another major organization in the secondary mortgage market. It was established in 1968, when the Federal National Mortgage Association (FNMA) was split into the current FNMA (Fannie Mae) and the Government National Mortgage Association (Ginnie Mae).

Description

Ginnie Mae is a corporation within the Department of Housing and Urban Development and as such is part of the federal government. It is headquartered in Washington, D.C. and operates through FNMA's regional offices.

Sources of Funds

Ginnie Mae finances its programs by borrowing money from the U.S. Treasury and selling securities to the public. From time to time, it may also use funds appropriated by Congress.

Uses of Funds

Ginnie Mae has two major functions: *the special assistance function* and the *management and liquidation function.* In its special assistance function, Ginnie Mae issues commitments to purchase mortgages secured by housing facilities for low-income and moderate-income families. It may also issue commitments to purchase other mortgages to promote home lending and construction in times of credit crunches or high interest rates. In its *tandem plan,* Ginnie Mae purchases mortgages at below market yields from lenders and sells them to investors at market yields, thereby absorbing the losses. In other words, it buys the mortgages at prices higher than their market prices and sells them at lower prices, absorbing the losses.

The purchase and sale program assists the housing industry. The sale of the mortgages by Ginnie Mae also frees funds for similar programs.

In its management and liquidation functions, Ginnie Mae can purchase residential mortgages from any government agency and manage them or liquidate them. This function also allows it to guarantee the timely payment of interest and principal on mortgage-backed securities. Ginnie Mae guarantees mortgage-backed certificates that are issued by approved lenders.

II MAJOR INSTRUMENTS AND TECHNIQUES OF FINANCING REAL ESTATE

Financing Instruments and Techniques: Conventional Programs

CHAPTER

6 Fixed-Rate Mortgages

Historically, the fixed-rate mortgage has been the most dominant type of mortgage. In recent years, however, its relative importance has fluctuated, depending largely on the level of interest rates, the spread between fixed-rate mortgage rates and adjustable-rate mortgage rates, and the availability of creative financing.

DESCRIPTION

In a typical fixed-rate mortgage, a mortgagor (borrower) borrows a given amount of money today at a given interest rate and for a given period of time.The loan is repaid in equal monthly installments during the life of the loan. With each monthly payment, the loan balance declines and by the end of the term of the loan, the loan balance goes down to zero or approximately zero.

HOW IT WORKS

For a good understanding of how the fixed-rate mortgage works, we will show the calculation of the monthly payment, the construction of the amortization schedule, the calculation of the mortgage balance at different points in time, and the effects of points and other financial charges on the annual percentage rate.

The Calculation of the Monthly Payment

The size of the monthly payment depends upon the loan amount, the annual interest rate and the term or life of the loan. Equation 6–1 shows the formula for calculating the monthly payment.

(6–1)
$$M = \frac{A*(i/12)}{1 - (1 + i/12)^{-12N}}$$

where: M = monthly mortgage payment
A = loan amount
i = annual interest rate
N = term of the loan in years
12 = number of months in a year

EXAMPLE: An individual buys a house at a price of $125,000. He or she puts down 20 percent or $25,000 and borrows $100,000 from a bank at an annual interest rate of 12 percent for a period of 30 years. What will his or her monthly payment be? The monthly payment will be $1028.61. It is calculated as follows:

$$M = \frac{100000*(.12/12)}{1 - (1 + .12/12)^{-12(30)}} = \$1028.61$$

The monthly payment covers principal and interest only. It does not include taxes and insurance. Assuming that the payments are made for 30 years or 360 months, the total payment over the life of the loan will be $370,299.60. This amount is obtained by multiplying the monthly payment of $1028.61 by 360. The interest portion is $270,299.61. This amount is obtained by subtracting the loan amount of $100,000 from $370,299.60.

The Amortization Schedule

The monthly payment is made up of interest and principal. For many years, the bulk of the payment is interest. Since the interest portion is tax-deductible, it is important to decompose the monthly payment into interest and principal. This can be done by constructing an amortization schedule. See Table 6–1. The amortization schedule shows not only the interest portion and the portion that reduces principal but also the mortgage balance at the end of the month.

Payments are, usually, due on the first day of each month, but the payments apply to the previous month. For example, if a payment is made on July 1, it is for June. Let's assume that the first payment was made on July 1, 1987. The monthly payment is shown in the second column. The interest portion (third column) is calculated by multiplying the loan amount (principal) by the monthly interest rate. For the first month, the loan amount of $100,000 is multiplied

TABLE 6–1 The Amortization Schedule

Month	*M*	*Interest Paid*	*Principal Paid*	*Mortgage Balance*
1.	$1028.61	$1000.00	$28.61	$99,971.39
2.	1028.61	999.71	28.90	99,942.49
3.	1028.61	999.42	29.19	99,913.30
4.	1028.61	999.13	29.48	99,883.82
5.	1028.61	998.84	29.77	99,854.05
6.	1028.61	998.54	30.07	99,823.97
.				
.				
360.	1028.61	10.18	1018.43	0.00
TOTAL	$370,299.60	$270,299.60	$1,000,000.00	

by the monthly interest rate of 1 percent (.12/12 = .01) to get $1000. The principal paid (column 4) is the monthly payment minus the interest for the same month ($1028.61 − $1000 = $28.61). This amount reduces the loan balance or principal to $99,971.39 (=$100,000−$28.61). This amount is, in turn, multiplied by 0.01 to get the interest of $999.71 for July (second month).

The interest that a taxpayer can deduct is determined by adding the numbers in the third column. If the taxpayer in this example uses the calendar year as the fiscal year, the total interest paid in the first six months—$5995.64—would be deducted in the taxpayer's 1987 tax return.

It is important to note that the monthly payments will, eventually, extinguish the loan balance. Every payment reduces the loan balance (fifth column). However, the principal reduction is small and for many years the loan balance will remain large. Even after 293 payments, the loan balance will be $50050.82, which is slightly more than half the original loan amount.

The Calculation of the Mortgage Balance

As we saw in the previous section, the mortgage balance declines every time a payment is made. A homeowner may want to know the exact balance at any given point of time for a variety of reasons. For example, he or she may need the balance to prepare a personal balance sheet or may need to know the balance to pay off the loan.

Whatever the reason, there are several ways of calculating the balance.

One way is to use the method we used in constructing the amortization schedule in the previous section. For example, the balance at the end of the sixth month is $99,823.97. That method is, however, tedious and time-consuming, especially if many years have elapsed since the first payment. A better way of determining the loan balance is by using Equation 6–2.

$$L_k = \frac{M}{i/12}[1 - (1 + i/12)^{k-12N}] \tag{6–2}$$

where: L_k = mortgage balance at the end of the kth month.

EXAMPLE: Consider the following data. Loan amount = $75,000, annual interest rate = 15 percent, and term of the loan = 30 years. What is the mortgage balance after 5 years?

The first step is to determine the monthly payment. It turns out to be $948.33. The next step is to calculate the loan balance using Equation 6–2.

$$L_{60} = \frac{948.33}{.15/12}[1 - (1 + .15/12)^{60-12(30)}]$$

$$= \$74,040.47$$

The balance can be calculated for any month. The only value that changes in Equation 6–2 is that of k.

Points and the Annual Percentage Rate

Nearly all institutional lenders seem to charge discount points to increase the yields on their loans. A discount point is one percent of the loan amount. For example, if a lender charges 2½ points on a loan of $100,000, the discount would be $2500. The lender subtracts $2500 and provides only $97,500 to the borrower. However, the monthly payments are based on the full amount of the loan ($100,000). As a result, the true interest rate, called the ***annual percentage rate*** (***APR***), will be higher than the stated annual interest rate. Thus for a 30-year, $100,000 loan with a stated interest rate of 12 percent per year and 2½ points the APR will be 12.3416%. The 2½ points (or the discount of $2500) increase the APR by .3416 percent. The calculation of the APR is explained in the section on "Financial Charges and the APR" (in this chapter).

Alternatively, if the lender wants to increase the APR from 12 percent to 12.3416 percent, for the same loan, the lender should charge 2½ points or $2500. If we denote the discount by D, the loan amount by A, the term of the loan, in years, by N, the APR by r and the stated annual interest rate by i, the discount D can be calculated by solving for D in Equation 6–3.

$$A - D = \frac{M}{r/12}[1 - (1 + r/12)^{-12N}] \qquad (6\text{–}3)$$

Equation 6–3 implies that the discount D is:

$$D = A - \frac{M}{r/12}[1 - (1 + r/12)^{-12N}] \qquad (6\text{–}4)$$

In the example given above, the discount was calculated as follows:

$$D = 100{,}000 - \frac{1028.61}{0.010284667}[1 - (1 + 0.010284667)^{-360}]$$

$$= \$2500$$

When the discount (D) is expressed as a percent of the loan amount A, we get the number of discount points as follows:

$$D/A = 2500/100{,}000 = 0.025 \text{ or } 2.5 \text{ points}$$

Points and the Prepayment of the Loan

If the loan is assumed to be paid off early, the lender would not have to charge as many points to increase the APR by 0.3416 percent. For example, if the loan is expected to be paid off in the 120th month, the number of points needed to increase the APR by 0.3416 percent would be only 1.92. To see this, we will first determine the mortgage balance in the month as follows:

$$L_k = \frac{M}{i/12}[1 - (1 + i/12)^{k-12N}]$$

The present value of this balance at a discount rate equal to the lender's required APR of r is:

$$L_k = \frac{M}{(1 + r/12)^k(i/12)}[1 - (1 + i/12)^{k-12N}] \qquad (6\text{–}5)$$

In addition, we have to discount the k monthly payments at r/12 and sum them to get the sum of the present values of the k payments (S) as follows:

$$S = \frac{M}{r/12}[1 - (1 + r/12)^{-k}] \tag{6-6}$$

The loan amount less the discount, (A − D), should be equal to S in Equation 6-6 plus L(k) in Equation 6-5 as follows:

$$A - D = \frac{M}{r/12}[1 - (1 + r/12)^{-k}] + \frac{M}{(1 + r/12)^{k}(i/12)}[1 - (1 + i/12)^{k-12N}] \tag{6-7}$$

Solving Equation 6-7 for the discount (D), we get Equation 6-8:

$$D = A - \frac{M}{r/12}[1 - (1 + r/12)^{-k}] - \frac{M}{(1 + r/12)^{k}(i/12)}[1 - (1 + i/12)^{k-12N}] \tag{6-8}$$

Using the example of the previous section and assuming an average loan life of 10 years (120 months), the discount would be $1918.42. This is calculated as follows:

$$D = 100{,}000 - \frac{1028.61}{0.01028469942}[1 - (1 + 0.01028469942)^{-120}] - \frac{1028.61}{(1 + 0.01028469942)^{120}(.12/12)}[1 - (1 + .12/12)^{120-360}]$$

When expressed as a percent of the loan amount, the discount turns out to be about 1.92 points.

Discount points are not the only finance charges paid by borrowers. There are several other charges that increase the true cost of credit. The next section discusses the most common finance charges.

Truth in Lending

Effective July 1, 1969, the Board of Governors of the Federal Reserve System issued Regulation Z to implement the provisions of the Truth in Lending Act, which is part of the Consumer Credit Protection Act. Essentially, Regulation Z requires lenders to disclose the conditions and costs of credit to borrowers who apply for credit. A borrower is also given the right to rescind a credit transaction within three business days, if the credit involves a lien on the principal residence of the borrower. However, this right does not apply to the purchase of a new home.

The regulation applies to any lender who makes loans to consumers for personal and household purposes on a regular basis and charges interest on the loan or requires repayment in at least five installments. The lender makes the disclosures before the transactions are completed and/or at closing. However, the applicant can also request disclosure of the APR and the finance charges at the time of application.

Regulation Z includes a loan model form that may be used as a truth in lending statement by lenders for making disclosures. The loan model is shown in Figure 6-1.

Among the items that should be disclosed are the finance charges, the amount financed, the total payments over the life of the loan, the payment schedule, late payment charges, and any prepayment penalties. The *finance charges* are the costs that are associated with the credit, that is, costs that the consumer would not have to pay in an all-cash transaction. They include all the interest payments during the life of the loan, loan origination fees, discount points, prepaid interest, tax service, assumption fees, and premiums for mortgage insurance required by the lender. Premiums for credit life, disability income and property insurance are not considered finance charges, if the lender discloses that they are not required for the credit or that the borrower can choose his/her own insurer.

The *loan origination fees* cover the lender's costs of processing the application, and commission for the loan officer who originated the loan. As explained in the previous section, the discount points are used to increase the lender's yield on the loan. Tax service fees are charged for checking the property tax records. If the borrower assumes the seller's loan, the lender may charge a loan assumption fee. This fee is also considered a finance charge.

If the downpayment made by the borrower on the property is less than 20 percent of the value of the property (that is, if the loan to value ratio is greater than 80 percent), the lender requires private mortgage insurance. The private mortgage insurance protects the lender against the borrower's default. The premiums for private mortgage insurance vary from one private mortgage insurer to another. The premiums are based on the loan amount and in general, they decline as the loan amount declines or as the borrower's equity in the property increases. In general, the premiums for the first year and premiums for the first two months of the second year that are placed in escrow are included in finance charges.

In the loan model form, the amount financed is the loan amount less the finance charges paid by the borrower at closing or the finance charges subtracted from the proceeds of the loan. Examples of such charges are loan origination fees, discount points, interest on the loan from the date of closing to the first day of the month to which the first payment applies, tax service and premiums for private mortgage insurance for about 14 months.

The total of the payments shown in the model form is the monthly payment for principal and interest times the total number of payments. The annual percentage rate (APR) is the true cost of the credit. It reflects all the finance charges. For this reason, it is higher than the stated annual interest rate on the loan.

The lender should also disclose the payment schedule, which shows the number of payments, the amounts of the payments, and when they are due. Finally, the insurance disclosure allows the lender to exclude the premiums from the finance charges.

Finance Charges and the Annual Percentage Rate

The prepaid finance charges (that is, the finance charges paid by the borrower at closing or that are subtracted from the proceeds of the loan) reduce the effective loan amount or the amount that is truly financed. However, the monthly payment is calculated on the basis of the full loan amount (that is, the amount financed plus the prepaid finance charges). So, the APR includes not only the interest payments that will be made during the life of the loan but also the prepaid finance charges.

EXAMPLE: A consumer buys a house for $125,000, makes a downpayment of $25,000 and borrows $100,000 from a savings and loan (S&L) association at an annual interest rate of 12 percent for a term of 30 years. The monthly payment for this loan is $1028.61. Since the downpayment is 20 percent, the borrower is not required to buy private mortgage insurance. However, the S&L association charges one point in loan origination fee, 1½ discount points, and a tax service fee of $35. The closing is set for May 12, 1988 and the payments are due monthly, beginning July 1, 1988.

Since the first payment is for June, 1988, the S&L will collect the interest on the loan from May 12, 1988 to May 31, 1988 at closing. This is what we called prepaid interest and it is equal to the daily interest rate times the loan amount times the remaining number of days in May or (0.12/365) × 100,000 × 20 = $657.40.

The total prepaid finance charges amount to $3192.40. This amount is the sum of the loan origination fee of $1000 (=$100,000×0.01), the discount points of $1500 ($100,000×0.015) the tax service fee of $35 and the prepaid interest of $657.40. The amount financed is $96,807.60 (=$100,000−3192.40).

To calculate the APR, we will need the monthly payment of $1028.61, the amount financed of $96,-807.60, the term of the loan, 30 years, and an assumed initial monthly interest rate of 1 percent.

The APR will be calculated using the Newton-Raphson method, which is explained in Appendix 2. It involves a series of iterations. Equations 6–8 and 6–9 will be used repeatedly until a stable value of i is obtained.

$$R(i_q) = \frac{1 - (1 + i_q)^{-n} - (L/M) * i_q}{n(1 + i_q)^{-n-1} - [1 - (1 + i_q)^{-n}]/i_q} \quad (6\text{–}9)$$

$$i_{q+1} = i_q - R(i_q) \quad (6\text{–}10)$$

where: i_q = the monthly interest rate in iteration q
L = amount financed
M = monthly payment
N = term of the loan in months

FIRST ITERATION: $i_0 = .01$.

$$R(.01) = \frac{1 - (1 + .01)^{-360} - (96807.6/1028.61) * .01}{360(1 + .01)^{-360-1} - [1 - (1 + .01)^{-360}]/.01}$$

$$= -0.000355468$$

$i_1 = i_0 + R(i_0) = .01 + .000355468 = .010355468$

SECOND ITERATION: $i_1 = .010355468$:

R(.0103 . . .)

$$= \frac{1 - (1.010355468)^{-360} - (96807.6/1028.61).010355468}{360(1.010355468)^{-361} - \dfrac{[1 - (1.010355468)^{-360}]}{.010355468}}$$

$= -.000010395$

$i_2 = i_1 - R(i) = .010355468 + .000010395 = .010365863$

THIRD ITERATION: $i_2 = .010365863$:

$$R(.010365863) = -.000000008$$

$i_3 = i_2 - R(i_2) = .010365863 + .000000008 = .010365871$

FOURTH ITERATION: $i_3 = 0.010365871$:

$$R(.010365871) \approx 0$$

$i_4 = i_3 - R(i_3) = .010365871 + 0 = .010365871$

The value of the monthly interest rate has converged to or stabilized at 0.0103655871. This monthly rate is annualized by multiplying it by 12 to get .124390452 or approximately 12.44 percent. This is the APR. The APR, the finance charge, the amount finance, the total payments and the payment schedule for this example are shown in Figure 6–1.

Obviously, the calculations we have done in this chapter are time-consuming and difficult to do manually. They can be calculated using a financial calculator or a computer. Appendix 4 shows a sample output of a loan amortization program written for the IBM PC or compatible. The actual program is listed in Appendix 5.

ADVANTAGES OF THE FIXED-RATE MORTGAGE

The major advantage of the fixed-rate mortgage is that the interest rate and the monthly payments remain the same until the loan is paid off. This aspect of the mortgage produces a peace of mind and a sense of ease for the borrower.

Related to the first advantage is the fact that with each monthly payment, the balance declines and results in the increase of the equity of the property owner. In some mortgage instruments, the loan balance may increase with each payment for some period of time. An example of such a mortgage is the graduated-payment mortgage.

FIGURE 6-1 H-2 Loan/Model Form

ANNUAL PERCENTAGE RATE The cost of your credit as a yearly rate.	FINANCE CHARGE The dollar amount the credit will cost you.	AMOUNT FINANCED The amount of credit provided to you or on your behalf.	TOTAL OF PAYMENTS The amount you will have paid after you have made all payments as scheduled.
%	$	$	$

You have the right to receive at this time an itemization of the Amount Financed.
☐ I want an itemization. ☐ I do not want an itemization.

Your payment schedule will be:

Number of Payments	Amount of Payments	When Payments Are Due

Insurance
Credit life insurance and credit disability are not required to obtain credit, and will not be provided unless you sign and agree to pay the additional cost.

Type	Premium	Signature
Credit Life		I want credit life insurance. Signature
Credit Disability		I want credit disability insurance. Signature
Credit Life and Disability		I want credit life and disability insurance. Signature

You may obtain property insurance from anyone you want that is acceptable to ______________ (creditor).
If you get the insurance from ______________ (creditor), you will pay $__________.

Security: You are giving a security interest in:

☐ the goods or property being purchased.

☐ ______________________________
(brief description of other property)

Filing fees $__________ **Non-filing insurance** $__________

Late Charge: If a payment is late, you will be charged $__________ __________ % of the payment.

Prepayment: If you pay off early, you

☐ may ☐ will not have to pay a penalty.
☐ may ☐ will not be entitled to a refund of part of the finance charge.

See your contract documents for any additional information about nonpayment, default, any required repayment in full before the schedule date, and prepayment refunds and penalties.

e means an estimate

Furthermore, as the loan balance declines, the value of the property may rise. Any appreciation in the value of the property would increase the equity of the property owner.

Finally, if the loan is assumable and the interest rate on the loan is low relative to current mortgage rates, the loan could speed up the sale of the property and increase its value.

DISADVANTAGES OF THE FIXED-RATE MORTGAGE

At low interest rates, the fixed-rate mortgage is attractive, but at very high interest rates, it may not be affordable. Other mortgage instruments may be more appealing. For example, the interest rates on adjustable-rate mortgages tend to be 1 percent or 3 percent lower than those of fixed-rate mortgages.

CHAPTER

7 ADJUSTABLE-RATE MORTGAGES

Until the second half of the 1970s, mortgage rates were relatively low and stable. As a result, the fixed-rate mortgage worked well for both lenders and borrowers. With the high and volatile rates of the second half of the 1970s, however, many thrift institutions were, financially, squeezed. The financial squeeze was the result of the high and volatile interest rates on the one hand and the mismatch between the asset and liability maturities of the thrifts on the other. Loan rates were fixed for 29–30 years while deposit rates increased at relatively short intervals. So they had to pay high interest rates on deposits but could not raise rates on existing loans.

In April 1981, federally chartered savings and loans associations were allowed to offer the adjustable-rate mortgage (ARM). This was one of a number of reforms that enabled the thrifts to cope with the new situation. The ARM allows a better match between the maturities of assets and those of liabilities. It also means borrowers now bear greater risks of interest rate fluctuations.

Within a short period of time, the ARM became the most dominant type of mortgage. The share of ARMs in the total mortgage market fluctuates from month to month, depending on the level of interest rates and the spread between rates on ARMs and rates on fixed-rate mortgages.

DESCRIPTION

The initial monthly payment of the adjustable-rate mortgage is calculated the same way the monthly payment of the fixed-rate mortgage is calculated. However, the monthly payments of the adjustable-rate mortgages are adjusted periodically. They may be adjusted every year, once every three years, once every five years, or at other frequencies. The monthly payments could go up or down. In some cases, the term of the loan could also be increased to up to 40 years. The loan balances could also rise. However, the adjustments are often subject to caps.

HOW THE ADJUSTABLE-RATE MORTGAGE WORKS

To gain a good understanding of how an ARM works, it is important to be familiar with its basic features. The features we will review are the index rate, the margin, periodic interest rate caps, lifetime interest rate caps, interest rate floors, payment caps, and negative amortization.

The Index Rate

The index rate is a measure of interest rates. It is used as a basis for adjusting mortgage rates. Several interest rates are used as index rates by different lending institutions. They include yields on Treasury securities adjusted to constant maturities, costs of funds to S&Ls, national average contract interest rates for major lenders on the purchase of previously occupied homes closed in the first five working days of each month and rates on certificates of deposit. The most widely used rates are yields on Treasury securities and costs of funds.

Although Treasury securities are issued in different maturities, yields of one-year, three-year and five-year Treasury securities are used. Of the three T-security yields, the yield on the one-year T-bill is the most commonly used interest rate.

The cost of funds is, basically, the ratio of interest (dividends) paid to deposits, FHLBB (Federal Home Loan Bank Board) advances, and other borrowed money. It is calculated for different periods. There is the national monthly median cost of funds ratio, the quarterly cost of funds index and the semiannual national average cost of funds to FSLIC (Federal Savings and Loan Insurance Corporation) insured institutions.

Borrowers can get rate information on T-securities and certificates of deposit from two statistical releases of the Board of Governors of the Federal Reserve System. The first release (H.15) is issued weekly and shows daily, weekly, and monthly rates on certificates of deposit, T-securities, bonds and mortgages. The other release (G.13) shows similar information but is issued monthly.

Sample Federal Reserve Statistical Releases are shown in Figures 7-1 and 7-2.

Information on the national average contract interest rate and the cost of funds may be obtained from a newsletter ("News") published by the FHLBB. Up-to-date recorded information on selected index rates may also be obtained by calling a toll-free number (1-800-424-5405). Samples of the rates published by the FHLBB are shown in Figures 7-3 and 7-4.

Margin

The *margin* is the number of percentage points that is added to the index rate to determine the note interest rate. It covers some operating expenses and some profit. The margin varies from lender to lender but is, usually, between 2 percent and 3 percent.

Interest Rate Caps

In general, new interest rates are determined by adding the index rate and the margin. However, if interest rates—as measured by the index rates—increase sharply, the monthly payments of the borrower could also increase sharply. Such a sharp payment increase, commonly called a "payment shock," could cause financial hardship to the borrower and possibly end in foreclosure. For this reason, most lenders, voluntarily, impose interest rate or payment caps.

There are two kinds of interest rate caps—periodic and lifetime. The periodic interest rate caps limit interest rate changes at the time the interest rate is adjusted. For example, suppose the annual interest rate cap is 2 percent, the current contract rate is 8.25 percent, the margin is 2.5 percent, and the new index rate is 8 percent. The sum of the index rate and the margin would be 10.5 percent but the new contract rate would be 10.25 because the contract rate cannot increase or decrease by more than 2 percent.

There may also be a lifetime interest rate cap. In other words, there would be an absolute ceiling over which the contract rate cannot go up. For example, if the initial interest rate is 9 percent and the lifetime cap is 5 percent, the contract rate cannot be higher than 14 percent (9 percent + 5 percent) at any time during the life of the mortgage.

The lender may also specify an interest rate floor. This is the lowest contract rate that can be used. For example, if the interest rate floor is 8 percent, the contract rate cannot be lower than 8 percent at any time during the life of the mortgage.

FIGURE 7-1 Selected Interest Rates on CDs, T-Securities, Bonds and Mortgages—Issued Weekly

FEDERAL RESERVE statistical release

These data are released each Monday. The availability of the release will be announced, when the information is available, on (202) 452-3206.

H.15 (519) For immediate release

SELECTED INTEREST RATES

Yields in percent per annum FEBRUARY 2, 1987

Instruments	1987 JAN 26	1987 JAN 27	1987 JAN 28	1987 JAN 29	1987 JAN 30	This week	Last week	1987 JAN
FEDERAL FUNDS (EFFECTIVE) 1/	6.14	6.15	6.50	6.22	6.28	6.13	6.01	6.43
COMMERCIAL PAPER 2/3/								
1-MONTH	5.90	5.93	5.96	5.94	5.98	5.94	5.87	5.95
3-MONTH	5.83	5.86	5.87	5.87	5.90	5.87	5.79	5.84
6-MONTH	5.75	5.77	5.80	5.78	5.80	5.78	5.71	5.76
FINANCE PAPER PLACED DIRECTLY 2/								
1-MONTH	5.77	5.88	5.86	5.89	5.91	5.86	5.75	5.86
3-MONTH	5.57	5.58	5.75	5.58	5.58	5.61	5.44	5.59
6-MONTH	5.54	5.55	5.55	5.55	5.55	5.55	5.41	5.60
BANKERS ACCEPTANCES (TOP RATED) 2/								
3-MONTH	5.76	5.79	5.82	5.80	5.90	5.81	5.69	5.74
6-MONTH	5.66	5.72	5.70	5.68	5.79	5.71	5.60	5.65
CDS (SECONDARY MARKET)								
1-MONTH	5.91	5.90	5.93	5.93	5.93	5.92	5.85	5.94
3-MONTH	5.86	5.87	5.89	5.88	5.89	5.88	5.82	5.87
6-MONTH	5.85	5.86	5.89	5.87	5.88	5.87	5.80	5.85
BANK PRIME LOAN 1/4/	7.50	7.50	7.50	7.50	7.50	7.50	7.50	7.50
DISCOUNT WINDOW BORROWING 1/5/	5.50	5.50	5.50	5.50	5.50	5.50	5.50	5.50
U.S.GOVERNMENT SECURITIES								
TREASURY BILLS								
AUCTION AVERAGE 2/ 6/								
3-MONTH	5.44					5.44	5.23	5.45
6-MONTH	5.43					5.43	5.27	5.47
1-YEAR								5.44
AUCTION AVERAGE(INVESTMENT) 6/								
3-MONTH	5.59					5.59	5.37	5.60
6-MONTH	5.66					5.66	5.49	5.71
SECONDARY MARKET 2/								
3-MONTH	5.49	5.49	5.47	5.48	5.60	5.51	5.35	5.43
6-MONTH	5.43	5.45	5.43	5.46	5.59	5.47	5.33	5.44
1-YEAR	5.47	5.49	5.47	5.48	5.60	5.50	5.38	5.46
TREASURY CONSTANT MATURITIES 7/8/								
1-YEAR	5.79	5.81	5.79	5.80	5.93	5.82	5.69	5.78
2-YEAR	6.26	6.24	6.24	6.24	6.33	6.26	6.18	6.23
3-YEAR	6.45	6.46	6.43	6.45	6.51	6.46	6.37	6.41
5-YEAR	6.67	6.66	6.63	6.65	6.71	6.66	6.58	6.64
7-YEAR	6.97	6.97	6.93	6.95	6.99	6.96	6.86	6.92
10-YEAR	7.17	7.16	7.13	7.13	7.18	7.15	7.03	7.08
30-YEAR	7.49	7.49	7.46	7.45	7.48	7.47	7.33*	7.39
COMPOSITE								
OVER 10 YEARS(LONG-TERM)9/	7.70	7.69	7.64	7.63	7.68	7.67	7.54	7.60
CORPORATE BONDS								
MOODY'S SEASONED								
AAA	8.33	8.40	8.40	8.37	8.36	8.37	8.31	8.36
BAA	9.67	9.68	9.70	9.68	9.68	9.68	9.65	9.72
A-UTILITY 10/					8.81	8.81	8.86	n.a.
STATE & LOCAL BONDS 11/				6.56		6.56	6.54	6.61
CONVENTIONAL MORTGAGES 12/					9.12	9.12	9.10	9.23

1. WEEKLY FIGURES ARE AVERAGES OF 7 CALENDAR DAYS ENDING ON WEDNESDAY OF THE CURRENT WEEK; MONTHLY FIGURES INCLUDE EACH CALENDAR DAY IN THE MONTH.
2. QUOTED ON BANK-DISCOUNT BASIS.
3. RATES ON COMMERCIAL PAPER PLACED FOR FIRMS WHOSE BOND RATING IS AA OR THE EQUIVALENT.
4. RATE CHARGED BY BANKS ON SHORT-TERM BUSINESS LOANS
5. RATE FOR THE FEDERAL RESERVE BANK OF NEW YORK.
6. AUCTION DATE. AUCTION DATE FOR DAILY DATA; WEEK AND MONTH AVERAGES ON ISSUE-DATE BASIS.
7. YIELDS ON ACTIVELY TRADED ISSUES ADJUSTED TO CONSTANT MATURITIES. SOURCE: U.S. TREASURY.
8. SEE REVERSE FOR A DESCRIPTON OF THE CONSTANT MATURITY SERIES. THE 20-YEAR CONSTANT MATURITY YIELD WAS DISCONTINUED AT THE END OF 1986 BECAUSE THE TREASURY NO LONGER ISSUES A 20-YEAR BOND.
9. UNWEIGHTED AVERAGE OF ALL ISSUES OUTSTANDING OF BONDS NEITHER DUE NOR CALLABLE IN LESS THAN 10 YEARS, INCLUDING ONE VERY LOW YIELDING "FLOWER" BOND.
10. ESTIMATE OF THE YIELD ON A RECENTLY-OFFERED, A-RATED UTILITY BOND WITH A MATURITY OF 30 YEARS AND CALL PROTECTION OF 5 YEARS; FRIDAY QUOTATIONS.
11. BOND BUYER INDEX, GENERAL OBLIGATION, 20 YEARS TO MATURITY, MIXED QUALITY; THURSDAY QUOTATIONS.
12. CONTRACT INTEREST RATES ON COMMITMENTS FOR FIXED-RATE FIRST MORTGAGES. SOURCE: FHLMC.

NOTE: WEEKLY AND MONTHLY FIGURES ARE AVERAGES OF DAILY RATES, EXCEPT FOR STATE & LOCAL BONDS, WHICH ARE BASED ON THURSDAY FIGURES, AND CONVENTIONAL MORTGAGES AND A-UTILITY BONDS, BOTH OF WHICH ARE BASED ON FRIDAY FIGURES.

*The 30-year Treasury constant maturity daily rate for January 23 was revised to 7.42.

FIGURE 7-2 Selected Interest Rates on CDs, T-Securities, Bonds and Mortgages—Issued Monthly

FEDERAL RESERVE statistical release

These data are scheduled for release on the first Tuesday of each month. The availability of the release will be announced, when the information is available, on (202) 452-3206.

G.13 (415)

For immediate release
JANUARY 6, 1987

SELECTED INTEREST RATES

Yields in percent per annum

Instruments	Week ending NOV 28	DEC 5	DEC 12	DEC 19	DEC 26	NOV	DEC
FEDERAL FUNDS (EFFECTIVE) 1/	6.00	6.25	5.97	6.30	6.31	6.04	6.91
COMMERCIAL PAPER 2/ 3/							
1-MONTH	5.88	6.02	6.03	6.59	7.39	5.84	6.63
3-MONTH	5.81	5.89	5.90	6.14	6.35	5.76	6.10
6-MONTH	5.72	5.75	5.77	5.92	6.05	5.69	5.88
FINANCE PAPER PLACED DIRECTLY 2/							
1-MONTH	5.84	5.92	5.96	6.33	6.79	5.79	6.32
3-MONTH	5.73	5.73	5.73	5.84	5.83	5.67	5.81
6-MONTH	5.60	5.64	5.65	5.74	5.82	5.58	5.74
BANKERS ACCEPTANCES (TOP RATED) 2/							
3-MONTH	5.71	5.73	5.82	6.02	6.21	5.67	5.96
6-MONTH	5.58	5.60	5.70	5.82	5.94	5.59	5.78
CDS (SECONDARY MARKET)							
1-MONTH	5.84	6.03	6.06	6.52	7.58	5.80	6.66
3-MONTH	5.76	5.83	5.88	6.08	6.27	5.76	6.04
6-MONTH	5.76	5.81	5.85	6.00	6.10	5.76	5.95
BANK PRIME LOAN 1/4/	7.50	7.50	7.50	7.50	7.50	7.50	7.50
DISCOUNT WINDOW BORROWING 1/5/	5.50	5.50	5.50	5.50	5.50	5.50	5.50
U.S. GOVERNMENT SECURITIES							
TREASURY BILLS							
AUCTION AVERAGE 2/ 6/							
3-MONTH	5.35	5.40	5.51	5.55	5.49	5.35	5.49
6-MONTH	5.39	5.46	5.50	5.58	5.56	5.42	5.53
1-YEAR	5.45				5.60	5.45	5.60
AUCTION AVERAGE(INVESTMENT) 6/							
3-MONTH	5.50	5.55	5.61	5.71	5.65	5.49	5.63
6-MONTH	5.62	5.69	5.74	5.82	5.80	5.65	5.76
SECONDARY MARKET 2/							
3-MONTH	5.39	5.42	5.49	5.57	5.56	5.35	5.53
6-MONTH	5.42	5.44	5.49	5.59	5.60	5.41	5.55
1-YEAR	5.45	5.47	5.51	5.57	5.59	5.48	5.55
TREASURY CONSTANT MATURITIES 7/							
1-YEAR	5.77	5.78	5.83	5.90	5.92	5.80	5.87
2-YEAR	6.21	6.21	6.22	6.30	6.30	6.28	6.27
3-YEAR	6.39	6.37	6.38	6.45	6.46	6.46	6.43
5-YEAR	6.66	6.61	6.62	6.68	6.69	6.76	6.67
7-YEAR	6.99	6.93	6.93	6.98	6.96	7.08	6.97
10-YEAR	7.14	7.09	7.09	7.12	7.08	7.25	7.11
*20-YEAR	7.31	7.26	7.26	7.29	7.25	7.42	n.a.
30-YEAR	7.42	7.35	7.35	7.39	7.35	7.52	7.37
COMPOSITE							
OVER 10 YEARS(LONG-TERM) 8/	7.71	7.64	7.67	7.69	7.61	7.81	7.67
CORPORATE BONDS							
MOODY'S SEASONED							
AAA	8.55	8.52	8.48	8.51	8.47	8.68	8.49
BAA	9.99	9.99	9.97	9.97	9.98	10.07	9.97r
A-UTILITY 9/	9.16	9.08	9.03	9.08	9.07	9.31	9.08
STATE & LOCAL BONDS 10/	6.74	6.77	6.94	6.92	6.83	6.85	6.86
CONVENTIONAL MORTGAGES 11/	9.50	9.30	9.35	9.30	9.30	9.70	9.31

1. WEEKLY FIGURES ARE AVERAGES OF 7 CALENDAR DAYS ENDING ON WEDNESDAY OF THE CURRENT WEEK; MONTHLY FIGURES INCLUDE EACH CALENDAR DAY IN THE MONTH.
2. QUOTED ON BANK-DISCOUNT BASIS.
3. RATES ON COMMERCIAL PAPER PLACED FOR FIRMS WHOSE BOND RATING IS AA OR THE EQUIVALENT.
4. RATE CHARGED BY BANKS ON SHORT-TERM BUSINESS LOANS.
5. RATE FOR THE FEDERAL RESERVE BANK OF NEW YORK.
6. RATES FOR AUCTIONS OCCURRING WITHIN THE CURRENT WEEK.
7. YIELDS ON ACTIVELY TRADED ISSUES ADJUSTED TO CONSTANT MATURITIES. SOURCE: U.S. TREASURY.
8. UNWEIGHTED AVERAGE OF ALL ISSUES OUTSTANDING OF BONDS NEITHER DUE NOR CALLABLE IN LESS THAN 10 YEARS, INCLUDING ONE VERY LOW YIELDING "FLOWER" BOND.
9. ESTIMATE OF THE YIELD ON A RECENTLY-OFFERED, A-RATED UTILITY BOND WITH A MATURITY OF 30 YEARS AND CALL PROTECTION OF 5 YEARS; FRIDAY QUOTATIONS.
10. BOND BUYER INDEX, GENERAL OBLIGATION, 20 YEARS TO MATURITY, MIXED QUALITY; THURSDAY QUOTATIONS.
11. CONTRACT INTEREST RATES ON COMMITMENTS FOR FIXED-RATE FIRST MORTGAGES. SOURCE: FHLMC.

NOTE: WEEKLY AND MONTHLY FIGURES ARE AVERAGES OF DAILY RATES, EXCEPT FOR STATE & LOCAL BONDS, WHICH ARE BASED ON THURSDAY FIGURES, AND CONVENTIONAL MORTGAGES AND A-UTILITY BONDS, BOTH OF WHICH ARE BASED ON FRIDAY FIGURES.

r=revised
*The 20-year constant maturity yield will be discontinued at the end of 1986 because the Treasury no longer issues a 20-year bond.

FIGURE 7-3 National Monthly Median Cost of Funds Ratio to FSLIC-Insured Institutions

Announcement Date[1]	Index Month*	Index Rate(%)	Announcement Date	Index Month	Index Rate(%)
N.A.	January 1979	N.A.	July 13, 1983	May 1983	9.62
N.A.	February 1979	N.A.	August 11, 1983	June 1983	9.54
N.A.	March 1979	N.A.	September 13, 1983	July 1983	9.65
N.A.	April 1979	N.A.	October 13, 1983	August 1983	9.81
N.A.	May 1979	7.35	November 15, 1983	September 1983	9.74
N.A.	June 1979	7.27	December 12, 1983	October 1983	9.85
N.A.	July 1979	7.44	January 13, 1984	November 1983	9.82
N.A.	August 1979	7.49	February 10, 1984	December 1983	9.90
N.A.	September 1979	7.38	March 13, 1984	January 1984	9.89
N.A.	October 1979	7.47	April 11, 1984	February 1984	9.73
N.A.	November 1979	7.77	May 11, 1984	March 1984	9.73
N.A.	December 1979	7.87	June 11, 1984	April 1984	9.64
N.A.	January 1980	8.09	July 12, 1984	May 1984	9.74
N.A.	February 1980	8.29	August 10, 1984	June 1984	9.67
N.A.	March 1980	7.95	September 12, 1984	July 1984	9.90
N.A.	April 1980	8.79	October 11, 1984	August 1984	10.01
N.A.	May 1980	9.50	November 15, 1984	September 1984	9.93
N.A.	June 1980	9.41	December 11, 1984	October 1984	10.15
N.A.	July 1980	9.18	January 14, 1985	November 1984	10.04
N.A.	August 1980	8.98	February 11, 1985	December 1984	9.92
N.A.	September 1980	8.78	March 13, 1985	January 1985	9.75
N.A.	October 1980	8.60	April 10, 1985	February 1985	9.40
N.A.	November 1980	8.68	May 10, 1985	March 1985	9.36
N.A.	December 1980	8.84	June 11, 1985	April 1985	9.29
N.A.	January 1981	9.50	July 12, 1985	May 1985	9.19
N.A.	February 1981	9.82	August 12, 1985	June 1985	8.95
N.A.	March 1981	10.24	September 13, 1985	July 1985	8.87
N.A.	April 1981	10.40	October 11, 1985	August 1985	8.77
N.A.	May 1981	10.59	November 13, 1985	September 1985	8.63
N.A.	June 1981	10.79	December 12, 1985	October 1985	8.59
N.A.	July 1981	10.92	January 13, 1986	November 1985	8.50
N.A.	August 1981	10.76	February 10, 1986	December 1985	8.48
N.A.	September 1981	11.02	March 12, 1986	January 1986	8.50
N.A.	October 1981	11.53	April 10, 1986	February 1986	8.29
N.A.	November 1981	11.68	May 12, 1986	March 1986	8.35
N.A.	December 1981	11.58	June 11, 1986	April 1986	8.22
N.A.	January 1982	11.44	July 11, 1986	May 1986	8.12
N.A.	February 1982	11.26	August 11, 1986	June 1986	7.95
N.A.	March 1982	11.37	September 11, 1986	July 1986	7.94
N.A.	April 1982	11.35	October 14, 1986	August 1986	7.80
N.A.	May 1982	11.39	November 12, 1986	September 1986	7.59
N.A.	June 1982	11.38	December 12, 1986	October 1986	7.50
N.A.	July 1982	11.54	January 13, 1987	November 1986	7.33
N.A.	August 1982	11.50	February 12, 1987	December 1986	7.28
N.A.	September 1982	11.17	March 23, 1987	January 1987	7.22
December 14, 1982	October 1982	10.91	April 15, 1987	February 1987	7.02
January 12, 1983	November 1982	10.62	May 15, 1987	March 1987	6.99
February 11, 1983	December 1982	10.43	June 15, 1987	April 1987	6.93
March 14, 1983	January 1983	10.14	July 15, 1987	May 1987	6.92
April 12, 1983	February 1983	9.75	August 14, 1987	June 1987	6.90
May 13, 1983	March 1983	9.72			
June 14, 1983	April 1983	9.62			

* Adjusted for variation in length of month.

FIGURE 7-4 National Average Contract Interest Rate for Major Lenders on the Purchase of Previously Occupied Homes

Announcement Date[1]	Index Month	Index Rate(%)	Announcement Date	Index Month	Index Rate(%)
April 3, 1980	January 1980	11.78	February 10, 1984	January 1984	11.70
April 7, 1980	February 1980	12.30	March 13, 1984	February 1984	11.73
May 7, 1980	March 1980	12.56	April 11, 1984	March 1984	11.69
May 21, 1980	April 1980	13.21	May 11, 1984	April 1984	11.61
June 11, 1980	May 1980	13.74	June 11, 1984	May 1984	11.63
July 11, 1980	June 1980	12.88	July 12, 1984	June 1984	11.79
August 11, 1980	July 1980	12.23	August 10, 1984	July 1984	12.03
September 11, 1980	August 1980	11.89	September 12, 1984	August 1984	12.24
October 10, 1980	September 1980	12.00	October 11, 1984	September 1984	12.43
November 10, 1980	October 1980	12.31	November 15, 1984	October 1984	12.52
December 11, 1980	November 1980	12.85	December 11, 1984	November 1984	12.38
January 13, 1981	December 1980	13.15	January 14, 1985	December 1984	12.26
February 11, 1981	January 1981	13.24	February 11, 1985	January 1985	12.09
March 12, 1981	February 1981	13.73	March 13, 1985	February 1985	11.90
April 10, 1981	March 1981	13.91	April 10, 1985	March 1985	11.72
May 12, 1981	April 1981	13.99	May 10, 1985	April 1985	11.62
June 10, 1981	May 1981	14.19	June 11, 1985	May 1985	11.62
July 13, 1981	June 1981	14.40	July 12, 1985	June 1985	11.29
August 12, 1981	July 1981	14.77	August 12, 1985	July 1985	11.02
September 14, 1981	August 1981	15.03	September 13, 1985	August 1985	10.87
October 13, 1981	September 1981	15.38	October 11, 1985	September 1985	10.76
November 12, 1981	October 1981	15.47	November 13, 1985	October 1985	10.86
December 14, 1981	November 1981	15.80	December 12, 1985	November 1985	10.80
January 12, 1982	December 1981	15.53	January 13, 1986	December 1985	10.70
February 12, 1982	January 1982	15.37	February 10, 1986	January 1986	10.40
March 12, 1982	February 1982	15.22	March 12, 1986	February 1986	10.46
April 12, 1982	March 1982	15.07	April 10, 1986	March 1986	10.24
May 12, 1982	April 1982	15.39	May 12, 1986	April 1986	10.00
June 11, 1982	May 1982	15.57	June 11, 1986	May 1986	9.80
July 13, 1982	June 1982	15.01	July 11, 1986	June 1986	9.83
August 12, 1982	July 1982	14.96	August 11, 1986	July 1986	9.88
September 13, 1982	August 1982	15.03	September 11, 1986	August 1986	9.88
October 13, 1982	September 1982	14.71	October 14, 1986	September 1986	9.71
November 12, 1982	October 1982	14.37	November 12, 1986	October 1986	9.59
December 14, 1982	November 1982	13.74	December 12, 1986	November 1986	9.48
January 12, 1983	December 1982	13.44	January 13, 1987	December 1986	9.29
February 11, 1983	January 1983	13.04	February 12, 1987	January 1987	9.19
March 14, 1983	February 1983	12.88	March 13, 1987	February 1987	8.89
April 12, 1983	March 1983	12.61	April 15, 1987	March 1987	8.80
May 13, 1983	April 1983	12.42	May 15, 1987	April 1987	8.79
June 14, 1983	May 1983	12.36	June 15, 1987	May 1987	8.93
July 13, 1983	June 1983	12.21	July 15, 1987	June 1987	9.02
August 11, 1983	July 1983	12.18	August 14, 1987	July 1987	9.05
September 13, 1983	August 1983	12.25			
October 17, 1983	September 1983	12.38			
November 15, 1983	October 1983	12.19			
December 12, 1983	November 1983	12.11			
January 13, 1984	December 1983	11.94			

[1] The National Average Mortgage Contract Interest Rate was introduced as an index in April, 1980.

Payment Caps

Some lenders leave the monthly payment unchanged or limit its increase when interest rates increase. Suppose the current monthly payment is $1000 and the new contract rate yields a monthly payment of $1100. If there is a payment cap of 7 percent, the new monthly payment will be $1070 and not $1100.

Negative Amortization

When there is a payment cap and the new monthly payment is smaller than the payment that is implied by the new contract rate, the new monthly payment may not cover interest on the loan. The portion of the interest that is not covered by the monthly payment may be added to the loan balance. As a result, the loan balance will rise despite the monthly payments. This situation is known as negative amortization or disamortization. In some cases, there may be a limit on negative amortization.

Initial Contract Rate

Many lenders use an initial contract rate that is lower than the sum of the index rate and the margin. This initial rate is sometimes called a promotional rate, a teaser rate or a discounted rate, the discount being the difference between the initial rate and the sum of the index rate and the margin. A discounted rate is used to attract more borrowers. The lower initial rate enables more borrowers to qualify for loans.

Other Features

Other features that ARMs may have are convertibility and prepayment penalties. The convertibility feature allows a borrower to convert the ARM into a fixed-rate mortgage at predetermined times. Conversion fees may apply. Finally, if the ARM is paid off at the time the interest rate is adjusted, there are no prepayment penalties. At other times, however, there may be prepayment penalties.

Now that we have discussed the basic features of ARMs, we can see how an ARM works. Typically, a lender announces an initial interest rate, a margin, interest rate caps or payment caps, if any, the index rate that will be used, and other features. While no one can say what the index rates will be in the future, one can calculate the monthly payments under various assumptions.

EXAMPLE: A home buyer wishes to borrow $100,000. He or she is interested in an ARM, and the ARM has the following features:

Initial contract rate	= 9%
Current index rate	= 8%
Margin	= 2.5%
Annual interest rate cap	= 2%
Lifetime interest rate cap	= 5%
Adjustment period (in years)	= 1
Interest rate floor	= 8.5%
Terms of Loan	= 30 years

The calculations are shown in Table 7-1. The second column shows the current index rate and the index rate for the next eight years. The third column shows the sum of the index rates and the margin of 2.5 percent. The fourth column shows the current contract rate less the annual interest rate cap of 2 percent. The fifth column shows the current contract rate plus the annual interest rate cap of 2 percent. The sixth column shows the new contract or note rate. The seventh column shows the loan balance, and the last column shows the monthly payment.

For the first year, the contract interest rate will be 9 percent, and when the loan is amortized over a period of 30 years, the monthly payment will be $804.62 (first number of column 8). The loan balance at the end of the first year will be $99,316.81 (second number of column 7). Thirty to 45 days before the anniversary date of closing, the lender will send the borrower a notice that shows the new monthly payment for the second year and other pieces of information. The monthly payment for second year will be $913.06. This monthly payment is based on a contract rate of 10.5 percent (second number in column 6), the loan balance of $99,316.81 and the remaining term of the loan (29 years or 348 months). The contract rate of 10.5 percent is the same as the second number in column 3. This rate is acceptable because it is greater than 7 percent (second number in column 4) and is smaller than 11 percent (second number in column 5). You should note here that although the index rate has remained unchanged at 8 percent, the contract rate has increased.

The sum of the index rate and the margin for the fourth period is 14.5 percent (fourth number in column 3) but the contract rate for the same period is 14 percent (fourth number in column 6) because the interest rate ceiling is 14 percent (9 percent + 5 percent). For the sixth period, the sum of the index rate and the margin is 10.5 percent

TABLE 7–1. Calculations for an ARM

(1) Adjustment Period	(2) Index Rate (%)	(3) = (2) + 2.5% Index Rate + Margin	(4) Old Note Rate (%) − Annual Rate Cap of 2%
0	8	10.5	9.0
1	8	10.5	7.0
2	10	12.5	8.5
3	12	14.5	10.5
4	14	16.5	12.0
5	8	10.5	12.0
6	6	8.5	10.0
7	4	6.5	8.0
8	2	4.5	6.5

(5) ONR (%) + AIRC of 2%	(6) Note Rate (%)	(7) Loan Balance	(8) Monthly Payment
9.0	9.0	100000.00	804.62
11.0	10.5	99316.81	913.06
12.5	12.5	98762.18	1061.41
14.5	14.0	98347.30	1174.79
16.0	14.0	97996.49	1174.79
16.0	12.0	97593.30	1027.88
14.0	10.0	96934.53	889.27
12.0	8.5	95910.69	792.31
10.5	8.5	94501.36	792.31

ONR = Old note rate
AIRC = Annual interest rate cap
NOTE: The amounts in columns 5–8 are for the adjustment periods in column 1.

but the contract rate is 12 percent, because the contract rate can't fall by more than 2 percent. Finally, the sum of the index rate and the margin for the eighth period is 6.5 percent but the contract rate is 8.5 percent, because the interest rate floor is 8.5 percent.

Table 7–2 shows the amortization schedule for the first 25 months. Note that the monthly payments for months 13 and 25 are higher than the monthly payment of the first year.

Appendix 6 shows a sample output of an ARM program, and Appendix 7 shows the actual program itself.

It is difficult to determine what the index rates will be in the fu-

TABLE 7-2 Amortization Schedule

Month	Monthly Payment	Interest Paid	Principal Paid	Mortgage Balance
1	804.62	750.00	54.62	99,945.38
2	804.62	749.59	55.03	99,890.34
3	804.62	749.18	55.44	99,834.90
4	804.62	748.76	55.86	99,779.04
5	804.62	748.34	56.28	99,722.76
6	804.62	747.92	56.70	99,666.06
7	804.62	747.50	57.13	99,608.93
8	804.62	747.07	57.55	99,551.38
9	804.62	746.64	57.99	99,493.39
10	804.62	746.20	58.42	99,434.97
11	804.62	745.76	58.86	99,376.11
12	804.62	745.32	59.30	99,316.81
13	913.06	869.02	44.04	99,272.78
14	913.06	868.64	44.42	99,228.35
15	913.06	868.25	44.81	99,183.54
16	913.06	867.86	45.20	99,138.34
17	913.06	867.46	45.60	99,092.74
18	913.06	867.06	46.00	99,046.74
19	913.06	866.66	46.40	99,000.33
20	913.06	866.25	46.81	98,953.52
21	913.06	865.84	47.22	98,906.31
22	913.06	865.43	47.63	98,858.68
23	913.06	865.01	48.05	98,810.62
24	913.06	864.59	48.47	98,762.16
25	1061.41	1028.77	32.64	98,729.52

ture. However, it would be a good idea to consider the worst situation that can happen before making a commitment and see if you can handle the resulting monthly payments. In this example, the worst situation results when the contract rate increases by 2 percent a year until it reaches the ceiling of 14 percent and then stays at that level for the rest of the life of the mortgage. This is unlikely, but possible.

Factors to Consider in Selecting an ARM

When ARMs were first introduced, they were generally misunderstood. Borrowers found the relatively low initial rates of ARMs attractive, but they did not realize that their contract rates would go up at the end of the adjustment period. As a result, the Federal Home Loan Bank Board and the Board of Governors of the Federal Reserve System prepared a handbook on ARMs to be distributed by lenders to borrowers. The Federal National Mortgage Association (Fannie Mae) and different lenders have also produced their own brochures on ARMs. The ARM seems to be better understood now.

Nonetheless, the following factors should be considered in selecting an appropriate ARM:

1. *Holding Period.* The ARM would be suitable for a borrower if he or she expects to pay off the loan within a relatively short period of time (say, within five years). The borrower could take advantage of the relatively low initial interest rate. People who are frequently relocated by their employers or investors who buy real properties for short periods could benefit from ARMs.
2. *Income Ratio.* The monthly payment should not exceed 28 percent of the borrower's gross monthly income. There should be a comfortable margin of safety. That way when interest rates rise in later years, the borrower would be in a better position to handle the increased payments. Of course, if income is expected to increase as fast or faster, the borrower can afford to have a smaller margin of safety.
3. *Volatility of the Index Rate.* For risk-averse borrowers, an ARM with a less volatile index rate might be advisable. Comparing the yield on one-year Treasury bills (adjusted to a constant maturity), the national median cost of funds ratio (NMCFR) and the national average contract interest rate (NACIR), the yield on one-year T-bills is the most volatile of the three. The coefficient of variation is used as a measure of volatility. The higher the value of the coefficient, the greater the volatility of the index rate. The coefficients of variation for the three index rates for the period January 1980 through October 1985 are shown in Table 7–3.

The coefficient of variation is calculated by dividing the standard deviation of the index rate by the mean of the index rate. The standard deviation, in turn, is calculated using the following formula:

$$SD = [\,\Sigma\,(I - AI)^2/(N - 1)]^{1/2}$$

where: SD = standard deviation

TABLE 7–3 Means, Standard Deviations and Coefficients of Variation of Index Rates

Index Rate	*Mean (%) (1)*	*Standard Deviation (2)*	*Coefficient of Variation (3) = (2)/(1)*
T-bill yield	11.43	2.52	0.22
NACIR	13.01	1.41	0.108
NMCFR	9.92	0.95	0.096

NACIR = National average contract interest rate
NMCFR = National median cost of funds ratio

I = index rate
AI = mean of the index rate
N = number of index rates

The interest rate caps reduce the effects of volatility of the index rates. However, even in the presence of caps, the choice of a less volatile index rate could reduce the risk of larger increases in the monthly payments. It should also be pointed out that the choice of a less volatile index rate also means smaller benefits when the index rate falls. In other words, the declines in the monthly payments would be smaller.

4. *Periodic and Lifetime Interest Rate Caps.* For borrowers, ARMs with annual (periodic) and lifetime interest rate caps are advisable. The smaller the caps the better, assuming all other factors are the same. However, smaller caps often mean higher initial interest rates. So, if the loan is expected to be paid off within a short period of time, lower initial interest rates with higher caps may have to be considered.
5. *Margin.* Assuming all other factors are the same, an ARM with a lower margin would be advisable for a borrower.

One might argue that the opposite would be good for a lender. To some extent this is true, but features that increase the probability of failure sharply would not be good for the borrower or the lender.

ADVANTAGES OF ARMS

Compared to fixed-rate mortgages, ARMs have lower initial interest rates. The difference is 1 percent to 3 percent. This difference allows more people to qualify for loans, because the monthly payment for the first adjustment period is lower. Moreover, for people who are relocated very frequently, the ARM may be cheaper.

Another advantage of ARMs is that they allow borrowers to benefit from declines in mortgage rates. As rates decline, monthly payments decline.

In some cases, points on ARMs may be lower than points on fixed-rate mortgages. Also, ARMs are not subject to prepayment penalties if the loan is prepaid at the end of an adjustment period.

DISADVANTAGES OF ARMS

The major objection to ARMs is the uncertainty associated with the monthly payments and the loan balances. If mortgage rates go up, the monthly payment will go up or the loan balance will go up, if the monthly payment is not raised. Unless there are interest rate and payment caps, the potential increases in the monthly payments are large. Large increases in monthly payments could cause major financial hardships on borrowers.

CHAPTER

8 GRADUATED-PAYMENT MORTGAGES

The graduated-payment mortgage (GPM) was introduced by the Department of Housing and Urban Development in the mid-1970s. It was designed to help families whose incomes were expected to increase to qualify more easily for mortgage loans. It may be insured by the Federal Housing Authority (FHA). It is also offered on a conventional basis, that is, without government insurance or guarantees.

DESCRIPTION

GPM is a fixed-rate mortgage; the overall note or contract rate is fixed. However, the monthly payment starts at a level that is lower than the monthly payment of a comparable fixed-rate mortgage, and then rises at a specified rate, called the *graduation rate,* for a defined period of time, called the graduation period, to a level higher than that of the comparable fixed-rate mortgage and then remains the same for the remaining term of the loan. The overall interest rate or note rate, the term of the loan, the graduation period, and the graduation rate are set at the time of application or loan approval. This way, the borrower knows in advance what the monthly payments and the loan balances will be.

In some cases, a lender may establish an overall rate and a corresponding initial interest rate for purposes of calculating the monthly payment for the first year. The interest rate is then increased each year during the graduation period by 1 percent, for example, for purposes of determining the new monthly payment for each year or the monthly payment may be increased at the graduation rate each year during the graduation period.

HOW GPM WORKS

At any given point in time, there may be several GPM plans. The plans may vary by graduation period, graduation rate, and term of the loan, but in all cases, the monthly payments increase at some specified graduation rate during the graduation period.

The Calculation of the Monthly Payments

The calculation of the monthly payments is rather time-consuming. First, the monthly payment for the first year is determined.Then the monthly payments for subsequent years are determined on the basis of the monthly payment for the first year.

The monthly payment for the first year is calculated using Equation 8-1. This formula takes into account the loan amount, the overall note rate, the graduation rate, the graduation period and the term of the loan. Monthly payments for subsequent years are calculated using Equations 8-2 and 8-3.

(8-1) $$M1 = A/[(B * C) + (1 + g)^T(D)]$$

where:

$$B = [(1 - (1 + i/12)^{-12})/(i/12)]$$

$$C = [(1 + k)^T - 1]/k$$

$$D = \frac{[1 - (1 + i/12)^{-12(N-T)}]/(i/12)}{(1 + i/12)^{12T}}$$

$$k = [(1 + g)(1 + i/12)^{-12}] - 1$$

A = loan amount
M1 = monthly payment for the first year
i = overall annual interest rate (note rate)
12 = number of months in a year
T = graduation period in years
g = graduation rate of the monthly payments
N = term of the loan in years

(8-2) $$Mi = M1(1 + g)^{i-1} \qquad \text{for } i = 2, \ldots, T + 1$$

where: Mi = monthly payment for the ith year

(8-3) $$M_{T+1} = M_{T+2} = \ldots = M_N$$

EXAMPLE: An individual wishes to borrow $100,000 to buy a $125,000 home. The homeowner chooses a GPM with an overall annual interest rate of 10.75 percent, a term of 30 years, a graduation period of 5 years, and a graduation rate of 7.5 percent.

The monthly payments will be as follows:

YEAR	MONTHLY PAYMENT
1	712.77
2	766.23
3	823.70
4	885.48
5	951.89
6–30	1023.28

The monthly payments are calculated as follows:

$$k = [(1 + 0.075)(1 + (0.1075/12))^{-12}] - 1$$
$$= -0.03410552$$

$$B = [1 - (1 + (0.1075/12))^{-12}]/(0.1075/12)$$
$$= 11.32950773$$

$$C = [(1 - 0.03410552)^5 - 1]/(-0.03410552)$$
$$= 4.670379632$$

$$D = \frac{[1 - (1 + (0.1075/12))^{-12(30-5)}]/(0.1075/12)}{[1 + (0.1075/12)]^{12(5)}}$$
$$= 60.86801941$$

$$M1 = \frac{100{,}000}{[(11.32950773)(4.670379632) + (1 + 0.075)^5(60.86801941)}$$
$$= 712.77$$

$$M2 = 712.77(1 + 0.075)^1 = 766.23$$

$$M3 = 712.77(1 + 0.075)^2 = 823.70$$

$$M4 = 712.77(1 + 0.075)^3 = 885.48$$

$$M5 = 712.77(1 + 0.075)^4 = 951.89$$

$$M6 \text{ to } M30 = 712.77(1 + 0.075)^5 = 1023.28$$

The interest rate corresponding to the monthly payment for the first year is 7.697 percent. In other words, this is the interest rate of a 30-year, $100,000 loan with a monthly payment of $712.77. It can be calculated using the trial and error method or the Newton-Raphson method, explained in Appendixes 1 and 2, respectively.

Sometimes, lenders quote the note rate and the initial interest rate. If the note rate, the loan amount, the term of the loan, the graduation rate, the graduation period, and the initial interest rate are given, the monthly payments can be easily calculated. The first monthly payment is calculated using the formula for the monthly payment from Chapter 6. However, the initial interest rate, not the note rate, should be used for this purpose. The other monthly payments are calculated as shown in the samples here.

The Amortization Schedule

The amortization schedule for a GPM is calculated the same way the amortization schedule for a fixed-rate mortgage is constructed. However, in a GPM, there may be negative amortization (rising loan balance) during the first few years. The monthly payment may not be large enough to cover the interest that accrues each month. The excess interest is added to the loan balance and the addition of the excess interest to the loan balance causes negative amortization.

The amortization schedule for the example given above is shown in Table 8–1. It shows negative amortization. Also note that the monthly payment increased in the 13th month and the 25th month.

As the loan balance increases, the loan-to-value ratio may increase, if the value of the house remains the same, declines, or does not increase as fast as the increase in the loan balance.

It should be pointed out, however, that negative amortization is not characteristic of all GPM plans. Many institutions offer 15-year GPMs with no negative amortization. It is possible to design a GPM plan such that the initial monthly payment is large enough to cover the interest that accrues each month in the first year. For example, the interest on the $100,000 loan discussed above is $895.83 in the first month (100,000 × 0.1075/12). A GPM with a monthly payment of at least $895.83 in the first year will prevent negative amortization. If the monthly payment is higher than $895.83, the loan balance will decline with each payment. The problem with this is that the borrower will have to pay a higher amount, $895.83 or more rather than $712.77 in the first year. This means some borrowers may not

TABLE 8–1 Amortization Schedule

Month	*Monthly Payment*	*Interest Paid*	*Principal Paid*	*Mortgage Balance*
1	712.77	895.83	−183.06	100,183.10
2	712.77	897.47	−184.70	100,367.80
3	712.77	899.13	−186.35	100,554.10
4	712.77	900.80	−188.02	100,742.10
5	712.77	902.48	−189.71	100,931.90
6	712.77	904.18	−191.41	101,123.30
7	712.77	905.90	−193.12	101,316.40
8	712.77	907.63	−194.85	101,511.20
9	712.77	909.37	−196.60	101,707.80
10	712.77	911.13	−198.36	101,906.20
11	712.77	912.91	−200.14	102,106.30
12	712.77	914.70	−201.93	102,308.30
13	766.23	916.51	−150.28	102,458.50
14	766.23	917.86	−151.63	102,610.20
15	766.23	919.22	−152.98	102,763.20
16	766.23	920.59	−154.36	102,917.50
17	766.23	921.97	−155.74	103,073.20
18	766.23	923.36	−157.13	103,230.40
19	766.23	924.77	−158.54	103,388.90
20	766.23	926.19	−159.96	103,548.90
21	766.23	927.63	−161.39	103,710.30
22	766.23	929.07	−162.84	103,873.10
23	766.23	930.53	−164.30	104,037.40
24	766.23	932.00	−165.77	104,203.20
25	823.70	933.49	−109.79	104,313.00

qualify for such a GPM plan even though their incomes are expected to increase in the future.

GPM may be appealing to borrowers if interest rates on fixed-rate mortgages are high. If interest rates on fixed-rate mortgages are low, there will be little interest in GPMs.

ADVANTAGES OF THE GRADUATED-PAYMENT MORTGAGE

The main advantage of GPM is that it enables more people to qualify for a loan. Borrowers are qualified at the initial monthly payment, which is lower than the payments in subsequent years or the monthly payment of a comparable fixed-rate mortgage.

The second advantage of a GPM is that the borrower knows what the payments will be at the time of application or loan approval.

Finally, there are several GPM plans from which a potential borrower can choose. The borrower can select the plan that matches his or her financial situation.

DISADVANTAGES OF THE GRADUATED-PAYMENT MORTGAGE

A major drawback of a graduated-payment mortgage is negative amortization. Despite the monthly payments, the loan balance rises to a certain point. That is why some lenders offer GPMs without this unpleasant feature.

The other drawback is that the expected increases in the borrower's income may not be large enough to cover the scheduled increases in the monthly payments.

CHAPTER

9 Growing Equity Mortgages

Growing equity mortgages (GEMS) are similar to GPMs in that the note rate is fixed and that the monthly payments increase periodically. However, GEMS and GPMs differ in other respects.

DESCRIPTION

A GEM is a fixed-rate mortgage in which the monthly payments increase at a predetermined rate for a specified period of time. The increases in the monthly payments are applied fully to the principal. As a result, the life of the mortgage is reduced.

HOW THEY WORK

The annual note rate, the graduation rate or rate of increase of the monthly payments and the graduation period are established at the time of application or approval. Given the note rate, the graduation rate, the graduation period, the loan amount and a term for amortization purposes, the monthly payment for the first period is calculated the same way the monthly payment of a fixed- rate, level-payment mortgage is calculated.The monthly payment formula described in Chapter 6 is used.

Because the note rate is used in the calculation of the monthly payment, there is no negative amortization. The monthly payment is high enough to cover the interest that accrues each month. In fact, the loan balance declines, because the monthly payments exceed the interest that accrues.

The monthly payment is increased at the predefined graduation rate at the beginning of each adjustment period for the entire graduation period. The graduation rate may vary from 2 percent to 5 percent per year and the graduation period could be as long as 10 years. Although the frequency of adjustment may vary, the adjustments are typically made once a year.

Because the increases in the monthly payments are used to reduce the loan balance, the life of the loan is reduced substantially.It must be pointed out, however, that a borrower need not use a GEM to pay off a mortgage loan more quickly. The borrower can get a standard fixed-rate, level-payment mortgage and make additional payments each period to reduce the loan balance. At his or her option, the borrower can, in fact, do exactly what the GEM requires in terms of payment increases. However, this requires discipline. Moreover, the interest rate on the GEM may be lower than the interest rate on a fixed-rate, level-payment mortgage.

EXAMPLE: A borrower wishes to get a GEM loan of $100,000. The annual interest rate is 10 percent, the graduation rate is 3 percent, and the adjustment period is 1 year. Using the monthly payment formula in Chatper 6 and assuming 30-year amortization, the monthly payment for the first year is $877.57. This payment rises to $903.90 (877.57 * (1 + .03)) in the second year, $931.03 (903.90 * (1 + .03)) in the third year, and so on.

The difference between the new monthly payment and $877.57 is used to reduce the loan balance. In the first year, the difference is $26.33; in the second year, it is $53.43, and so on. These differences accelerate the equity buildup, and the life of the loan is cut to 194 months.

Table 9-1 shows the monthly payments for the different years, and Table 9-2 shows the amortization schedule for the first 25 months.

ADVANTAGES OF GEMs

First, the interest rate, the graduation rate, and the graduation period are determined at the time of origination. For this reason, the borrower knows in advance what the monthly payments will be and when the loan will be paid off. There is no uncertainty about payment amounts.

TABLE 9-1 GEM: Monthly Payments

Year	*Monthly Payment*
1	877.57
2	903.90
3	931.02
4	958.95
5	987.72
6	1017.35
7	1047.87
8	1079.30
9	1111.68
10	1145.03
11	1179.38
12	1214.76
13	1251.21
14	1288.74
15	1327.41
16	1367.23

Second, although the monthly payments go up from year to year, the applicant is qualified using the monthly payment of the first year. However, there should be reasonable expectation that the income of the borrower will increase.

Third, unlike a GPM, a GEM does not generate negative amortization.

Finally, the GEM accelerates the equity buildup and the mortgage is paid off more quickly. This feature may be attractive to the lender also because the faster equity buildup could reduce the probability of default.

DISADVANTAGES OF GEMs

The major problem with GEMs is that the borrower may not be able to handle the increases in the monthly payments. The borrower's income may not increase as fast as the increase in the payments, or other expenses of the borrower may increase.

There may also be uncertainties if the increases in the monthly payments are not predetermined.

TABLE 9–2 Amortization Schedule

Month	*Monthly Payment*	*Interest Paid*	*Principal Paid*	*Mortgage Balance*
1	877.57	833.33	44.24	99,955.76
2	877.57	832.96	44.61	99,911.15
3	877.57	832.59	44.98	99,866.18
4	877.57	832.22	45.35	99,820.81
5	877.57	831.84	45.73	99,775.08
6	877.57	831.46	46.11	99,728.97
7	877.57	831.07	46.50	99,682.47
8	877.57	830.69	46.89	99,635.58
9	877.57	830.30	47.28	99,588.30
10	877.57	829.90	47.67	99,540.62
11	877.57	829.51	48.07	99,492.56
12	877.57	829.10	48.47	99,444.09
13	903.90	828.70	75.20	99,368.89
14	903.90	828.07	75.83	99,293.06
15	903.90	827.44	76.46	99,216.60
16	903.90	826.81	77.09	99,139.51
17	903.90	826.16	77.74	99,061.77
18	903.90	825.51	78.38	98,983.38
19	903.90	824.86	79.04	98,904.34
20	903.90	824.20	79.70	98,824.65
21	903.90	823.54	80.36	98,744.29
22	903.90	822.87	81.03	98,663.26
23	903.90	822.19	81.71	98,581.55
24	903.90	821.51	82.39	98,499.16
25	931.02	820.83	110.19	98,388.97

FINANCING INSTRUMENTS AND TECHNIQUES: Government Programs

CHAPTER 10 FHA-Insured Loans

The Federal Housing Administration (FHA) was established in 1934 to promote the ownership of safe and sanitary homes by prescribing minimum housing standards and developing suitable financing methods. FHA has been a major influence in the development of the mortgage market. For example, it introduced long-term, fully amortizing, level-payment mortgages. In the 1930s, mortgage loans were, typically, balloons. As you will see later in the chapter, FHA loans are also assumable, and there are no prepayment penalties.

The FHA is now part of the Department of Housing and Urban Development (HUD).

Although there are a variety of HUD-FHA programs, the focus here is on a few of the currently available programs.

DESCRIPTION

HUD/FHA insures loans made by commercial lenders to homebuyers. The loans may be used to finance purchases of existing homes or newly constructed homes in urban or rural areas. Anyone with good credit, enough cash for a downpayment, and the ability to repay the loan is eligible. Note that the FHA itself does not make loans. The funds come from private, primary lenders such as banks, savings and loans, or mortgage banks. If the lender defaults, the FHA takes over the property and pays the lender in cash or government securities.

The HUD-FHA insures fixed-rate, level-payment mortgages (Section 203), graduated-payment mortgages (Section 245) and adjustable-rate mortgages (Section 251). The level-payment mortgages may be for 15 years or 30 years. The adjustable-rate mortgages (ARMs) have annual and lifetime interest rate caps of 1 percent and

5 percent, respectively. The note rate changes of ARMs depend on movements in the one-year Treasury constant maturity yield. Lenders set the initial interest rate, the discount points and the margin.

HUD-FHA has seven graduated-payment mortgage (GPM) plans. The plans differ in graduation rates, graduation periods and downpayment requirements. Section 245-a plans require higher downpayments than Section 245-b plans or Section 203 (level- payment plans). Furthermore, Section 245-b plans are available to borrowers who do not qualify for Section 245-a plans and who have not owned property in the preceding three-year period. The different GPM plans are shown in Table 10-1.

HOW THEY WORK

A potential borrower who is interested in a HUD-FHA loan completes an application for a loan at an FHA-approved lending institution. If the lender has been approved for HUD Direct Endorsement, the lender qualifies the applicant and the property as required by HUD-FHA rules and regulations. This means the applicant should have good credit, enough money for a downpayment, and the ability to repay the loan. The appraised value of the property has to be determined and the property should meet the minimum standards set by HUD-FHA.

If the underwriter at the lending institution who handles HUD-FHA loans determines that the loan package meets HUD-FHA requirements for insurance, the loan is closed and the documents are sent to a HUD office in the area for review. If the review does not un-

TABLE 10-1 GPM Plans

Section	*Plan Type*	*Graduation Rate per Year(%)*	*Graduation Period in Years(%)*
245-a	I	2.5	5
	II	5.0	5
	III	7.5	5
	IV	2.0	10
	V	3.0	10
245-b		4.9	10
		7.5	5

cover omissions or departures from HUD-FHA requirements, a certificate of mortgage insurance is issued to the lender.

For a lending institution to be approved for HUD Direct Endorsement, the underwriters, appraisers and other personnel who handle HUD-FHA loans have to meet HUD-FHA requirements. If a lending institution is not approved for Direct Endorsement, the institution has to request an appraisal from HUD-FHA, and all the relevant information about the applicant has to be sent to the area office of HUD-FHA for approval. If HUD-FHA approves the loan application, it issues a commitment for insurance and the loan is closed. After the loan is closed, the certificate of insurance is issued by HUD-FHA and sent to the lending institution.

The Maximum Loan Amount and the Downpayment

The maximum loan amount in an area is set in terms of the median price of new homes in the area. Given the maximum mortgage amount, the mortgage amount for a specific property and the amount that qualifies for HUD-FHA mortgage insurance is the acquisition cost minus the required downpayment, where the acquisition cost is the sum of the lesser of the purchase price or the appraised value and the closing costs. The required downpayment depends on the classification of the property. For example, if the structure is over a year old, or its construction was approved before its construction started, the downpayment is 3 percent of the first $25,000 and 5 percent of the excess of the acquisition cost over $25,000. Different percentages apply for loans to veterans, homes with acquisition costs of $50,000 or less, homes that are not occupied by the borrowers, or homes that are less than one year old and that were not approved by HUD-FHA before construction began.

EXAMPLE: Suppose the purchase price of a home is $56,000 and closing costs are $1500. For simplicity, we will assume that the maximum mortgage amount for the area is higher than $60,000. The acquisition cost is $57,500 (56,000 + 1,500). The required downpayment is $2375, calculated as follows:

0.03 * 25,000 =	750
0.05 *(57,500 − 25,000) =	1625
Total	2375

The maximum loan amount that HUD-FHA will insure is $55,125, which is $57,500 − $2375. This amount can also be calculated, directly, as follows:

0.97 * 25,000 =	24,250
0.95 * (57,500 − 25,000) =	30,875
Total	55,125

This example applies to homes that are over one year old or homes that were constructed with prior approval of HUD-FHA.

The required downpayment for Section 245-a GPM plans is higher than the downpayment for level-payment mortgages (Section 203). A higher downpayment is required because with negative amortization, the loan balance may increase during the graduation period and HUD requires that the ratio of the highest loan balance to the original acquisition cost not exceed 97 percent. This implies that the mortgage amount will be smaller than that of the level-payment mortgage.

The maximum loan amount is the smaller of the two amounts calculated using the two criteria. Criterion 1 is the same as the example. Criterion 2 establishes the loan amount that corresponds to the highest loan balance of the GPM, given the acquisition cost and the interest rate.

EXAMPLE: Consider the example given above, in which the acquisition cost was $57,500. Assuming a 30-year GPM with a graduation rate of 7.5 percent per year for 5 years and a note rate of 10.75 percent, the highest loan balance is reached in the 60th month, regardless of the loan amount. The loan balance factor per thousand, from a table of loan balance factors prepared by HUD, is 1063.5966. To determine the loan amount, we apply the two criteria as follows:

Criterion 1:

0.97 * 25,000	$24,250
+ 0.95 * (57,500 − 25000)	30,875
= Criterion 1 loan amount	$55,125

OR

0.97
* 57,500 (acquisition cost)
= 55,775
/ 1063.5966 (loan balance factor per 1000)
= 52.43999
* 1000
= 52,439.99 (Criterion 2 loan amount)

Since the Criterion 2 loan amount is smaller than the Criterion 1 loan amount, the Criterion 2 loan amount of $52,439.99 is used. This amount is rounded down to the nearest 50 to yield $52,400. The highest loan balance corresponding to this amount is $55,732.46 ($52400/1000 * 1063.5966). This amount is smaller than 97 percent of the acquisition cost ($55,775 = 0.97 * 57,500).

Given an acquisition cost of $57,500 and a loan amount of $52,400, the required downpayment will be $5100 ($57,500 − $52,400) or about 8.87 percent of the acquisition cost.

The size of the required downpayment for Section 245-a GPM plans may disqualify some potential borrowers. Borrowers who cannot qualify for Section 245-a GPM plans can apply for Section 245-b GPM plans. These plans require downpayments that are as low as those of the level-payment mortgages (Section 203).

Mortgage Insurance Premium

The borrower has to pay a price for FHA mortgage insurance. The price or premium is, currently, a flat percentage of the loan amount (not the acquisition cost). This premium can be paid in cash at closing or it can be added to the loan amount. For mortgages with terms of 30 years, the premium is 3.8 percent of the loan amount, if the entire premium is added to the loan amount (that is, if the premium is financed). If the premium is paid in cash at closing, it is 3.661 percent of the loan amount.

For the example given in the previous section, the premium would be $1991.20 (=0.038 * $52,400) if the premium is financed, and the total loan amount would be $54,391.20 (=$52,400+$1991.20). The highest loan balance corresponding to this loan would be $57,850.30 [=($54,391.20/1000) * 1063.5966]. This is 100.61 percent of the acquisition cost. It exceeds the 97 percent limit, but it is acceptable.

If the loan is prepaid, the borrower is entitled to a refund of the unearned premium. In principle, since the premium is for the entire term, there is some unearned premium until the term of the loan ends.

ADVANTAGES OF HUD-FHA LOANS

HUD-FHA loans offer a number of advantages to the borrower. First, the required downpayment is low. For borrowers who have the ability to repay the loan but do not have large amount of cash now, this is a major advantage.

Second, the HUD-FHA loans can be paid at any point in time during the term of the loan without prepayment penalty. This feature is important for people who move or for homeowners who wish to refinance at lower interest rates.

Third, HUD-FHA loans are assumable. This feature of FHA loans is especially important to the seller if the existing loan's interest rate is much lower than current mortgage rates and the loan balance is high. Assumability speeds up the sale of the property and, possibly, increases the sales price of the property. A buyer may be willing to accept a higher price if there is an assumable low interest loan with a balance that is large relative to the price of the home.

However, unless the seller gets a release of liability from HUD-FHA, the seller would still be liable if the buyer defaults and the net proceeds from reselling the house are not large enough to cover the loan balance. To get the release from liability, the seller's buyer has to meet the requirements of the HUD-FHA.

Finally, properties financed with FHA loans have to meet FHA's minimum standards. If the house does not meet the standards, it has to be brought up to the minimum standard before the loan can be approved and closed.

DISADVANTAGES OF HUD-FHA LOANS

One drawback of FHA loans has been the time it takes to get approval. With the Direct Endorsement Plan, the time it takes to close loans has been cut substantially.

Another problem is that there are absolute ceilings to FHA loans. For example, if the ceiling for a single-family dwelling is $73,500 and the price of the property is $123,500, the homebuyer has to pay the difference of $50,000 out of pocket. This amount is in addition to the downpayment on the loan and the closing costs.

Finally, the requirement that a house has to meet minimum standards may be seen as a drawback by sellers who wish to sell their properties as is.

CHAPTER

11 VA-Guaranteed Loans

The Veteran's Administration (VA) offers a variety of benefits to veterans. One of the benefits that it offers is the Loan Guaranty Program. This program was established in 1942.

DESCRIPTION

In its Loan Guaranty Program, VA guarantees a portion of the loan amount provided by a commercial lender to an eligible veteran. As in the HUD-FHA loans discussed in Chapter 10, the loans are funded by private lenders—banks, savings and loans, mortgage companies, and others. The loans are used to finance properties that will be occupied by the veteran. If the property has four units, the veteran has to live in one of them. The VA guarantees level-payment as well as graduated-payment mortgages. The interest rate is set by VA, but the lender may charge discount points to earn competitive yields on loans. The monthly payments include property taxes and homeowner's insurance premiums.

HOW THEY WORK

This section discusses the procedure for obtaining a VA loan and Loan Guaranty Entitlements.

VA-guaranteed loans are available only to veterans of certain wars or veterans who meet certain service requirements. In order to obtain a VA loan, the veteran first submits to the VA's regional office a completed Request for Determination of Eligibility and Available Loan Guaranty Entitlements form and discharge or separation papers. If the veteran is eligible, a Certificate of Eligibility for Loan Guaranty Benefits is issued to the veteran.

In the second step, the veteran takes the Certificate of Eligibility and a fully executed purchase agreement to a lending institution and applies for a VA loan. If the applicant has a good chance of qualifying for the loan, the lender requests an appraisal of the property from the VA and starts collecting information about the applicant.

In the meantime, if an appraisal report ordered by VA shows no defects, it issues a Certificate of Reasonable Value, a copy of which is sent to the lender and the loan applicant. This value defines the maximum amount of the loan. The veteran can pay a price that is higher than the appraised value of the property, but the excess money has to come out of his or her pocket.

What happens after this step depends on whether the lender can make VA loans on an automatic basis or can process loans only after prior VA approval. Lenders that can make loans automatically perform the underwriting function. That is, they determine if the applicant and the property qualify for a VA loan. If both the applicant and the property satisfy the VA's requirements, the lender closes the loan and then sends a report to the VA. The VA reviews the report and if there are no problems with the loan, it issues a Loan Guaranty Certificate to the lender.

If the lender cannot make VA loans automatically, the lender sends the loan data to VA and if the loan applicant meets VA's standards, VA issues a Certificate of Commitment to the lender, authorizing the lender to close the loan. After closing, the lender submits a Certificate of Loan Disbursement and other required documents to get the Loan Guaranty Certificate.

Automatic versus Prior Approval Basis Loan Processing

All supervised lenders can make VA loans on an automatic basis. Supervised lenders are lenders that are supervised by a federal or a state agency. Examples are banks, savings and loans, and mutual savings banks. Nonsupervised lenders have to be approved by the VA for automatic processing of VA loans. For approval, they have to meet a number of specific requirements with respect to assets, experience, servicing, and other factors. Examples of nonsupervised lenders are mortgage companies. Nonsupervised lenders that have not been approved by the VA for automatic loan processing have to process loans only on a prior approval basis.

Loan Guaranty Entitlements

The VA does not insure or guarantee the entire loan amount given by a lender. The maximum amount that VA guarantees is currently limited to the smaller of $27,500 or 60 percent of the appraised value. This amount is the veteran's entitlement. So, if a veteran borrows $57,500 and then defaults, VA would pay the lender a maximum of $27,500 and then collect the $27,500 from the veteran.

The entitlement is like a downpayment, although the veteran does not have to pay a downpayment. Assuming an entitlement of $27,500 the veteran can borrow up to $110,000 (4 * $27,500) without making any downpayment, provided the veteran and the property qualify for the loan. This is like a $110,000 loan with a 25 percent downpayment, because the VA guarantees the $27,500.

If the veteran has used the entitlement before, the available entitlement will be smaller than $27,500 or 60 percent of the appraised value of the property and the maximum amount that the lender would allow would be 4 times the unused entitlement. However, the veteran can have the entitlement that was used before restored under certain conditions. The VA will restore entitlement if the veteran sells the property to another veteran who:

- Qualifies for assuming the loan
- Has entitlement that is at least equal to that of the selling veteran and agrees to substitute his/her entitlement for the entitlement of the selling veteran
- Certifies that he or she will live in the property

In this sense, the entitlement can be used again and again. It should also be pointed out that the selling veteran should get VA approval for the substitution of entitlement or release of liability, in writing, from the VA to protect himself or herself. The release of liability is important when a mortgage is assumable because without the release or grant of substitution, the selling veteran is still liable for the loan. If the buyer defaults and VA ends up paying the lender, VA will collect the money from the selling veteran.

Although the veteran does not have to pay a downpayment, he or she may have to pay closing costs. There is also a funding fee of 1 percent of the loan amount, which may be paid in cash or added to the loan amount. This fee is a user's fee.

ADVANTAGES OF VA LOANS

The major advantages of VA loans are little or no downpayment, assumability, and prepayment without prepayment penalties.

DISADVANTAGES OF VA LOANS

There are two disadvantages of VA loans. First, lenders may charge several discount points to earn competitive yields on their loans, especially if the interest rate set by VA is much lower than conventional rates. Second, the time to get a VA loan may be relatively long if the lender is not approved for or does not qualify for automatic processing.

Financing Instruments and Techniques: Other Primary Residential Programs

CHAPTER

12 Graduated-Payment Adjustable Mortgage Loans

The graduated-payment adjustable mortgage loan (GPAML) combines features of the graduated-payment mortgage (GPM), adjustable-rate mortgage (ARM), and a renegotiable-rate mortgage (not covered here).

DESCRIPTION

As in a GPM, the initial monthly mortgage payment is smaller than the monthly payment of a comparable, level-payment mortgage, but rises at the graduation rate during the adjustment period. At the end of the first adjustment period, the monthly payment could increase at a rate higher than the graduation rate, if interest rates increase and there are no additional caps on payment increases. After the graduation period, any increases in the monthly payments reflect increases in the note rate. Furthermore, every five years, the payment may increase to a level that would fully amortize the loan balance over the remaining term of the loan. This adjustment is called a "catch up" payment.

HOW THEY WORK

In a GPAML, the initial note rate, the graduation period, the graduation rate, the adjustment period, the catch up period, and the method for determining the changes in the note rate and any other caps on payments are established at the time of application or loan approval. To show how GPAMLs work, review the following example.

EXAMPLE: Consider a $100,000, 30-year GPAML with an initial note rate of 10.75 percent, a graduation rate of 7.5 percent per year for a graduation period of 5 years, an interest adjustment period of 3 years, a catch up period of 5 years and a periodic payment cap of 15 percent. The payment cap applies to the payment increase at the beginning of each adjustment period. Furthermore, the note rate cannot increase by more than 3 percent per adjustment period.

Table 12-1 shows the monthly payments and note rates for different years. The monthly payments for the first three years are the same as that of a regular GPM with the same features. Once the first payment is calculated, the second payment is calculated by multiplying the first by 1.075, the third payment is 1.075 times the second payment, and so on.

If interest rates do not change throughout the term of the loan, the monthly payments would rise by 7.5 percent per year for the first 5 years (graduation period), and the payment from the sixth to the thirtieth year would be $1023.28. The GPAML would be the same as the regular GPM. However, if the note rate increases at the beginning of the second adjustment period, as it did in the example, the payment will increase further. Since the loan balance at the end of the third year is $105,587.51 and the remaining term is 27 years, the monthly payment at a note rate of 11.4 percent would be $1052.25. However, the payment for the fourth year cannot exceed $947.26 ($823.70 * 1.15), because the periodic payment cap is 15 percent. So, the payment for the fourth year is $947.26.

TABLE 12–1 GPAML: Payments and Note Rates

Year	*Note Rate(%)*	*Monthly Payment*
0	—	—
1	10.75	712.77
2	10.75	766.23
3	10.75	823.70
4	11.40	947.26
5	11.40	1018.30
6	11.40	1094.68

The payment for the fifth year ($1018.30) is 1.075 times $947.26, because the graduation rate is 7.5 percent and the graduation period has not yet ended. Normally, the payment for the 6th year would also be 1.075 * $1018.30. However, because of the catch up payment feature, a new monthly payment that amortizes the loan balance at the end of year 5 over the remaining term of the loan (25 years) at a note rate of 11.4 percent is calculated. If the new monthly payment is higher than $1094.68 (= 1.075 * $1018.30), the lender could require payment of the new monthly payment.

After the sixth year, the graduation rate does not apply. Increases in the monthly payments reflect only increases in the note rate, and the payment adjustment occurs at the beginning of each adjustment period, subject to the 15 percent cap. The payment could also be adjusted every five years to a level that would amortize the loan balance over the remaining term of the loan.

ADVANTAGES OF GPAML

One advantage of this type of loan to the borrower is the relatively low initial monthly payment. The borrower can thus qualify for a larger loan. Also, if the note rate declines, the monthly payments could go down. From the lender's point of view, the risk of interest rate changes is, largely, shifted to the borrower.

DISADVANTAGES OF GPAML

The major disadvantage of GPAML is the fact that the monthly payments increase during the graduation period. Negative amortization is another problem. Finally, increases in future interest rates could cause further increases in monthly payments. To a large extent, the borrower bears the risk of interest rate fluctuations.

CHAPTER

13 BALLOON MORTGAGES

Balloon mortgages (BMs) are intermediate-term mortgages. They may be used by investors in income properties or by individuals who wish to buy homes.

DESCRIPTION

A balloon mortgage involves level payments for a specified period of time—usually three to five years—and a large lump-sum payment or balloon at the end of the period. The level payments may include principal and interest or just interest.

HOW THEY WORK

Balloon loans may be obtained from primary lenders such as banks and savings and loans. In periods of high interest rates, developers also offer low-interest balloon loans to induce potential buyers to buy homes or condominiums.

The lender specifies the interest rate, downpayment, and term of the loan. If the payments are to include principal and interest, the monthly payment is calculated using the monthly payment formula described in Chapter 6. The calculation assumes 20 to 30 year amortization even though the life of the loan is 3 to 5 years. The borrower makes monthly payments of principal and interest during the term of the loan and the remaining balance is paid in full at the end of the term of the loan.

EXAMPLE: Consider a $100,000, 5-year balloon mortgage with an annual interest rate of 12 percent. Assuming 30-year amortization, the monthly payment turns out to be $1028.61. The balance at the end of the sixtieth month, using the loan balance formula in Chapter 6, is $97,663.22. Thus, the borrower pays $1028.61 monthly for 5 years, and then makes a lump-sum payment of $97,663.22 at the end of the five-year period. Table 13-1 shows a portion of the amortization schedule. This schedule is similar to that of the fixed-rate, level-payment mortgage discussed in Chapter 6.

Note that amortization of the $100,000 over a period of 5 years would have resulted in monthly payments of $2,224.44. The balloon mortgage produces a lower monthly payment.

In some cases, the balloon mortgage requires payments of interest only during the term of the loan and payment of the full amount of the loan at the end of the term. For this example, the borrower would pay $1000 each month for five years and then pay $100,000 at the end of the five-year period. The monthly interest payment is simply the monthly interest rate times the loan amount: $1000 = ((.12/12) * $100,000).

ADVANTAGES OF BALLOON MORTGAGES

The major advantage of a balloon mortgage is that it allows relatively low payments for the term of the loan. The low payments result from amortization over 20 to 30 years, when the term of the loan is, in fact, 3 to 5 years. This is convenient for investors who buy properties with the intention of selling them within a relatively short period of time. This type of mortgage may also be attractive to people who move frequently. Furthermore, interest rates on balloon mortgages may be lower than interest rates on long-term, fixed rate, level-

TABLE 13-1 Amortization Schedule for a Balloon Mortgage

Month	*Monthly Payment*	*Interest Paid*	*Principal Paid*	*Mortgage Balance*
1	$1028.61	$1000.00	$28.61	$99,971.39
2	1028.61	999.71	28.90	99,942.49
3	1028.61	999.42	29.19	99,913.31
4	1028.61	999.13	29.48	99,883.83
5	1028.61	998.84	29.77	99,854.06
6	1028.61	998.54	30.07	99,823.99

payment mortgages. Since the term of the mortgage is smaller, less risk is involved. In addition, when mortgage rates are high, developers may offer balloon mortgages at relatively low interest rates to promote sales of new properties. However, the buyer should compare balloon mortgages with adjustable-rate mortgages before making a decision.

DISADVANTAGES OF BALLOON MORTGAGES

The main disadvantage of a balloon mortgage is that the balloon payment has to be paid at the end of the term of the loan. This would be a problem if the borrower does not sell the property. He or she must then get a new loan to pay off the balloon loan at the prevailing interest rate for new loans, which may be very high. The original lender may be willing to refinance the loan, but there is no guarantee that the lender will agree to a refinancing.

CHAPTER

14 Reverse Annuity Mortgages

Many individuals or couples own homes free and clear or have a very low outstanding balance on their mortgages. They are, generally, people over 60 who have lived in their homes for 15 to 30 years and have paid off their mortgage loans. Many of these homeowners are retired, and they may be low on cash. The reverse annuity mortgage (RAM) allows such individuals or couples to use the equity in their homes without selling their homes or getting new loans that require monthly payments.

DESCRIPTION

In a reverse annuity mortgage, a lending institution agrees to make a loan to a homeowner. The loan amount (including interest) depends on the current estimated value of the property and the amount of mortgage loan outstanding, if any. The lending institution pays the homeowner a monthly annuity for a specified period of time until the total payments and accrued interest amount to the amount established at the time the loan was approved. The loan is paid off when the property is sold, the owners die, or some other event causes the property to change hands.

HOW THEY WORK

A reverse annuity mortgage is a loan. However, it is more or less the reverse of a fixed-rate, level-payment mortgage, in which the borrower receives a lump-sum today and then repays the loan in equal installments over a specified period of time. In a RAM, the borrower receives the loan in equal installments over a defined period of time and then makes a lump-sum payment at the end of the loan period. The lump-sum payment includes principal and interest.

There are different forms of RAMs, but only one type is explained here. The future amount that the borrower has to pay in a lump sum is based on the current estimated market value of the property. Assuming that the borrower owns the home free and clear, the lender may agree to a loan of approximately 70 percent of the appraised value of the home. Depending on the expected appreciation of the property value, the proportion could be much lower than 70 percent.

If there is already a loan against the property, the sum of the new loan and the existing loan would be limited to 70 percent or less of the current appraised value.

If the homeowner sells the house or dies, the mortgage ends. Other events, such as nonpayment of taxes, may also end the mortgage. In the event of death, the lender collects the money from the estate of the borrower. However, to speed up collection, the lender may require life insurance in which the lender is named the beneficiary. After the term of the RAM ends, the same arrangement can be made again, if the homeowner still has large equity in the house.

EXAMPLE: Mrs. Brown owns a home free and clear. The current appraised value of the home is $142,860. Mrs. Brown can obtain a $100,000, 12 percent RAM with a term of 10 years. The $100,000 is roughly 70 percent of the appraised value. Given these terms, Mrs. Brown would receive $430.41 every month for 10 years. This amount is not taxable, because it represents a loan disbursement. At the end of the tenth year, she would sell the house and pay off the $100,000 loan or obtain another RAM. Assuming an average annual appreciation rate of 7 percent, the estimated market value of her home in 10 years would be $281,027.40 (=$142,860 * $(1.07)^{10}$) and her net equity in the house would be $181,027.40 (=$281,027.40−$100,000).

Using the 70 percent ratio used earlier, Mrs. Brown could obtain another RAM with a face amount of about $126,720.

Table 14-1 shows the accumulation schedule on a monthly basis. The monthly amount received (M = $430.41) is calculated as follows:

TABLE 14-1 Accumulation of Debt Schedule of a RAM (Monthly)

(1) Month	*(2) Amount Received*	*(3) Amount Received (Cummulative)*	*(4) Accrued Interest (Cummulative)*	*(5) = (3) + (4) Loan Balance (Accumulated Debt)*
1	430.41	430.41	4.30	434.71
2	430.41	860.81	12.96	873.77
3	430.41	1291.22	26.00	1317.21
4	430.41	1721.62	43.47	1765.10
5	430.41	2152.03	65.43	2217.46
6	430.41	2582.43	91.90	2674.34

$$(14\text{-}1) \qquad M = \frac{F*i/12}{[(1 + i/12)^{12*n} - 1]*(1 + i/12)}$$

where: F = face value of RAM
i = annual interest rate on the loan
n = term of RAM in years

$$M = \frac{100{,}000*(.12/12)}{[(1+(.12/12))^{12*10} - 1]*(1+(.12/12))}$$

$$= 430.4057 \text{ or about } 430.41$$

Equation 14-1 assumes that Mrs. Brown will receive the monthly amount at the beginning of each month. If the amount is received at the end of each month, it would be $434.71 and not $430.41.

The third column shows the cumulative amount received and the fourth column shows the cumulative interest that accrues. For example, at the end of the second month, the cumulative interest consists of interest on the first payment for two months ($8.6082 = 2 * ($430.41 * .01)), interest on the first month's interest in the second month (0.043041 = 4.3041 * .01) and interest on the second payment ($4.3041 = $430.41 * .01). That is a total of $12.96 (rounded).

The fifth column shows the accumulated debt or loan balance. For each month, it is the sum of the total payments received by Mrs. Brown plus the cumulative interest. For example, in the first two months, Mrs. Brown will receive $860.82 (=2 * $430.41). The two-month, cumulative interest on this amount is $12.96. Thus, the total debt or loan balance at the end of the second month is $873.78. The small difference is due to rounding.

Table 14-2 shows the accumulation schedule on an annual

TABLE 14–2 Accumulation of Debt Schedule of a RAM (Annually)

(1) Year	(2) Amount Received	(3) Amount Received (Cummulative)	(4) Accrued Interest (Cummulative)	(5) = (3) + (4) Loan Balance (Accumulated Debt)
1	5164.87	5164.87	348.34	5513.21
2	5164.87	10,329.74	1395.88	11,725.62
3	5164.87	15,494.61	3231.33	18,725.93
4	5164.87	20,659.47	5954.58	26,614.05
5	5164.87	25,824.34	9678.24	35,502.59
6	5164.87	30,989.21	14,529.19	45,518.40
7	5164.87	36,154.08	20,650.40	56,804.48
8	5164.87	41,318.95	28,202.97	69,521.91
9	5164.87	46,483.82	37,368.43	83,852.25
10	5164.87	51,648.68	48,351.32	100,000.00

basis. Note that at the end of the 10-year period, the total debt is $100,000. This amount includes principal and interest. The total principal is the monthly payment ($430.4057) times 120 or $51,648.68 (last number of column 3). This is the amount that Mrs. Brown will receive from the lender over the 10-year period.

The total interest on all the payments is $48,351.32. This is the last number in column 4 of Table 14–2. The sum of the total payments and the total interest is $100,000.

ADVANTAGES OF RAM

First, the RAM enables individuals who own homes free and clear or with substantial equity to receive a limited-period annuity that is tax free. Second, the homeowner continues to live in the house, so he or she continues to benefit from the appreciation of the home and property deductions. Third, the homeowner does not have to make any payments until the term of the RAM ends. With refinancing, there would be monthly payments and the owner may not have income large enough to pay the monthly payments. Moreover, the lump-sum amount that the homeowner receives may not earn a return that is higher than the interest rate on the loan. There is also the risk of spending the proceeds from the refinancing quickly.

DISADVANTAGES OF RAM

The major disadvantage of the RAM is the accumulation of debt. If the homeowner outlives the RAM and there is little equity left for another RAM, the house must be sold and the homeowner has to find another residence.

From the point of view of the lender, the interest that accrues may be taxable, if the lender uses the accrual method of accounting, even though the interest is not received until the RAM expires. In the accrual method of accounting, income is recognized when it is earned rather than when it is received.

CHAPTER 15 PRICE-LEVEL ADJUSTED MORTGAGES

Inflation reduces the purchasing power of money, and unless there is indexing of some sort, inflation benefits borrowers at the expense of lenders. A borrower who repays a loan principal of $100 after prices have increased is actually returning a smaller amount in terms of goods or services. The price-level adjusted mortgage (PLAM) protects lenders against inflation.

DESCRIPTION

In a PLAM, the monthly payment for each year is calculated using the *real* interest rate rather than the *nominal* interest rate. Moreover, the mortgage balance is adjusted for inflation. If prices increase, the balances are revised upwards, resulting in higher monthly payments.

HOW THEY WORK

Since the monthly payments are based on the real interest rate, the monthly payment for the first year is relatively low. The *real interest rate* is approximately equal to the nominal interest rate minus the inflation rate. It is also called the *inflation-adjusted interest rate*. It measures the lender's required rate of return in the absence of inflation.

In subsequent years, however, the monthly payments can rise, possibly, sharply if prices rise rapidly. The balances on which they are based are adjusted upwards to reflect the increase in prices. The inflation adjustment is made by multiplying the year-end balance by one plus the inflation rate. This adjustment preserves the real value of the loan balance.

The new monthly payment is calculated using the adjusted balance, the real rate of interest, and the remaining term of the loan. This process continues until the loan is paid off.

EXAMPLE: Consider a 30-year, $100,000 PLAM with a real interest rate of 3 percent. The monthly payment for the first year would be $421.60. The unadjusted balance at the end of the twelfth month would be $97,912.20. Assuming an inflation rate of 4 percent for the year, the adjusted balance would be $101,828.70 (=$97,912.20 * 1.04). The monthly payment for the second year ($438.47) is based on $101,828.70, a real interest rate of 3 percent and a term of 29 years. Table 15–1 shows an amortization schedule for a PLAM for the first 25 years. Table 15–2 shows a 5-year amortization schedule on an annual basis. It required forecasts of 5 annual inflation rates: 4 percent for the first year, 5 percent for the second, 6 percent for the third, 7 percent for the fourth, and 8 percent for the fifth year.

ADVANTAGES OF PLAMS

From the point of view of the borrower, the main advantage of a PLAM is the relatively low payment in the first year. If prices remain stable, the low payments continue, although the likelihood of stable prices over a long period of time is slim.

From the point of view of the lender, the primary advantage of this type of mortgage is protection against inflation. The real rate of return on the loan is stable.

DISADVANTAGES OF PLAMS

In times of high inflation (hyperinflation), PLAMs spell disaster for borrowers. The loan balance and the monthly payments rise sharply and unless incomes rise proportionately, borrowers may not be able to handle the increases in payments. This situation also increases the riskiness of the lender's portfolio, because the probability of default rises.

TABLE 15-1 Amortization Schedule of a PLAM (Over 25 Years)

Month	(1) Monthly Payment	(2) Interest Paid	(3) Principal Paid	(4) Mortgage Balance
1	421.60	250.00	171.60	99,828.40
2	421.60	249.57	172.03	99,656.37
3	421.60	249.14	172.46	99,483.91
4	421.60	248.71	172.89	99,311.02
5	421.60	248.28	173.32	99,137.69
6	421.60	247.84	173.76	98,963.93
7	421.60	247.41	174.19	98,789.74
8	421.60	246.97	174.63	98,615.11
9	421.60	246.54	175.06	98,440.05
10	421.60	246.10	175.50	98,264.55
11	421.60	245.66	175.94	98,088.61
12	421.60	245.22	176.38	101,828.70
13	438.47	254.57	183.89	101,644.80
14	438.47	254.11	184.35	101,460.50
15	438.47	253.65	184.81	101,275.60
16	438.47	253.19	185.28	101,090.40
17	438.47	252.73	185.74	100,904.60
18	438.47	252.26	186.20	100,718.40
19	438.47	251.80	186.67	100,531.70
20	438.47	251.33	187.14	100,344.60
21	438.47	250.86	187.60	100,157.00
22	438.47	250.39	188.07	99,968.93
23	438.47	249.92	188.54	99,780.38
24	438.47	249.45	189.01	104,570.90
25	460.39	261.43	198.96	104,372.00

TABLE 15-2 Amortization Schedule (For Five Years, Annually)

Year	(1) Monthly Payment (Nominal)	(2) Monthly Payment (Real)	(3) Interest Paid	(4) Principal Paid	(5) Mortgage Balance (Nominal)
1	421.60	421.60	2971.45	2087.77	101,828.70
2	438.47	417.59	3024.26	2237.32	104,570.90
3	460.39	409.74	3104.02	2420.64	108,279.30
4	488.01	398.36	3212.22	2643.93	113,029.80
5	522.17	383.81	3351.03	2915.05	118,924.00

CHAPTER

16 SHARED-APPRECIATION MORTGAGES

In times of high mortgage rates and relatively high property values, many individuals or families are unable to qualify for the homes that they would like to purchase. A shared-appreciation mortgage (SAM) is one device that enables individuals that have been priced out of the mortgage market to buy homes.

DESCRIPTION

In a SAM, a lender makes a loan to a homebuyer at a rate below the market interest rate. The discount in the interest rate may be substantial, say 30 percent of the current mortgage rate. In return, the lender shares in the appreciation of the property. The life of the loan may be 10 years, but it is amortized over a period of 20 to 30 years. There may be substantial prepayment penalties, and the borrower is required to make a substantial downpayment, say 30 percent of the price of the property.

HOW THEY WORK

A homebuyer uses his or her own money and a loan from a lender, seller, or investor to buy a home. The buyer has to put down 20 to 40 percent of the price of the home, and the rest is borrowed at 20 to 40 percent below current market interest rates. The buyer/borrower lives in the property and makes monthly payments to the lender. When the term of the SAM ends—say after 10 years, or if the property is sold before the term of the loan ends—the lender receives the "contingent interest." That is 20 percent to 40 percent of the appreciation in the value of the home.

The lender may or may not refinance the loan when the term of the SAM ends, and the property may or may not be sold. The owner/borrower has to pay the lender the agreed upon portion of the appreciation.

EXAMPLE: Consider a homeowner who puts down $30,000 and obtains an 11.2 percent, $70,000 SAM for 10 years to buy a $100,000 home. The current mortgage rate is 16 percent. Because the downpayment is 30 percent and the interest discount is 30 percent of the current interest rate, the lender will get 30 percent of the gain from the sale of the property.

Assuming 20-year amortization, the borrower's monthly payment would be $732.08, and the loan balance at the end of the 10-year period would be $52,711.68.

If the value of the property appreciates at an average annual rate of 7 percent, the value at the end of the 10-year period would be $196,715.14 ($= \$100,000 * 1.07^{10}$). This implies a gross gain or appreciation of $96,715.14 ($= \$196,715.14 - 100,000$) and the lender would be entitled to $29,014.54 ($= 0.3 * \$96,715.14$). Thus, the borrower has to pay the lender not only the loan balance ($52,711.68), but also 30 percent of the gain ($29,014.54), a total of $81,726.22. With a regular 16 percent, 20-year, $70,000 fixed-rate mortgage, the borrower's monthly payment would have been $973.88, or $241.80 higher than the monthly payment of the SAM.

ADVANTAGES OF SAM

A SAM enables some potential homeowners with substantial cash but limited income to buy homes. Without the discounted rate, they would not qualify for the loans they need to buy comparable homes. SAM allows lower monthly payments.

From the point of view of the lender, the large downpayment reduces the probability of default. The shorter term (10 years) also reduces uncertainties of interest rate movements. Also, the potential for appreciation is unlimited. Finally, if the lender is the seller, it speeds up the sale of the property.

DISADVANTAGES OF SAM

Many homeowners do not like the idea of sharing profits from the sale of their home with someone else. Furthermore, the homeowner may not wish to sell the property when the term of the SAM ends, but if the homeowner is not able to refinance or the contract requires the sale of the property, it has to be sold. Even if refinancing is available, the interest rates could be very high. Finally, there may be substantial prepayment penalties, for those who wish to sell or refinance before the term of the SAM ends.

From the point of view of the lender, the expected appreciation (and the contingent interest or profit) in the property may not be realized. This is the major risk that the lender takes. Other problems also may arise if the borrower defaults.

CHAPTER

17 MORTGAGE ASSUMPTIONS

Chapters 10 and 11 described mortgage assumptions for FHA and VA loans. This chapter discusses assumptions in greater detail.

DESCRIPTION

A mortgage assumption refers to a situation in which the seller of a property transfers or assigns a mortgage loan to the buyer of his or her property. The buyer of the property agrees to make the payments on the existing mortgage to the lender of the seller.

HOW THEY WORK

A mortgage assumption is part of the sale of a property. The buyer pays the difference between the price of the property and the balance on the existing mortgage to the seller and takes over payments on the existing mortgage. In addition to taking over the payments on the existing mortgage, the buyer may have to borrow additional money from another lender or from the seller to complete the purchase.

Whether the new borrower (buyer) is personally liable for the existing mortgage on the property depends on the type of assumption. If the buyer purchases the property *subject to the mortgage,* the buyer is not personally liable for the mortgage. The seller continues to be liable for the mortgage until it is completely paid off. In other words, if the buyer defaults, the lender forecloses upon the property. If the proceeds from the sale of the property are not large enough to cover the balance, a *deficiency judgment* is entered against the seller of the property. For this reason, it's advisable for the seller to insist on the second type of assumption.

In the second case, the buyer *assumes* the mortgage. In other words, the buyer promises, in writing, to make the payments on the existing mortgage. Even in this situation, the seller may be liable if the lender is not able to collect the balance from the buyer unless the seller obtains a *release of liability* from the lender. To release the seller, the lender can sign a *novation contract.*

An assumption can take place if the mortgage is freely assumable. FHA and VA loans are assumable. However, conventional loans (loans that are not insured by the FHA or guaranteed by the VA) may not be assumable. The mortgage note may contain a *due on sale clause.* This clause allows the lending institution to accelerate the debt if the property is sold. In other words, the entire debt becomes due immediately. The due on sale clause or *acceleration clause* prevents mortgage assumption.

The due on the sale clause allows the lending institution to qualify the buyer of the property and to raise the interest rate on the loan. If the lender is able to do both, it may allow an assumption and release the seller from liability. The lender may also charge the buyer an assumption fee.

The value of an assumption depends on the spread or difference between the interest rate on the existing loan and current mortgage rates, the size of the balance relative to the price of the property, and the remaining term of the loan. The larger the interest rate difference, the larger the balance of the loan, and the longer the remaining term of the loan, the greater the potential benefits of the assumption to the buyer and the seller.

EXAMPLE: Suppose the selling price of a property is $65,000 and the balance on the existing 7 percent mortgage is $40,000. The remaining term of the mortgage is 15 years. The current mortgage rate on 15-year loans is 10 percent. If the buyer puts down $25,000, he or she could get a new, 15-year loan at 10 percent. If the existing loan is assumable, the buyer could assume the mortgage at 7 percent.

Because the monthly payment on the new loan is $429.84 and the monthly payment of the existing mortgage is $359.53, the assumption would save the buyer $70.31 each month for 15 years. Assuming that the buyer can earn 9 percent per year on the savings, the present value of monthly savings of $70.31 would be $6932.10, before taxes. Had the interest rate differential been larger, the monthly savings would have been larger.

Had the interest rate differential been larger, the

monthly savings would have been larger.

Obviously, the monthly savings have value to the buyer. For this reason, the buyer may be willing to pay a higher price for the property, but the increase in the price has to be smaller than the present value of the monthly savings.

The higher selling price benefits the seller. So, an assumable mortgage has value not only to the buyer but also to the seller.

ADVANTAGES OF ASSUMPTIONS

For the borrower, the main advantage of a mortgage assumption is lower monthly payments, resulting in some savings. The buyer realizes the full benefits of assumption (lower payments) if the price is not increased above what the price of the property would be without an assumption.

From the point of view of the seller, an assumable mortgage can speed up the sale of the property. The seller may also be able ask a higher price for the property. If the increase in the price is lower than the present value of the expected monthly savings of the assumption to the buyer, both the buyer and the seller benefit from the assumption.

DISADVANTAGES OF ASSUMPTIONS

From the buyer's point of view, the benefits of lower monthly payments could be partially offset by a higher price for the property. The monthly savings could also be reduced further if the lender raises the interest rate on the assumed mortgage loan. Moreover, if the buyer does not have enough cash to pay the difference between the price of the property and the balance on the assumable loan, he or she may have to get another loan (second mortgage) from a different lender, and the interest rate on second mortgages is higher than the interest rate on first mortgages. This situation would be more serious if the equity of the seller is large and the buyer's downpayment is small. Finally, the value of the assumption would be small if the interest rate spread is small and the remaining term of the assumable mortgage is short.

From the seller's point of view, the seller's personal liability will not vanish if the buyer buys the property subject to the mortgage.

The liability continues to exist even if the buyer assumes the loan and the seller does not get a release of liability from the lender. However, if the property values are rising rapidly and the buyer is creditworthy, this liability may not be a problem. The problem is that no one can be sure at the onset about these factors.

CHAPTER

18 SECOND MORTGAGES

When a property owner gets more than one mortgage loan, backed by the same property, the loans are classified as first, second, and third mortgages (and so on). All the mortgages other than the first are *junior* or *subordinated mortgages*. The first mortgage is senior to all the other mortgages, and the second mortgage is senior to the third mortgage, and so on. Usually, the time sequence in which each loan is obtained establishes the classification of the loan.

Although there are several types of loans backed by real estate, the second mortgage is more common than the other junior mortgages. This chapter covers second mortgages.

DESCRIPTION

A second mortgage or a second trust is a loan secured by a property that is already used as security for another mortgage loan—a first mortgage. The second mortgage may be used to finance the purchase of a property or to finance improvements. The term of the loan generally, varies from 3 years to 15 years. The interest rate on a second mortgage loan from a financial institution is higher than the interest rate on a first mortgage, because it is riskier. In the event of default and foreclosure, the property is sold and the proceeds of the sale are used to pay off the balance of the first mortgage first and then the balance of the second mortgage.

HOW THEY WORK

A second mortgage may be used with an assumable mortgage to buy property. The second mortgage supplements the buyer's downpayment to pay for the equity of the seller in the property. The buyer can obtain a second mortgage from a financial institution, or the seller may be willing to take back a second mortgage, if he or she does not need the cash now. In the latter case, the interest rate, the term of the loan and the payments are negotiated between the buyer and the seller.

The loan can be structured in a variety of ways. For example. The loan may be *fully amortized* over a period, say over 10 years. However, full amortization increases the amount of monthly payments, and the buyer may not be able to handle the higher payments. An alternative way of structuring the loan is to make it *partially amortizing*. The payments can be calculated assuming 30-year amortization to reduce the monthly payments. The unpaid balance would be due after a fixed time—say 5 or 7 years. The contract may also call for just interest payments during the life of the loan and the payment of the entire loan amount at the end of the loan period.

EXAMPLE: The market price of a house is $75,000. The balance of an assumable mortgage on the house is $35,000. If the buyer has only $20,000 for a downpayment, the buyer can arrange for a second mortgage to get the remaining $20,000. Suppose the seller is willing to take back a $20,000 second mortgage for 5 years with an interest rate of 12 percent. If the loan is fully amortized, the monthly payments on the second mortgage would be $444.89. If the monthly payment of the assumed mortgage is $334.48, the total monthly payment would be $779.37.

If the monthly payment of the second mortgage is based on 30-year amortization, it would be $205.72 and the pay off balance at the end of 5 years would be $19,532.64. The buyer would have to obtain another second mortgage to pay off the loan at that time.

The second mortgage may also be used even if there is no assumable mortgage. A lending institution may be willing to approve a first mortgage for 90 percent of the price of the property. If the buyer does not have 10 percent of the price in cash but is able to handle large monthly payments, the seller may be willing to take back a second mortgage.

EXAMPLE: Suppose the price of the house is $200,000. A lending institution is willing to approve a first mortgage loan of $180,000 (= .9 * $200,000). The buyer has $10,000 and he or she obtains a second mortgage loan of $10,000 from the seller.

In this example, a second mortgage was linked to the purchase of a property. It is called a *purchase money mortgage.* However, a second mortgage can also be used by a property owner who has substantial equity in his or her property. For example, a second mortgage from a lending institution or other source can be used to finance home improvements.

In a home equity loan, which is a variation of a second mortgage, the loan may be used for a variety of other purposes—travel, education, loan consolidation, purchasing an automobile, and so on. A lending institution may be willing to approve a loan or credit limit of up to the difference between 70 percent of the current appraised value of the home and the current balance of the mortgage on the house. If a credit limit is approved, the homeowner could use the money as needed up to the credit limit. The homeowner is given a checkbook or a credit card to obtain the credit. He or she pays interest only on the amount used. The interest rate on home equity loans is variable. It may be linked to a short-term interest rate, such as the prime rate.

EXAMPLE: The current appraised value of the house and the current mortgage balance on a house are $100,000 and $30,000, respectively. If the lender uses a 70 percent loan to value (L/V) ratio, the credit limit is calculated as follows:

Appraised value	=	$100,000
* L/V	=	.7
= Maximum total loan	=	$70,000
− Mortgage balance	=	$30,000
= Credit limit (home equity loan)	=	$40,000

The interest rate on the loan may be specified as the prime rate plus 1.5 percent, 2 percent, and so on.

ADVANTAGES OF A SECOND MORTGAGE

The second mortgage helps the buyer purchase a property or the seller sell a property. Furthermore, the second mortgage enables property owners to use the accumulated equities in their properties to buy other properties or for other purposes without selling their properties.

DISADVANTAGES OF SECOND MORTGAGES

From the point of view of the borrower, the interest rate on a second mortgage tends to be higher than the interest rate on a first mortgage. The term of a second mortgage is also shorter. If the loan is fully amortized, the monthly payment becomes relatively large. If it is partially amortized or is interest-only, the borrower has to look for other sources of funds within a relatively short period of time.

With the home equity loan, there is a risk that a homeowner with little discipline will use all or a portion of his or her equity in the property quickly.

From the point of view of the lender, a second mortgage is riskier than a first mortgage. The lender could reduce this risk by qualifying the borrower and the property carefully.

CHAPTER

19 Wraparound Mortgages

A wraparound mortgage contains an existing mortgage and is used in connection with the sale of a property. It can be structured to benefit both the seller and the buyer.

DESCRIPTION

A wraparound mortgage is a mortgage that includes or is wrapped around an existing first mortgage. The buyer purchases a property subject to an existing first mortgage and gives the seller a wraparound mortgage with a face amount that is larger than the balance on the existing loan. The difference between the face amount and balance is the amount financed by the seller. The seller continues to make payments on the first mortgage but retains the difference between the monthly payment on the wrap and the monthly payment on the first mortgage.

HOW THEY WORK

The wraparound mortgage is used when the interest rate on the existing mortgage is lower than current mortgage rates. In this case, the seller takes advantage of the difference in interest rates by taking back a wraparound mortgage from a buyer at an interest rate that is higher than that of the first mortgage but lower than current mortgage rates. The face amount of the wraparound mortgage consists of the balance of the existing mortgage and the amount financed by the seller. Since the interest rate on the wraparound mortgage is higher than the interest rate on the existing mortgage, the seller earns extra interest on the existing mortgage.

The term of the wraparound mortgage is, usually, the same as that of the remaining term of the existing mortgage, but it can also be different.

The buyer or wraparound borrower sends monthly payments to the seller (wrap lender) and the seller sends the payment on the first mortgage to the original lender and keeps the difference.

Although the buyer gets title to the property, the seller is still responsible for making the payments to the original lender.

The wraparound mortgage should not be used without the original lender's knowledge. If there is a due on sale clause in the mortgage, a wraparound mortgage is not likely to be used, because the original lender will want a higher interest rate and some fees.

EXAMPLE: Suppose a seller and buyer agree on a price of \$100,000. The current balance on the 7.5 percent mortgage is \$30,000, the remaining term is 15 years, and the monthly payment is \$278.10. The mortgage has no due on sale clause. The buyer has \$20,000 for a downpayment. If current mortgage rates are around 12 percent, both the buyer and seller could benefit from a wraparound mortgage with an interest rate of between 12 percent and 7.5 percent. If the seller takes a 15-year, \$80,000 wraparound mortgage with an interest rate of 10 percent, the buyer's monthly payment will be \$859.68. The seller receives \$859.68 every month, sends \$278.10 to the original lender, and keeps \$581.58 (= \$859.68 − 278.10). In effect, the seller loaned \$50,000 (= \$80,000 − 30,000) to the buyer and expects to receive \$581.58 each month for 15 years. The seller's yield on the \$50,000 loan is 11.42 percent. This yield is higher than the rate on the wraparound (10 percent) because the seller is also earning additional interest on the original loan.

The yield of 11.42 percent is the interest rate that equates the current loan of \$50,000 to the discounted sum of the monthly payments (\$581.58). It is the rate used for discounting the payments and can be calculated using the trial and error method or the Newton-Raphson method.

ADVANTAGES OF WRAPAROUND MORTGAGES

From the point of view of the buyer, the wraparound mortgage is attractive because the interest rate is, generally, lower than current mortgage rates.

From the seller's point of view, the wraparound mortgage facilitates the sale of the property, and the seller is able to earn additional interest on the first mortgage.

DISADVANTAGES OF WRAPAROUND MORTGAGES

If the existing mortgage has a due on sale clause, the seller should not take back a wraparound mortgage. Today it may be difficult to find a mortgage without such a clause. Thus, the use of wraparound mortgages is limited. It is also of limited value if the balance of the existing mortgage is low, the difference between the interest rate on the existing mortgage and current mortgages is small, and the remaining term of the existing mortgage is short.

In addition, the buyer faces the extra risk that the seller may not make timely payments on the original mortgage. The original lender could foreclose upon the property, which is now owned by the buyer, if the seller fails to make the required payments. So, it is not enough for the buyer to make timely payments to the seller. The seller should also make timely payments to the original lender.

CHAPTER 20 LAND CONTRACTS

A land contract is another example of seller financing. It is used in financing unimproved land, as well as improvements such as residential properties. It is also called a *contract for deed* or *installment sale.*

DESCRIPTION

A land contract is a contract or agreement in which a seller agrees to deliver marketable title to the buyer after the buyer makes all the payments required by the contract. The buyer makes a downpayment at the time the contract is signed, and the rest of the price is paid in installments over a specified period of time. The repayment period could be longer than 10 years, but it can also be relatively short (3 or 5 years). The contract specifies the terms of the sale, including the price of the property, the sizes and frequencies of the payments, the payment period, and other conditions that the buyer and the seller agree on.

The land contract is different from a purchase money mortgage. In a purchase money mortgage, the buyer obtains title to the property at the time agreement is signed. Also, in a purchase money mortgage, a default leads to a foreclosure; in a land contract, the seller sues either for specific performance (enforcement of the contract) or eviction of the buyer and repossession of the property.

HOW THEY WORK

The land contract is used for different reasons. For example, the buyer may not qualify for a loan from a bank or a savings and loan and the seller may want to use a land contract for tax reasons. In other words, the seller may want to spread the gain on the sale of the property over several years to defer payment of income taxes and reduce income taxes.

Whatever the reason, the terms of the sale and the financing of the property are spelled out in the land contract. The interest rate on the loan may or may not be explicitly stated in the contract, but the amount of each payment, the frequency of payments, and the length of the contract are explicitly stated. The loan may be fully amortized or partially amortized with a balloon.

Unless the agreement prohibits it, the buyer should have the contract recorded and have the deed to the property placed in escrow. Because the seller retains title to the property until full payment for the property is received, these measures would protect the buyer, especially if the seller dies or moves after the last payment is received.

The buyer has equitable title to the property after the contract is signed. Usually, he or she gets possession and pays property insurance premiums and property taxes. Both the seller and the buyer can assign their interests to others. There are investors who buy land contracts at substantial discounts.

What happens in the event of default depends on state laws. The seller may be able to sue for repossession of the property and retention of all the payments made by the buyer. If the contract is rescinded, the buyer gets a refund of the payments less estimated rental payments, and the property is returned to the seller. Some states may require foreclosure.

EXAMPLE: A buyer agrees to pay $100,000 for a house. The buyer also agrees to assume a mortgage with a current balance of $30,000, interest rate of 7.5 percent and remaining term of 7 years. The buyer has $20,000 for a downpayment and signs a land contract for $50,000 with an interest rate of 10 percent. The payments are amortized over a period of 30 years, and the balance is due at the end of 7 years. The monthly payment of the assumed mortgage is $460.15, and the monthly payment of the land contract is $438.79. The buyer will send $460.15 to the original lender, $438.79 to the seller. The buyer's total monthly payment is $898.94. The payoff balance (balloon) of the land contract at the end of the seventh year is $47,324.68.

If current mortgage rates are 14 percent to 15 percent, the land contract would enable the buyer to purchase the property and the seller to sell it now. However, the seller delivers a marketable title at the end of the seventh year when all required payments are made by the buyer.

ADVANTAGES OF LAND CONTRACTS

In times of high interest rates or when a potential borrower cannot qualify for a loan from a lending institution, a land contract in which the interest rate is lower than current mortgage rates may be one way of purchasing a property. The method would be more attractive if there is a low-interest rate, assumable mortgage on the property.

Another advantage to the buyer is that there may not be a deficiency judgment with a land contract if the buyer defaults and there is no assumed mortgage.

From the seller's point of view, the major attraction of the land contract is the fact that the lender retains title to the property until all payments are received from the buyer. In case of default, the seller is able to regain possession of the property relatively quickly, if foreclosure is not required. The land contract also facilitates the sale of property.

DISADVANTAGES OF LAND CONTRACTS

The main disadvantage to the buyer is buying a property for which he or she does not hold title for some time. Unless an escrow is set up for the title, problems could also arise from death and other factors. There could also be a problem if the seller does not deliver a marketable title.

From the seller's point of view, there may not be a deficiency judgment in the event of default.

CHAPTER

21 Buy Downs

Previous chapters covered assumptions, wraparounds, and land contracts. These techniques are useful in promoting sales of properties. Another technique that can be used to increase sales in times of slow sales is the buy down.

DESCRIPTION

A buy down is a technique of reducing the interest rate on a mortgage loan. The reduction in the interest rate results in lower monthly payments. With lower payments, more people qualify for loans and sales of properties increase.

The buy down may be temporary or permanent and the buy down may be financed by the seller of the property or by others who are related to the buyer. The buyer can also buy down the interest rate.

HOW THEY WORK

In times of high interest rates, sales of properties slow down and sellers, like developers, may buy down mortgage rates to lower monthly payments. If the buy down is temporary, the interest rate is reduced for the first few years. If the buy down is permanent, the interest rate is lowered for the entire life of the mortgage.

The seller finances the buy down by making a lump sum payment at closing or by depositing an amount in an interest- bearing account with the lender at time of closing. In the latter, the amount deposited plus interest earned on the amount should be large enough to cover the reduction in the monthly payments resulting from the buy down. If the buyer prepays the loan during the buy down period, the seller may be able to get the unused portion of the deposit from the lender.

The amount of the lump sum payment at closing will be larger than the amount deposited in the second method, because interest earnings are not counted. Moreover, there is no refund of the lump-sum payment or portion of it if the buyer prepays the loan during the buy down period. So, the first method is more costly for the seller than the second method.

However, the seller may not, really, bear the cost of the buy down. The seller may increase the price of the property by an amount equal to the present value of the cost of the buy down. In such a case, the buyer would bear the cost and the buy down may not increase sales.

A buyer can also buy down the interest rate on a mortgage but this arrangement is between the buyer and the lender. The buyer can pay more points at closing for a lower interest rate. The lender may have several options. For example, a lender may offer 15 year fixed-rate mortgages at 11 percent with zero points, 10.75 percent with 1 point, 10.5 percent with 1.5 points, and 10.25 percent with 2 points. This type of buy down does not involve third parties. It is not a sales technique used by sellers. There is no subsidy.

In the example that follows, we will see how sellers use temporary buy downs to attract buyers and increase sales.

EXAMPLE: Suppose the current mortgage rate on a 30-year, level-payment, fixed-rate mortgage is 12 percent. The price of the property is $125,000, the loan amount is $100,000 and the developer arranges for a 3-2-1 buy down with a lender. A 3-2-1 buy down means the interest rate will be 3 percent lower than the current mortgage rate of 12 percent in the first year, 2 percent lower in the second year and 1 percent lower in the third year. From the fourth year on, the payments are based on the current mortgage rate (the note rate) of 12 percent.

Given the information we have, the buyer's monthly payment will be $804.62 in the first year, $877.57 in the second year, $952.32 in the third year and $1028.61 for years four through 30. Without the buy down, the monthly payment would have been $1028.61 each year for 30 years. So, the buy down saves the buyer $223.99 per month in the first year, $151.04 per month in the second year and $76.29 per month in the third year.

What is the cost of the buy down to the seller? If interest is ignored, the lump-sum payment at closing would be the undiscounted sum of the differences between the monthly payments during the buy down period. The undiscounted sum is equal to (12 * $223.99) + (12 * $151.04) + (12 * $76.29) or $5415.84.

If the lender allows the seller to deposit a specific amount into an account with the lender that earns, say 5.5 percent, the amount that has to be deposited today to cover the payment differences would be the sum of the present values of the payment differences, discounted at the monthly interest rate of 0.45833 percent (.055/12) or $5071.55.

Note that the lender receives $1028.61 every month during and after the buy down period. The lender's yield on the loan is also the same at 12 percent.

The seller could also offer the buyer a lower price instead of a payment subsidy. The price of the property can be reduced by an amount equal to the cost of the buy down. This option may be better for buyers who plan to hold the property for a relatively long period of time.

ADVANTAGES OF BUY DOWNS

In a buy down in which a third party (like a seller/developer or relative of the property buyer) truly pays for the buy down, the seller, the lender, and the buyer benefit. The seller will be able to sell properties and the buyer would be in a better position to buy. The lender is able to make loans without any reduction in cash inflow or yield.

DISADVANTAGES OF BUY DOWNS

Unless the cost of the buy down is reflected in the price of the property, the buy down reduces the sales proceeds to the seller/developer. From the point of view of the buyer/borrower, the increases in the monthly payments during the buy down period could create financial problems for the buyer unless his or her income rises by an amount large enough to cover payment increases. This problem is particularly serious if the interest rates/payments increase sharply. The increased likelihood of default could, in turn, be of concern to the lender.

CHAPTER

22 ZERO INTEREST MORTGAGES

Zero interest mortgages (ZIMs) are usually used by builders of new homes, but potentially they can be used by any seller. Used correctly, they can be an effective sales tool.

DESCRIPTION

As the name suggests, a ZIM is a mortgage in which the interest rate on the loan is zero percent. The loan's term is less than 10 years, and all monthly payments go to principal reduction.

HOW THEY WORK

In a typical ZIM, the downpayment is rather high. It may be 30 percent or more of the sales price of the property. The buyer makes the downpayment and the difference between the price of the property and the downpayment is paid in equal installments over a fixed period—generally not more than 10 years, but possibly as short as 5 years.

If the builder/seller needs the money, he or she can sell the note to a lender or investor. The proceeds from the sale of the note will depend on the rate of return required by the lender or investor. The higher the lender's required rate of return, the lower the price of the notes will be.

EXAMPLE: Suppose the price of a property is $142,857.14. The builder requires a 30 percent downpayment or $42,857.14. The balance of the price (or $100,000) is received in equal monthly installments of $1666.67

> over a period of five years. If the builder needs the money, she or he can sell the loan to a lender or investor. Assuming that the required rate of return of the lender/investor is 12 percent per year, the builder would receive \$74,925.21. This amount is the present value of the stream of 60 monthly payments of \$1666.67 discounted at the monthly required yield of 1 percent (12 percent/12). This example assumes that the note will be sold right away. However, the seller of the property can sell the note at any time during the life of the loan.

The price of the note is calculated as follows:

$$NP = \frac{1 - (1 + d)^{-N}}{d} * M$$

$$= \frac{1 - (1 + .01)^{-60}}{.01} * 1666.67$$

$$= \$74,925.21$$

Where: NP = price of the note
M = monthly payment on ZIM
d = investor's monthly yield
N = total number of monthly payments

Note that as long as the buyer of the note requires a positive yield, and one can safely assume that he or she will, the price of the note will be smaller than the loan amount agreed upon by the seller and the buyer of the property. In the example given previously, the loan amount was \$100,000, but the price of the note was only \$74,925.21. That is a discount of \$25,074.79, or 25 percent of the loan amount.

The effective price of the property was really \$117,782.34. This is the sum of the downpayment (\$42,857.14) and the price of the note (\$74,925.21). If the value of the property was \$142,857.14, the seller of the property would sustain a loss. Thus ZIM results in a loss for the seller. For this reason, the seller will try to sell the property at a higher price than the price at which the property would sell with conventional fixed-rate financing.

The real issue then becomes how much higher the price should be. If the seller wishes to receive cash that is equal to the price that goes with conventional fixed-rate financing, the selling price associated with ZIM should be high enough such that the sum of the downpayment and the price of the note is equal to the price that would be associated with conventional fixed-rate financing.

The ZIM price would then be calculated as follows:

$$P = \frac{V}{\left[k + \frac{(1-k)/N}{(1+d)^1} + \frac{(1-k)/N}{(1+d)^2} + \cdots + \frac{(1-k)/N}{(1+d)^N}\right]}$$

OR

$$P = \frac{V}{\left[k + \frac{(1-k)/N}{d}\{1-(1+d)^{-N}\}\right]}$$

where: P = ZIM price
V = price with conventional fixed-rate financing
k = downpayment as percent of ZIM price
N = total number of monthly payments
d = investor's monthly required yield

EXAMPLE: Suppose the price with conventional fixed-rate financing is \$142,857.14, the required downpayment is 30% of the ZIM price, the investors annual yield is 12% and the term of ZIM is 5 years. If the seller wishes to receive cash of \$142,857.14 for the property, the ZIM price should be \$173,270.34. The seller would then receive a downpayment of \$51,981.10 (=.3 * 173,270.34) and the face value of the 5-year ZIM would be \$121,289.24 (=173,270.34 − 51,981.10) and the buyer's monthly payment would be \$2,021.49 (= 121,289.24/60). When the seller of the property sells the ZIM to an investor, S/he will get \$90,876.61 for it. That is a total of \$142,857.93 (= \$51,981.32 + 90,876.61). This amount is slightly higher that \$142,857.14 due to rounding.

The ZIM price is calculated as follows:

$$P = \frac{142{,}857.14}{\left[0.3 + \frac{(1-0.3)/60}{0.01}\{1-(1+0.01)^{-60}\}\right]}$$

$$= 173{,}270.34$$

As you can see, the ZIM price is \$30,413.20 higher than the price with conventional fixed-rate financing. That is a premium of 21.29

percent over the latter price. This premium may not be acceptable to the buyer. So, the seller may have to accept a price somewhere between \$142,857.14 and \$173,270.34. If the demand for housing is weak, the actual selling price would be closer to the lower price.

Although the interest rate of a ZIM is zero percent, for tax purposes, a portion of the monthly payments is considered interest. In other words, an estimated interest rate is applied to determine the interest component.

ADVANTAGES OF ZIMS

Unless the price at which the property is purchased contains a premium, the effective price of the property is lower than the price that corresponds to conventional fixed-rate financing. This is a plus for the buyer. The other advantage for the buyer is that the property can be owned free and clear within 5–10 years.

From the seller's point of view, ZIM may increase sales. Many buyers are attracted to zero interest financing.

Finally, for lenders or investors, ZIM has a low risk because the terms are relatively short and the downpayments are relatively high.

DISADVANTAGES OF ZIMS

In a weak market, ZIM can reduce the seller's return on the property. However, the return could be worse without a ZIM. Moreover, if the note is not sold right away and the seller plans to sell it at some point in the future, the seller bears the risk of a lower price for the note as investors' required yields rise. If required yields fall, the note will be worth more.

From the borrower's/buyer's point of view, the downpayment may be too large. Because the term of ZIM is relatively short, the monthly payment may also be too high for some potential buyers. These problems get worse if the stated selling price of the property includes a large premium.

A price that includes a premium may also result in higher property taxes for the buyer. Finally, although the buyer/borrower may deduct imputed interest as an itemized deduction, the imputed rate may be lower than the market rate.

APPENDIX: DERIVATION OF THE PRICE OF A PROPERTY FINANCED WITH A ZERO INTEREST MORTGAGE

$$V = kP + \frac{(P - kP)/N}{(1 + d)^1} + \cdots + \frac{(P - kP)/N}{(1 + d)^N}$$

$$\Rightarrow P = V/\left[k + \frac{(1 - k)/N}{(1 + d)^1} + \cdots + \frac{(1 - k)/N}{(1 + d)^N}\right]$$

$$\Rightarrow \quad P = V/\left[k + \frac{(1 - k)/N}{d}\{1 - (1 + d)^{-N}\}\right]$$

where: V = price with conventional financing
P = ZIM price
k = downpayment as percentage of ZIM price
d = monthly yield of investor
N = total number of monthly payments (= life of ZIM in months)

CHAPTER

23 Lease With Option to Purchase

Often, potential buyers have the capacity to repay mortgage loans, but they have little or no money for a downpayment. One solution to this problem may be a lease with option to purchase (LOP). For sellers/developers, LOPs are effective techniques for selling properties.

DESCRIPTION

In an LOP, the tenant/buyer leases a property for a specified period of time. During that period, the lessee has the option of buying the property. If he or she does not exercise the option, the option to purchase expires. For short-term options, the option period could be any period up to 5 years, but most likely less than 20 years. For long-term options, it could be more than 20 years. This chapter covers short-term options only.

HOW THEY WORK

LOPs may be useful when potential buyers have little or no downpayment. They could also be useful when mortgage rates are high and there is expectation they will come down.

The prospective buyer leases the property for one to five years and takes possession. During this period, the tenant/prospective buyer pays rent. Also, at the time the lease is signed, the tenant pays a price for the option to purchase (premium or deposit).

The price of the option depends on the length of the exercise period, the volatility of the property, the price at which the property can be purchased (exercise price), and the level of the interest rate.

In some cases, the price of the option (deposit) may not be paid at the time the contract is signed. Instead, the tenant may have to pay rent that is higher than the market rent for the property.

The tenant/prospective buyer may get credit for all or part of the rent paid. In other words, if the tenant decides to buy the property, all or part of the rent may be applied to the price of the property. If the option to purchase expires unexercised, the tenant loses the premium or deposit and the rental payments.

The price at which the property can be purchased during the exercise period is usually specified at the time the contract for the LOP is signed. In some cases, however, the price may be left open to be determined through appraisal at some point in the future.

If the market value of the property rises to a level higher than the exercise price of the property plus their costs, the option is likely to be exercised. Otherwise, the option holder (buyer) is likely to let the option expire. The owner of the property keeps the property, the deposit, and rental payments.

EXAMPLE: A developer offers a lease with option to purchase contract for a one-bedroom condominium unit. The option expires in six months, and the price at which the property can be purchased (exercise price) is $75,000. The monthly rent is $600 and the deposit (price of the option or premium) is $2000. Should the holder of the option decide to buy the property within the six-month exercise period, all the rental payments and the deposit will be applied to the purchase price (exercise price) of the property.

Over a period of six months, the holder of the option will have paid $3600. If the option is exercised, the buyer's total credit will be $5600. If closing costs amount to $2600, the buyer has to come up with $72,000 (= $75,000 + $2600 − $5600) to buy the property. For simplicity, the time value of money is ignored.

The lease with option to purchase may be structured in different ways. The example just given would be suited to buyers with relatively small amounts of money for a downpayment. The rental payments and the deposit are applied toward the purchase price. In this case, the exercise price would, presumably, be higher than what it would be if the seller does not allow rent credit or allows only partial credit. In the following example, the option holder receives credit only for the deposit.

EXAMPLE: Consider an LOP contract that is the same as the previous example except that the exercise price is $70,000 and there is no rent credit. This type of option may be suited to a buyer who has enough money for a downpayment.

The amount that the option holder has to pay for the property if he or she exercises the option is $70,600 ($70,000 − $2000 + $2600). If the market value of the property exceeds $74,600 (= $70,000 + $2,000 + $2,600) during the exercise period, the option holder should buy the property. If the market value of the property remains below $74,600, it may not pay to exercise the option.

ADVANTAGES OF AN LOP

An LOP is a useful technique for selling properties to people with little or no money for a downpayment, but incomes large enough to handle the rental payments during the exercise period and the mortgage payments thereafter. This is particularly true when the seller allows full or partial credit for rental payments and full credit for the deposit. The arrangement benefits the owner of the property and the option holder.

If interest rates are expected to come down, the LOP gives the potential buyer time to get a mortgage loan at a lower interest rate. Furthermore, the option holder could get additional benefits, if the market value of the property rises to a level higher than the exercise price minus the deposit minus the rental payments plus the closing costs.

From the seller's point of view, the LOP facilitates the sale of the property. If the property is not sold, the owner keeps the deposit. In fact property owners can use LOPs to increase incomes from their properties by setting the exercise prices at levels higher than the expected market values of their properties. For example, the price of the property may be $60,000 and the owner may expect the price to remain the same a year from now. The owner could offer an LOP with a deposit of $2000 and an exercise price of $63,000, which assumes an appreciation rate of 5 percent. This way the LOP is not likely to be purchased. If the LOP expires, the owner keeps the $2000 in addition to the usual rental income.

Moreover, the owner continues to benefit from tax writeoffs, such as deduction of property taxes and depreciation. To offset losses from rental properties against incomes from other sources, certain requirements have to be met.

DISADVANTAGES OF AN LOP

For an owner who is interested in selling the property, an LOP is not a sale. There is the risk that the option holder will not purchase the property. The longer the exercise period, the greater the risk.

From the point of view of the option holder, there are no deductions of property taxes until the option holder purchases the property. Interest rates could also rise during the option period, and the option holder may not qualify for a loan. This situation creates a problem for both the owner and the option holder.

CHAPTER

24 PLEDGED ACCOUNT MORTGAGES

Structurally, pledged account mortgages (PAMs) are similar to a buy down. However, the PAM is generally an arrangement between the borrower/buyer and the lender only.

DESCRIPTION

In a PAM, a borrower pledges or deposits a portion of his or her downpayment into an interest-bearing account with the lender. This money is used to supplement direct payments made by the borrower for a specified period of time. In other words, the lender collects money from the borrower, but because the payments made by the borrower are initially smaller than the monthly mortgage payments on the loan, the lender takes out the difference from the pledged account. This process continues until the money in the pledged account is exhausted.

HOW THEY WORK

The PAM could be appealing to potential buyers with substantial money for a downpayment but incomes that are not high enough for the types of properties that they wish to purchase. By placing a portion of the downpayment money into an interest-bearing account with the lender rather than using the entire amount for a downpayment, the borrower can reduce the monthly out-of-pocket payment for a specified period of time. Because of the lower payment, the borrower is able to qualify for a larger loan initially. The out-of-pocket payments may increase at a specified rate for a specified period of time and then remain level at the amount that amortizes the loan over its life. The difference between the payment that amortizes the loan and the out of pocket payments are taken out of the pledged account. The balance in the pledged account will be zero when the out-of-pocket payment equals the amount that amortizes the loan.

Before, it is depleted down to zero, the pledged account serves as additional security for the loan. If the borrower defaults, the remaining balance in the account goes to the lender.

PAMs can be structured in different ways. The following example shows one possible structure of PAM.

EXAMPLE: Suppose a home buyer has $15,733.69 and wishes to buy a house at a price of $105,263.16, using a PAM. The closing costs amount to $3000. The buyer puts down $5263.16 (5 percent of $105,263.16), places $7,470.53 ($11,495.16 − $5263.16 − $3000) into a pledged account that earns 5.5 percent and gets a $100,000, 30-year loan at 12 percent.

The monthly payment that fully amortizes the $100,000 is $1028.61. However, let's assume that PAM allows an initial out-of-pocket monthly payment that grows to $1028.61 in 5 years at the rate of 5 percent per year. The initial out-of-pocket payment will be $805.94. This is the monthly out-of-pocket payment for the first year. It is equal to $1028.61/(1 + .05).[5] So in the first year, the lender will collect $805.94 from the borrower each month. The difference between $1028.61 and $805.94 (=$222.67) will be taken out from the pledged account.

In the second year, the out-of-pocket payment will be $846.24 (=$805.94 * 1.05) and the lender will take out $182.37 each month from the pledged account. The out-of-pocket payments by the borrower, the amounts taken out of the pledged account by the lender, and the amounts received by the lender will look like the figures in Table 24–1.

Now, suppose the buyer uses all his or her money except $3000 ($12,733.69 = $15,733.69 − 3,000) for closing costs to make a down-payment on the $105,263.16 house and gets a $92,529.47, 30-year loan at 12 percent. The monthly payment would be $951.77. Although this is

Table 24-1 Breakdown of Out-of-Pocket Payments for a Pledged Account Mortgage

Year	*Monthly Out-of-Pocket Payment*	*Monthly Amount from Pledged Account*	*Monthly Amount Received by Lender*
1	$ 805.94	$222.67	$1028.61
2	846.24	182.37	1028.61
3	888.55	140.06	1028.61
4	932.98	95.63	1028.61
5	979.63	48.98	1028.61
6–30	1028.61	0	1028.61

lower than $1028.61, it is higher than the monthly payments for the first five years with a PAM.

ADVANTAGES OF PAMS

A PAM benefits sellers of properties because they increase sales. More people are able to qualify. They are also appealing to borrowers with substantial cash now and incomes that are expected to rise in the future.

From the lender's point of view, the PAM results in larger loans. Moreover, the interest charged on the loan is higher than the interest paid on the pledged account.

DISADVANTAGES OF PAMS

If the borrower's income does not increase as expected, he or she may not be able to handle the payment increases in the first few years. This situation would not be good for the borrower or the lender.

Furthermore, because the interest rate on the pledged account is lower than the interest rate on the loan, the borrower has to deposit a relatively large amount into the pledged account at closing. If the interest rate on the pledged account in the PAM example had been 12 percent, the required deposit would have been only $1737.75 instead of $3232. The required deposit is simply the present value of the monthly amounts taken out of the pledged account, discounted at a monthly interest rate of 1 percent.

Financing Instruments and Techniques: Secondary Mortgage Market Programs

CHAPTER

25 Mortgage Pass-Through Securities

The issuance of the first Government National Mortgage Association (GNMA) mortgage pass-through securities in 1970 marked a major phase in the development of the secondary mortgage market. The pass-through securities contributed significantly to the liquidity of mortgage products. They also increased the flow of funds from other segments of the capital market to the mortgage industry.

DESCRIPTION

A mortgage pass-through is a security backed by a pool or group of mortgages. It represents undivided interest in a pool of mortgages. It is sold to an investor and in a typical situation, the originators of the mortgages collect the scheduled monthly payments of interest and principal and any prepayments from the mortgagors, deduct mortgage servicing and guarantee fees, and forward the remaining amounts to the investors (security holders) directly or through a conduit.

HOW THEY WORK

The way pass-through securities work depends on the type of pass-through. There are four major types of pass-throughs: Ginnie Mae (GNMA) pass-through, the Freddie Mac mortgage participation certificate (PC), the Fannie Mae mortgage-backed security (MBS) and the private pass-through.

Ginnie Mae Pass-Through

Ginnie Mae pass-through securities (GMNA) are issued, mainly by mortgage companies but they may also be issued by other FHA and VA approved lenders. Basically, the lender applies for a commitment from GNMA to guarantee securities backed by a pool of federally insured or guaranteed mortgages. If GNMA approves the application, it issues a commitment and the lenders send the appropriate mortgage documents to custodial agents. The lenders also send documents about the pool to GNMA for further review. If there are no problems with the pool, the lender issues certificates backed by the mortgages and GNMA guarantees them. After they are guaranteed by GNMA, the lenders sell the certificates to investors.

The minimum pool size for family mortgages is $1 million, and the pools could consist of FHA, VA, or Farmers Home Administration (FmHA) mortgages. Initially, mortgages were assembled into a pool only by one issuer of certificate and the mortgages included were of the same type, interest rate, and maturity. Moreover, the issuers of the certificates forwarded the scheduled payments (principal and interest) and prepayments to the investors directly. Some investors received multiple checks every month, if their certificates were backed by different pools of underlying mortgages.

In 1983, GNMA introduced the GNMA II program. This program allows different lenders to form one pool of underlying mortgages. In addition, the monthly payments collected by the servicers are forwarded to a central paying agent (Chemical Bank), and the central paying agent sends single monthly checks to each investor even if the investor owns several certificates backed by different pools of mortgages.

Ginnie Mae pass-throughs are fully modified pass-throughs. That means investors receive monthly payments of principal and interest, even if the servicer does not receive payments from the mortgagors. Ginnie Mae guarantees the timely payment of principal and interest. Since Ginnie Mae is part of the Department of Housing and Urban Development (HUD), the guarantee represents the full faith and credit of the U.S. government. For this reason, Ginnie Mae pass-throughs are high quality securities.

Ginnie Mae charges a small fee (currently .06 percent of the balance) for guaranteeing the certificates, and the servicers receive .44 percent of the remaining mortgage balance. Both the guarantee fee and the mortgage servicing fees are deducted from the interest portion of the monthly payments.

Given the guarantee and servicing fees of .5 percent, the stated certificate would be the rate on the underlying mortgages less the fees. The stated certificate rate is what the investors earn on their investments.

Freddie Mac Participation Certificates

Freddie Mac PCs were introduced in 1971. They are the main source of funds for Freddie Mac. The PCs are sold to security dealers through auctions held each business day. Freddie Mac announces the PC amounts, certificate rates, and other criteria and dealers submit competitive and noncompetitive bids. In the competitive bids, the dealers specify prices, whereas in the noncompetitive bids, the PCs are sold at the weighted average price of the accepted competitive bids.

Freddie Mac confirms accepted bids and on the settlement date, and it deposits the PCs at financial institutions specified by the dealers.

Freddie Mac PCs are backed by pools of conventional, FHA, and VA loans. For this purpose, Freddie Mac purchases whole loans and participation interests in loans with cash. Under the guarantor program, however, lenders sell conventional and seasoned FHA and VA loans to Freddie Mac in exchange for Freddie Mac's PCs.

As in Ginnie Mae pass-throughs, payments collected by servicers from mortgagors, less servicing fees, are forwarded to investors. Freddie Mac guarantees the timely payment of interest and the eventual payment of principal.

Fannie Mae Mortgage-Backed Securities

Fannie Mae (Federal National Mortgage Association) introduced its Mortgage-Backed Securities (MBSs) in 1981. The MBSs are backed by a pool of conventional or FHA/VA loans. Although the loans in each pool have to be of the same type, the interest rates on the loans can vary. The maximum range between the lowest and highest mortgage rates in a pool is 2 percent (200 basis points). The minimum pool size is $1 million.

As in GNMA II, servicers forward scheduled payments and prepayments, less servicing fees, to a central paying agent (Chemical Bank) and the central paying agent sends single monthly checks to investors. Fannie Mae guarantees the timely payment of interest and principal. In other words, Fannie Mae pass-throughs are fully modified pass-throughs.

Fannie Mae charges fees for the payment guarantees. The fees depend on the servicing option selected by servicers. Under the Regular Servicing Option, servicers are responsible for foreclosure losses, and the fee is lower than the fee under the Special Servicing Option in which servicers do not assume responsibility for foreclosure losses.

Private Pass-Throughs

Pass-throughs guaranteed by GNMA, Freddie Mac, and Fannie Mae are called agency pass-throughs. Other pass-throughs issued by banks, savings and loans, or conduits are called *private pass-throughs.* The first such pass-through was issued by Bank of America in 1977.

Private pass-throughs are also backed by pools of conventional mortgages. The pass-throughs may be placed privately or offered publicly. Public offerings require registration with the Securities and Exchange Commission and state securities bureaus.

The pools consist of conventional mortgages with sizes of $10 million or more. The pool mortgage insurance policies and possibly advances from the issuers ensure timely payment of interest and eventual payment of principal.

PREPAYMENT MODELS

Homeowners can and do prepay loans before the stated term of the loan ends. Such prepayments cause irregularities in cash flows to investors in mortgage pass-throughs. The investors receive not only the scheduled payments of interest and principal but also prepayments.

Loan prepayments may be caused by a variety of factors—declines in mortgage rates, job transfers (relocation), changes in family situation, unemployment, divorce, and a desire for a better home. Although some factors may be less important than others, all have some effect on prepayments. The extent of impact from these factors is not easy to predict, especially over a long period of time. Nonetheless, estimates of prepayments have to be made. Prepayments affect the cash flows and the lives of pass-throughs.

There are several prepayment models or approaches described in this section.

Twelve-Year Prepayment

The easiest way of dealing with prepayment is to assume that all the 30-year fixed-rate mortgages in a pool would be prepaid in the twelfth year. In this approach, there are level cash flows (consisting of scheduled payments) up to the twelfth year, and then the entire balance is assumed to be paid all at once. This is very much like a balloon mortgage. This is the basis for the calculation of what is called the *mortgage yield.*

For 15-year fixed rate mortgages (midgets), the number of years to prepayment is assumed to be 7 years.

FHA Experience

The assumption that all prepayments occur at one time, in the twelfth or seventh year, is not very realistic. A more realistic model is the FHA prepayment model. FHA developed survival probabilities for mortgages over a 30-year period. For example, if the FHA rate for year 5 is 79.771 percent, it means in year 5, 79.771 percent of the mortgages will still be outstanding. In year zero, 100 percent (that is, all) of the mortgages would be outstanding.

The prepayment rates can be estimated from those proportions. For example, if the proportion of mortgages outstanding is 79.771 percent in year 5 and 74.343 percent in year six, the prepayment rate for the sixth year would be 7 percent (1 − .74343/.79771). A pool with a prepayment rate of 7 percent in the sixth year would be described as a 100 percent FHA pool. If a pool prepays 1.5 times faster than an FHA pool, it would be a 150 percent FHA pool, and the prepayment rate in year 6 corresponding to that pool would be 10 percent. This is calculated as follows:

$$\text{Prepayment Rate} = [1 - (.74343/.79771)^{1.5}] = 0.10$$

Although the FHA model is the oldest, it is not suitable for pass-throughs backed by conventional mortgages that are, generally, not assumable.

Constant Prepayment Rate (CPR)

FHA prepayment rates vary from year to year, but in this model a constant prepayment rate is used each month. The rate is expressed as a percent and is applied to the outstanding balance of the pool. The prepayment rate is based on prepayment experience over the preceding months.

The Public Securities Association (PSA) Standard Prepayment Model

While the CPR model offers simplicity and may be better than the FHA model for securities backed by conventional mortgages, it is not realistic. Prepayment rates of mortgage pools tend to rise initially and then remain fairly stable. They do not remain constant throughout the life of the pass-through.

The PSA model reflects the rise in prepayment rates in the first few years. The rate for the first month is 0.2 percent (annualized) and increases by 0.2 percent per month until it reaches 6 percent in the 30th month and then remains level.

Prepayment rates for mortgage-backed securities can be expressed as multiples of PSA rates. If the prepayment rates are equal to those of the PSA model, the pool would be 100 percent PSA. The multiple would be greater than 100 percent if the pool prepays faster and less than 100 percent if the pool prepays more slowly.

Although this model seems better than the previous models, it is not likely to represent actual prepayments well.

Salomon Brothers Prepayment Model

Salomon Brothers has developed a statistical model for projecting prepayment rates based on interest rates, types and ages of loans, and seasonal factors. The model is based on the major determinants of mortgage prepayments, but even with this model it would be difficult to generate long-term projections.

MEASURES OF THE LIFE OF A MORTGAGE PASS-THROUGH

In the absence of prepayments, the actual life of a pass-through would be equal to the stated term of the mortgages included in the pool, assuming all the mortgages in the pool have the same term. With prepayments, the actual life of the security will be shorter. However, because it is difficult to estimate prepayments, it is difficult to determine the true life of the security in advance. In this section, measures related to the term of the security will be presented briefly.

1. Half Life. This is the time it takes the loan balance to fall to 50 percent of the original amount.
2. Weighted Average Life (WAL). This is the average number of

of years it takes to receive a dollar of principal. For example, if the principal repayments of a 3-year security are 20, 30, and 50 in the first, second, and third years, the weighted average life of the security would be 2.3 years. This is calculated as shown in Table 25–1.

The weighted average life is useful in estimating cash flow yield.

3. Duration (D). This is a measure of the average number of years it takes a dollar of cash flow (principal and interest) to be prepaid. Assuming a discount rate of 10 percent, and interest payments of 35, 25, and 5 for the first, second and third years respectively, the duration of the 3-year security given above would be 1.9367 years. This is calculated as shown in Table 25–2. Note that if the entire cash flow were received in the third year, the duration of the three-year security would have been 3.

PAYMENT DELAY

There is a stated payment delay with each pass-through security. The stated payment delays for Ginnie Mae pass-throughs, Fannie Mae mortgage-backed securities, Freddie Mac PCs, and private pass-throughs are 45 days, 55 days, 75 days, and 55 days, respectively.

When the pass-through is issued, the investor may have to wait for up to the stated payment delay to receive the first payment. For example, if a Ginnie Mae pass-through is issued on the first day of a particular month, the payment from the mortgagor (homeowner/borrower) would be due on the first day of the following month, and the payment to the investor would be due on the fifteenth of the same month (second month). Assuming a 30-day month, the total payment delay would be 45 days. Because the payments on mortgages

Table 25–1 Weighted Average Life Calculations

(1) Year	*(2) Principal Repayment (PR)*	*(3) PR/100*	*(4) = (1) * (3) Weighted PR*
1	20	.2	.2
2	30	.3	.6
3	50	.5	1.5
	100		WAL = 2.3

Table 25-2 Calculating Duration

(1) Year	*(2) I*	*(3) P*	*(4) = (2) + (3) Cash Flow*
1	35	20	55
2	25	30	55
3	5	50	55
			165
(5) DF @ 10 percent	***(6) PV of (4)***	***(7) (6)/136.78***	***(8) = (1) • (7)***
0.9091	50.00	0.3656	0.3656
0.8265	45.46	0.3324	0.6648
0.7513	41.32	0.3021	0.9063
	136.78	1.0000	D = 1.9367

I = Interest
P = Principal
DF = Discount factor
PV = Present value
D = Duration

are in arrears, the true delay is only 15 days, including the payment day.

Using the same example, the first payment to the investor in Fannie Mae MBSs would be due on the twenty-fifth of the second month and the payment delay would be 55 days. For investors in Freddie Mac PCs, the first payment to the investor would be made on the fifteenth of the third month.

PASS-THROUGH YIELDS

Three types of yields are used in the secondary mortgage market. They are the mortgage yield (quoted yield), the cash flow yield (Honest to God or simply HTG yield), and the bond-equivalent yield.

The mortgage yield is calculated on the assumption that there will be level payments for a specified period of time and prepayment at the end of that period. The period used is 12 years for 30-year mortgages and 7 years for 15-year mortgages. The calculation of the mortgage yield takes into account the stated payment delay and the mortgage servicing fee.

The model on which the mortgage yield is based is not realistic. In practice, prepayments occur in different years. A better measure of yield is the cash flow yield. This yield takes into account not only scheduled payments but also prepayments based on some prepayment model. It also takes into account payment delay and mortgage servicing fees.

The payment delay and servicing fees are included because longer delays and larger servicing fees reduce yields.

Pass-through securities provide monthly payments, and the cash flow yield is not comparable to the yield to maturity of a bond. The cash flow yield can be converted into a bond-equivalent yield as follows:

$$BEY = 2[(1 + CFY/1200)^6 - 1] * 100$$

where: BEY = annual bond equivalent yield in percentages
CFY = annual cash flow yield in percentages
CFY/1200 = monthly cash flow yield

PURCHASING PASS-THROUGHS

Investors can buy pass-through securities through securities dealers. The minimum denomination is $25,000. For small investors, there are mutual funds and unit trusts that specialize in Ginnie Mae securities. The minimum denomination is, usually, $1000.

ADVANTAGES OF PASS-THROUGH SECURITIES

There are a number of advantages of pass-throughs. First, pass-throughs attract funds to the primary mortgage lenders from other segments of the capital market. The increased availability of mortgage credit benefits homebuyers (homeowners).

Second, pass-throughs are high-quality securities that yield competitive returns. Payment guarantees and pool insurance ensure high quality.

Third, pass-throughs increase the liquidity of lending institutions like savings and loans. It is easier to sell pass-throughs than individual loans.

Fourth, pass-throughs offer diversification. There may be hundreds of mortgages in the pools that back them. The mortgages may also be from different geographical areas. This diversification may reduce prepayment risk.

Finally, depository institutions can use pass-through securities as collateral for CMOs, repurchase agreements, and advances from the Federal Home Loan Banks or the Federal Reserve Banks.

DISADVANTAGES OF PASS-THROUGHS

The main disadvantage of a pass-through security is the prepayment risk. Prepayments occur at different points during the life of the security and they are difficult to predict. Some investors are not comfortable with irregular and unpredictable cash flows and uncertain maturities of the securities they hold. In other words, they want "call protection." Prepayments are, essentially, calls.

In addition to the irregularity of cash flows caused by prepayments, investors face reinvestment risks. The principal repayments may have to be reinvested at lower rates. This is particularly true when mortgage rates decline and homeowners refinance.

Because pass-throughs pay monthly, processing expenses are high relative to securities (bonds, for example) that generate less frequent cash flows.

Finally, holders of pass-throughs face some market and liquidity risks. As interest rates rise the prices of the securities decline and investors could experience losses on sale.

CHAPTER 26 COLLATERALIZED MORTGAGE OBLIGATIONS AND REMICS

For reasons that were presented in the previous chapter, pass-through securities have attracted investors that were not traditional investors in mortgages. Examples are pension funds and mutual funds. However, the appeal that pass-throughs have to such investors is limited by the prepayment risks and the resulting uncertainties of cash flows and maturities.

Collateralized mortgage obligations (CMOs) were introduced to reduce the prepayment risks. Real estate mortgage investment conduit (REMIC) securities represent a further development in mortgage-backed securities.

DESCRIPTION

CMOs are mortgage-backed securities or bonds with different maturity classes or *tranches*. All or most of the classes pay interest, but all principal payments including prepayments are paid to holders of bonds with the shortest maturity class first. When the bonds in that class are paid off, all the principal payments are paid to holders of bonds with the second shortest maturity class, and so on.

HOW THEY WORK

CMOs were first introduced by Freddie Mac in 1983. Subsequently, investment banks, savings and loans associations, and home-builders started to issue CMOs.

Issuers use pass-through securities or pools of mortgages as collateral for CMOs. Pass-through securities are the most widely used collateral. The value of the collateral is larger than the amount of the debt. If the collateral value is 1.4 times larger than the debt, it is called 140 percent over-collateralization. The overcollateralization increases the quality of the CMO.

Although the number of maturity classes in a CMO varies among the various CMOs, the most common number of classes is four. Investors and issuers use letters to identify the maturity classes. For a CMO with four classes, the bonds are called A bonds, B bonds, C bonds, and D bonds. The A bonds are the bonds with the shortest maturity, and the D bonds are the bonds with the longest maturity.

Sometimes, one or more classes of bonds may be accrual or Z bonds. In a typical case, the last maturity class consists of Z bonds. The interest that accrues on those bonds is used to increase the principal balance on a coupon date. The principal balance increases, but the interest on the Z bonds is, actually, used to retire bonds in the preceding classes until all the bonds in the preceding classes are retired. Thereafter, holders of the accrual bonds receive both interest and principal payments.

Each class has its own coupon rate, which may be the same for all the classes or may increase with the stated maturity of the class. In addition, each class has a stated maturity, projected maturity, and a weighted average life. Its duration can also be computed. The stated maturity is generally determined on the assumption that there will be no prepayments. The projected maturity is determined on the assumption that there will be prepayments. The prepayments are estimated on the basis of the Public Security Association (PSA) prepayment rates or multiples of those rates. The weighted average life and duration were explained in the preceding chapter.

Payments from the mortgagors are received monthly, but payments to CMO holders are made quarterly or semiannually. The funds are invested until the payments are made to the CMO holders.

The funds from the underlying collateral are first used to pay interest to holders of nonaccrual or non-Z bonds. The rest of the funds is used to retire the bonds sequentially.

Suppose there are four maturity classes: A, B, C, and Z. Initially, only the holders of A, B, and C bonds receive interest. Holders of Z bonds do not receive interest until bonds A, B, and C are retired. However, the principal balances of the Z bonds are increased on each coupon date.

The interest that would have been paid to the fourth class of bonds if they had not been Z bonds, the principal payments, and all prepayments are paid to holders of A bonds. Only holders of A bonds receive principal. When the A bonds are retired, interest is paid to holders of B and C bonds and all principal payments, including prepayments, are paid to holders of B bonds. This payment system continues through the remaining classes. When A, B, and C are retired, holders of Z bonds start to receive payments.

CMOs can be purchased from security dealers. Minimum investments vary from $1000 to $25,000.

CMO Equity

Sometimes, the funds that are available for payments to the CMO holders may exceed the required payments. In such a situation, the issuer will accumulate equity and this equity may be sold to other investors.

The equity may be due to actual reinvestment earnings that are higher than assumed reinvestment earnings. Payments that are received from mortgagors monthly are invested temporarily until the payments to the CMO holders are due. If the interest rate on those payments exceeds the reinvestment rate that was assumed at the time the CMO was issued, the issuer will have excess funds. Additional funds may be generated if the coupon rates on the underlying mortgages exceed the coupon rates on the CMOs.

CMOs are liabilities of the issuer. The issuer still owns the underlying mortgages or pass-throughs. They are used as collateral for the CMOs. With pass-throughs, the investors own the underlying mortgages, not the issuer, and the pass-through securities are not liabilities of the issuer.

Real Estate Mortgage Investment Conduit Securities

The Tax Reform Act of 1986 introduced a new conduit called the Real Estate Mortgage Investment Conduit (REMIC). The act allowed the issuance of REMIC securities effective January 1, 1987. This legislation allows issuers of mortgage-backed securities to get around the obstacles that limited the spread of CMOs. Issuers can elect to be treated as REMICs.

With REMICs, an issuer does not need to set up a subsidiary to issue a mortgage-backed security with multiple maturity classes. The issues may be considered sales or debt. The payments can be made monthly like pass-throughs, quarterly or semiannually, and overcollateralization is not required. REMIC securities can also be structured to have junior and senior classes and they may be backed by residential or commercial mortgages. Thus, REMIC securities provide greater flexibility to the issuers and increase the appeal of mortgage-backed securities to investors.

ADVANTAGES OF A CMO

The main advantage of CMOs is the protection against calls. They reduce the risks of prepayments through the multiclass structure and the payments of principal to only holders of one class of bonds at a time. The protection is greater for holders of C and Z bonds.

The multiclass structure with different maturities of bonds also appeals to different types of investors. For example, savings and loans and banks prefer to invest in the short maturity classes, while life insurance companies and pension funds prefer the classes with the longest maturities.

CMOs are also of high quality, because they are backed by high-quality pass-throughs or by insured pools of mortgages. There is also overcollateralization.

Because of the call protection, investors are willing to accept lower yields on CMOs relative to pass-throughs. The yields are still competitive to those of other securities. As a result, issuers are able to lower costs of their funds by issuing CMOs rather than pass-throughs. Furthermore, the CMOs allow mortgage lenders to raise funds without selling their mortgages at losses. The CMOs have the added benefit of lengthening the average maturities of the liabilities of mortgage lenders—especially savings and loans. Since CMOs are not deposits, they are not subject to reserve requirements.

Finally, CMOs increase the flow of savings into the mortgage business and may help in lowering mortgage rates for homebuyers.

DISADVANTAGES OF A CMO

First, although CMOs reduce prepayment risk, they do not eliminate it. So, investors still face some degree of cash flow and maturity uncertainty.

Second, since payments from mortgagors are received monthly and payments to investors are made quarterly or semiannually, there is some reinvestment risk.

Third, overcollateralization is required for higher quality rating.

CHAPTER

27 DISCOUNT MORTGAGES

In times of high mortgages rates, sellers of real properties may use seller-financed techniques to sell their properties. Examples of seller-financed techniques were given in previous chapters. They include land contracts, purchase money mortgages, and second mortgages.

Sometimes, a seller needs the money for other purposes before the term of the loan ends. In such a situation, the seller can sell the mortgage to an investor. There are many investors who would be willing to buy the mortgage.

DESCRIPTION

A *discount mortgage* is a mortgage loan that is sold at a price that is lower than the outstanding mortgage balance of the loan. When the price of the loan is smaller than the balance, the yield on the loan will be higher than the coupon rate or note rate on the loan.

HOW THEY WORK

A lender who wants to sell a mortgage loan can sell it directly to investors through loan brokers. It is fairly easy to find loan brokers who can arrange the sale of the loan. Loan brokers advertise in newspapers.

Investors who buy mortgages generally require relatively high yields. For this reason, they offer to buy mortgages at substantial discount. For example, if the balance of the loan is $25,000, the investors may offer to buy the loan at $17,000. The difference of $8,000 would be the discount.

In order to determine the price of the loan, the investor specifies a required yield first. Once the yield is established, the investor needs to know the remaining number of payments, the monthly payment and the balloon payment, if any. The price is then calculated as the present value of the monthly payments and the balloon payment, if any, discounted to the present at the investor's yield. Obviously, the price has to be acceptable to the seller also for the transaction to take place.

A computer program for calculating the price of a mortgage in the secondary mortgage market is included in the appendix.

Example: Consider a 10-year, $20,000 balloon loan with a 30-year amortization. The monthly payment is $205.72 and the remaining term of the loan is 72 months. The current balance is $19,649.65. The balance of the loan at the end of the 10-year period will be $18,683.60. If the investor's annual required yield is 16 percent, the corresponding price would be $16,683.09.

Needless to say, the investor should perform careful analysis of the mortgagor (borrower) and the property before purchasing the mortgage. The mortgagor/owner of the property should have good credit, adequate income, and substantial equity in the house. To determine equity in the property, an appraisal should be made, and the property's appraised value should be much higher than the existing loan balance.

The investor should require title insurance and hazard insurance. The legal documents such as the note and the mortgage should be carefully examined. Finally, the investor should be familiar with state foreclosure laws.

ADVANTAGES OF DISCOUNT MORTGAGES

First, the yield on discount mortgages is relatively high. Second, a discount mortgage can be fairly safe. Moreover, the investor can reduce risk further through diversification. He can invest small amounts in several mortgages rather than invest a big amount in one or two mortgages. Third, geographical diversification is also possible. The investor can buy mortgages in any state, although this is not advisable. There could be major complications if some of the out-of-state properties have to be foreclosed upon.

DISADVANTAGES OF DISCOUNT MORTGAGES

First, the borrower can default, which complicates the investment for the investor. Second, the seller may have to accept a substantial discount, especially if he or she needs to sell the mortgage quickly.

Financing Instruments and Techniques: Commercial Properties

CHAPTER

28 Land Development Loans

Some investors buy land as an investment. They plan to hold the land for some years and then sell it. Because raw land does not generate current income but property taxes have to be paid on it annually, the investor will experience negative cash flow during the holding period. If the gain from the sale of the land is large enough, however, the investor's rate of return could be good.

Other investors buy land to develop it with buildings. Developers buy land for this purpose, and they generally borrow money to buy the land and develop it. This chapter deals with such land development loans.

DESCRIPTION

A *land development loan* is a loan for purchasing land and developing it. The developer uses the loan in conjunction with his or her own funds to buy land, remove trees, build streets, add utilities, and the like. The lots are subdivided and sold to builders.

HOW THEY WORK

The developer could borrow money from a bank to buy land and develop it. In some cases, the developer may buy land by giving the seller a purchase money mortgage and then borrow more money from a bank or another lender to develop the land. In a situation like this, the bank requires the purchase money mortgage to be subordinated to the land development loan. The seller may agree to the subordination of the purchase money mortgage. This is generally done by inserting a clause to that effect in the purchase money mortgage at the time of purchase of the land.

The bank does not pay the developer the entire amount of the loan at the time it is approved. The proceeds of the loan are disbursed in stages. The lender will make the payments only when specified percentages of work are completed. By making payments in stages, the lender makes sure that the loan proceeds disbursed will not exceed the lender's loan to value ratio.

The land development loan is not repaid at one time. It is repaid as completed lots are sold. As a lot is sold, the developer pays the lender an amount equal to the release price. With the payment of the release price, the lender releases the lot and the buyer gets clear title to the lot.

The release price is, usually, 10 percent to 20 percent more than the amount of the loan (including accrued interest) per lot. The 10 percent to 20 percent is a safety margin. Because the lender receives more than the loan amount plus interest per lot, the loan can be repaid before all the lots are sold. Toward the end of this process, all the sales proceeds go to the developer. The return to the developer depends partly on the difference between the price at which the lot is sold and the release price.

The interest rate on the loan could be fixed or floating. If it floats, it is usually indexed to the prime rate. For example, a loan may be prime plus 2 percent. The term of the loan is short—up to 3 years. If the developer experiences difficulties in selling the lots, it may take longer to repay the loan.

Before a lender makes a loan commitment, the lender evaluates the developer and the proposed land development very carefully. The lender examines the financial condition, experience and track record of the developer. Experience and good track records indicate a strong likelihood that the developer will complete the development on time and with reasonable departures from original estimates of costs and plans.

Often the developer has to guarantee a land development loan. In addition, lenders may require that the developer make a substantial downpayment. This is especially true if the developer is not well-known and the proposed development does not look very attractive. In this case, the financial strength of the developer will be an important factor in the evaluation of the loan. The developer has to submit financial statements that show net income and net worth (assets – liabilities).

The lender also evaluates the proposed development very

closely. For this purpose, the lender requires appraisal reports, market analyses, surveys, site plans, photographs, soil tests, cost estimates, and permits or approvals for the proposed development from government units.

If the developer is experienced, has good track records, and is strong financially, and if the development project looks attractive, the lender makes a commitment for the loan. The loan commitment specifies the terms and conditions of the loan. Specifically, it contains the loan amount, the interest rate and how it will be determined, the term of the loan, the disbursement and repayment procedures, conditions (such as title insurance policy payment and completion bonds), evidence of proper zoning and permits, evidence of payment of property taxes, payment of commitment fee, and the date for commencing development work.

The lender usually requires a continuous title search during the development period to make sure that no liens are filed on the property. Other liens would endanger the seniority of the loan.

ADVANTAGES OF LAND DEVELOPMENT LOANS

The land development loan offers some benefits to the lender. First, the land development loan is a relatively short-term loan. The lender's funds are not usually tied up for years and years. Second, the yield on a land development loan is high because it is very risky. Third, if the interest rate on the loan is indexed to the prime-rate, the lender's yield tends to reflect current money market conditions.

From the borrower's point of view, the loan provides leverage. In many cases, the loan also makes land development possible. In addition, the fact that repayment of the loan (and maybe accrued interest) is linked to sales of lots makes the repayment of the loan convenient for the borrower.

DISADVANTAGES OF LAND DEVELOPMENT LOANS

From the lender's point of view, even after careful evaluation of the developer and the project, there is risk that the development work may not be completed or that there may be considerable delays in completion. However, this risk may be reduced by requiring payment and completion bonds. If the developer is unable to pay for labor and materials, the bonding company would make the payments and complete the development work. The bonding company may not be able to prevent delays caused by natural factors, supply problems or labor problems.

Even if the project is completed, the developer may have difficulties selling the lots. Economic conditions may have changed. There may also be zoning changes. Because the repayment of the loan depends on lot sales, any delays in sales could delay repayment of the loan.

Delays in completion, cost increases, and difficulties in selling the lots are also major risks for the borrower.

CHAPTER 29 CONSTRUCTION LOANS

The preceding chapter discussed land development loans. Once the land is developed, developers/builders can construct detached single-family homes, townhouses, condominiums, apartment buildings, office buildings, shopping centers, warehouses, hotels, or other structures. This chapter deals with the financing of construction activity, that is, construction loans.

DESCRIPTION

Construction loans are loans for financing the construction of residential, commercial, industrial, or agricultural buildings. The loans are relatively short-term. They are repaid when the construction of the buildings is completed.

HOW THEY WORK

A developer/builder can finance construction by obtaining a line of credit from a bank if the loan amount needed is relatively small and if the developer/builder has a very high credit standing. Generally, however, a construction mortgage is required for financing construction activity. The loan becomes a first lien on the property.

The construction loan is repaid with proceeds from a permanent loan at completion. The same lender could make both the construction loan and the permanent loan. More typically, however, a construction loan is made by one lender and a permanent loan by another lender.

Banks, savings and loans, and mortgage companies make construction loans. These institutions are close to the site of the construction activity and they are in a better position to evaluate the proposed construction and the progress made during the construction phase. Life insurance companies make permanent loans. Banks and savings and loans could also make permanent loans.

Loan Commitments

Because the construction loan is repaid with proceeds from a permanent loan, a construction (interim) lender requires that the borrower get a commitment for a permanent loan from another lender. This way, the construction lender would be assured that the construction loan will be repaid at completion.

The developer/builder applies for a permanent loan, and if the developer/builder is strong financially and has a good track record and the proposed construction looks good, the permanent lender makes a commitment for a permanent loan. This is called a *take-out commitment.* The funding will take place at some point in the future, so the commitment is a forward rather than an immediate commitment. If this commitment is a firm commitment, the permanent lender is expected to pay off the construction loan. On the other hand, if the commitment is a standby commitment, the permanent lender takes over the construction mortgage only if the borrower cannot find another permanent lender. The standby commitment allows the borrower to get a construction loan and look for another permanent lender with better terms. However, because a standby commitment is not a strong commitment, some construction lenders may not accept it. The permanent lender may find reasons not to honor it.

A take-out commitment from a permanent lender is a conditional commitment. In other words, the lender agrees to make the loan only if the permanent lender's conditions are met. The conditions may be that construction be completed on time and according to the approved plans and specifications, that there is a minimum percent of the funds lease-up, or other terms. The permanent lender may specify a floor loan amount to apply if the lease-up does not reach the required minimum level. The floor amount is less than the amount that would be loaned out if all the conditions are met.

Gap (or Bridge) Financing

Suppose the construction loan is $20 million, but the floor amount is $15 million. The builder has to find a temporary loan to finance the gap of $5 million. The builder could use his or her own funds or get a junior (second) mortgage loan until the required minimum lease-up is reached. This type of financing is called *gap* or *bridge financing.*

Buy-Sell Agreements

A *buy-sell agreement* is a three-way agreement among the borrower, the construction lender, and the permanent lender. The permanent lender agrees to provide the permanent loan at completion of the project, and the borrower and the construction lender agree not to find another permanent lender. This way, the permanent lender is assured that the borrower will not forfeit the commitment fee and find another lender with lower interest rates at the time of completion of the construction.

Applying for a Construction Loan

Once the commitment for a permanent loan is obtained, the builder can apply for an interim or construction loan. The construction lender carefully evaluates the builder and the proposed construction of the buildings. For this reason, the lender will require financial statements from the borrower, market studies, plans and specifications, cost estimates, surveys, soil tests, appraisal reports, and permits and approvals from government units. The construction lender may also require payment and completion bonds.

Once the loan is approved, a loan commitment is issued and must be accepted within a defined period of time. The loan commitment spells out the terms and conditions of the loan. If the loan commitment is accepted, a formal construction loan agreement is signed by the borrower and lender. The agreement contains the terms of the loans and the duties of each party.

Disbursement of the Loan

The lender disburses the loan in stages. At each stage, advances are made only if the builder is making progress satisfactory to the lender. The lender requires progress reports and inspections are made during the construction phase to make sure that construction is proceeding according to plans and specifications.

In addition to inspection and reports, the lender also requires title examination before each advance is made to make sure that no other liens are filed on the property. If the builder fails to pay subcontractors or suppliers of materials, they can file liens on the property. To reduce this risk, the lender may:

1. require proof of payments to subcontractors and suppliers of materials.

2. pay subcontractors and suppliers directly or through title companies.
3. require the builder to get a waiver from the subcontractors and suppliers. In this case, the subcontractors and suppliers waive their rights to file liens on the property.

The lender may also hold back 10 percent to 15 percent of the advances for unforeseen contingencies until the construction is completed. As mentioned earlier, payment bonds may also be required.

ADVANTAGES OF CONSTRUCTION LOANS

First, the construction loan is a relatively short-term loan, usually for less than three years. For this reason, the lender's money is not tied up for a long period of time.

Second, the yield on a construction loan is relatively high. The yield is high because the loan is very risky.

Third, the interest rate is usually indexed to the prime rate. As a result, the lender's yield reflects current money market conditions.

Fourth, the loan commitment from the permanent lender assures the construction lender that the loan will be repaid at completion.

For the borrower, the loan provides leverage. Also, without the loan, construction may not take place.

DISADVANTAGES OF CONSTRUCTION LOANS

A construction loan is a very risky loan. First, despite careful evaluation of the builder and of the project, the construction of the buildings may not be completed. However, this risk may be reduced by requiring completion bonds. If the builder is unable to complete the project, the bonding company completes it.

Second, there may be considerable delays in completing the construction project, even if it is eventually completed. The delays may be caused by natural forces such as adverse weather conditions or supply and labor problems.

Third, changes in economic and environmental factors could make the completed projects less desirable.

Fourth, there is the risk that the permanent lender will not make the permanent loan because of changes in plans and specifications or because other requirements are not met. It is important that the builder and construction lender try to meet the permanent lender's conditions.

CHAPTER 30 LEASE FINANCING

A *lease* is a contract between the owner of the property (lessor) and a tenant (lessee). In exchange for periodic lease payments, the lessor agrees to let the lessee occupy and use the property.

Leases may be classified according to the type of property leased. If the property is land, the lease is called a *ground lease;* if the property is a commercial property, such as an office building or a shopping center, it is called a *commercial lease;* and if the property is a residential property, it is called a *residential lease.*

The leases can also be classified according to the method of payment. A *gross* or *flat lease* is a lease in which the lessee pays a flat amount and the lessor pays expenses such as property taxes and insurance. In a *net lease,* the lessee pays the property taxes, insurance, maintenance, and utilities and pays a net amount to the lessor. Finally, in a *percentage lease,* the lessee pays a flat amount plus some amount that is indexed to sales or net income of the lessee. In long-term leases covering a period of 20 years or more, there may be provisions for periodic evaluations of the lease payments.

Given the definitions of basic leasing terms, the rest of the chapter will deal with sale-leasebacks and ground leasing.

DESCRIPTION

A sale-leaseback is a transaction in which an owner of a property sells the property and then leases it back from the purchaser. The property can be land or buildings or both. If the property is land and the seller/lessee erects buildings on it, it is called a ground lease. In a ground lease, the lessee could also lease land from an owner who owned the land for years. In other words, a ground lease may not involve a sale-leaseback.

HOW THEY WORK

In a sale-leaseback, a property owner sells the property and leases back the property. The lease is, generally, a long-term lease and it could involve land, buildings, or both. The interest of the buyer/lessor in the leased property is called the *underlying fee* or *leased fee*, and the interest of the seller/lessee is called a *leasehold*. The sale-leaseback benefits both parties. The benefits are discussed later.

In a ground lease, a landowner leases land to a developer/builder for a long period of time (30 or more years), and the developer/builder constructs buildings or other structures on the land. If the builder leases the building, the lease is called a *space lease*.

In order to construct buildings on the land, the developer/builder borrows money from a lending institution and pledges the land and improvements (buildings) as collateral. Because lenders require that long-term ground leases be subordinated to the loans they make, the developer/builder should have a ground lease that allows the subordination of the ground lease to the construction loans. This should be done at the time the ground lease is signed.

The lessor generally allows subordination of the lease to the loan. As a measure of protection, however, the lessor may demand the right to make the mortgage payments to the lender in the event the borrower is not able to make the payments.

Without this right to step in an make the payments, the lessor could lose the land. In a *subordinated ground lease*, both the land and buildings are used as collateral and if the borrower defaults, the lender forecloses upon the property and the lease is canceled.

Obviously, a lessee that allows subordination of a lease to a loan is assuming a relatively high risk. This risk can be eliminated by requiring a *lease insurance policy*. With a lease insurance policy, the insurance company makes the payments in the event the lessee is not able to do so. The lessee should also reduce the risk by evaluating the lessor very carefully. The lessor can also require higher lease payments in exchange for the subordination of the ground lease to the loan.

ADVANTAGES OF LEASE FINANCING

Leases offer advantages to lessors and lessees. The advantages to the lessee are the following:

1. The lease frees funds, which can be used for other purposes. Little or no money is tied up in the leased property.
2. Because of the lease, the lessee does not have to borrow money to buy the land. As a result, the debt/equity ratio of the lessee will be lower than it would have been with a leveraged purchase of land.
3. The closing costs associated with leases are smaller than those associated with purchases.
4. Lease payments are usually tax deductible. For owners, land is not depreciable.
5. In areas where the value of land is very high, it may be cheaper to lease land rather than buy it.

Leases also offer benefits to lessors. First, the lessors receive stable income. They can rely on the income, especially if the lessee is of high credit standing or the lease is backed by lease insurance. Second, lessors are able to postpone income taxes on the gains from land by leasing the land. With a sale, substantial income tax may have to be paid. Finally, after the lease period, the lessor may keep the improvements.

DISADVANTAGES OF LEASE FINANCING

For the lessee, the main disadvantage of lease financing is that the lessee will not own the building at the end of the lease period. To continue the occupancy, the lease must be renewed and the lessee must continue making lease payments. Furthermore, the lessee cannot depreciate the building, although the lease payments are deductible.

From the point of view of the lessor, the fact that a lease involves very little downpayment increases the chance that the lessee will walk away from the lease. Also, if the lessee declares bankruptcy, the amount of payments the lessor can receive is very limited.

CHAPTER 31 REAL ESTATE LIMITED PARTNERSHIPS

Real estate syndications may take the form of corporations or partnerships. In the corporate form, they are entities different or separate from those who own it—the stockholders. The corporation raises funds by selling shares to investors and uses the proceeds to buy real estate. The stockholders enjoy limited liability but they face double taxation.

Because of the double taxation, the partnership form has been the most widely used vehicle for real estate syndications. This chapter deals with real estate limited partnerships.

DESCRIPTION

A real estate partnership exists when one or more people raise money to invest in real estate for profit. If all the partners have management responsibilities, it is called a *general partnership.* If some of the partners do not have a say in the management and control of the partnership, the partnership is called a *limited partnership.* The partners with management responsibility are called the *general partners* and those without it are called the *limited partners.*

HOW THEY WORK

An individual with experience and expertise in the real estate field but with limited funds organizes a limited partnership and offers interests in the partnership to investors. Since the minimum investments are relatively small (usually $5000), the interests can be sold to a large number of small and large investors. This way the partnership is able to raise large amounts of capital.

SEC Registration

Before a partnership starts selling interests, it may have to file a registration statement with the Securities and Exchange Commission (SEC). An interest in a limited partnership is considered a security and if the interests are offered to the public, the partnership may have to register the security with the SEC. The registration is intended to ensure that issuers of securities make full disclosures and to prevent fraud, but the SEC does not approve or disapprove the investment merits of the security.

Once the registration is effective, any offer of sale of the security has to be accompanied by a prospectus. The prospectus is part of the registration statement filed with the SEC and provides detailed information about the offering.

The security may have to be registered with state securities bureaus also. States have blue sky laws that govern the sale of securities within their jurisdictions.

The broker/dealers and the agents that sell the securities should also be licensed.

Exemption from SEC Registration

Sales of real estate partnership interests may be exempt from registration with the SEC if they represent intrastate offerings or are privately placed.

In an intrastate offering, a domestic partnership sells interests only to residents of the state in which the partnership is located. A *domestic partnership* is defined as a partnership in which 80 percent of its assets are located in the state in which it sells the interests and 80 percent of its revenues are generated within the state.

In a private placement, the partnership cannot sell interests to more than 35 accredited investors. Accredited investors are wealthy or high-income individuals. Investors who do not meet minimum net worth, income, or investment requirements are called nonaccredited investors.

The Certificate of Limited Partnership and the Partnership Agreement

The partnership should also file the certificate of limited partnership with the appropriate state agency. Among other things, this document includes the purpose of the partnership, the duration of the partnership, list of partners, investments by partners, and sharing of profits and losses.

It is important that this certificate be filed. If it is not, the limited partners may not have limited liability.

The partnership agreement provides a detailed explanation of the purpose of the partnership, how the partnership will raise capital, the allocations of profits and losses, rights and duties of the general partners, transferability of limited partners' interests, books and accounting of the partnership, and dissolution of the partnership.

Types of Limited Partnerships

In some cases, the properties that the partnership plans to purchase are known in advance and investors can, if they choose, inspect the properties before they invest in the partnership. In addition, financial information about the properties may be available for evaluating the economic soundness of the investments.

In other cases, the properties that the partnerships will be buying are not known in advance. The partnerships raise funds and then identify suitable properties and purchase them. These types of partnerships are called blind pools.

Since the properties are not known in advance, stricter requirements apply to blind pools. For example, there are minimum experience requirements for general partners, and the partnership has to publish and distribute periodic reports to the partners.

Operation of a Limited Partnership

The general partners raise capital by selling partnership interests to investors who become limited partners in the partnership. The general partners then borrow money and use the loan proceeds and the funds received from the limited partners to buy real properties such as apartment and office buildings, shopping centers, and hotels and motels.

They manage the properties for a limited period of time and sell them. During the holding period, operating profits or losses are distributed to the limited partners. The general partners may also share in the profits.

When the property is sold, the profits or losses are allocated among the limited partners and the general partners. The limited partners may receive 85 percent of the profits, and the general partners may get the rest of the profits.

In addition to sharing in the profits from operations and sale, the general partners may receive brokerage fees for buying or selling properties, management fees, and insurance commissions.

Purchases of limited partnership interests are subject to loads or commissions. The loads are, typically, 8 percent of the investment.

Tax Aspects of Limited Partnerships

A limited partnership is not a taxable entity. The profits are distributed to the partners and the partners report their partnership income as part of their incomes from other sources. If the partnership is treated as a corporation for tax purposes, the partnership cannot pass the profits and losses to the partners.

A partnership may be treated as a corporation for tax purposes if it possesses at least three of the following features:

- continuity of life
- centralized management
- limited liability
- free transferability of interests

ADVANTAGES OF LIMITED PARTNERSHIPS

The advantages to the limited partners are:

1. Limited liability. If the partnership fails, the limited partners lose only their investments in the partnership. For this feature to exist, the certificate of limited partnership has to be filed with the state, and the limited partners should not participate in the management and control of the partnership.
2. Small minimum investment requirement. With small investments of $5000 (possibly less), investors are able to acquire interests in large multimillion dollar buildings.
3. Diversification. If the partnership invests in different types of real estate (residential, commercial, and so on) and in different parts of the country, investors benefit from product and geographical diversification.
4. Professional management. Limited partners do not have to worry about identifying good properties, buying them, managing them, and finally selling them.

The general partners also benefit from the partnership. First, they receive a variety of fees. Second, they are able to raise large amounts of capital to buy large properties.

DISADVANTAGES OF LIMITED PARTNERSHIPS

There are major drawbacks to investing in real estate limited partnerships. First, a partnership's interests are highly illiquid. They are difficult to sell. Where it is possible to sell interests, they have to be sold at big discounts. The partnership interests can be sold to the general partners of the partnership or to investment companies. They can also be sold through securities brokers. In 1984, the National Partnership Exchange was established in St. Petersburg, Florida. It handles the sale of partnership interests in approved public partnerships through a computer network of brokers who are members of the Exchange. National Association of Securities Dealers (NASD) broker/dealers and registered representatives can become members of the exchange.

The development of master limited partnerships has also contributed to greater liquidity of partnership interests. Their shares are freely traded on a major exchange.

Second, the variety of fees and size of fees may discourage some investors.

Third, projections of rental incomes could be overstated and/or projections of costs could be understated. It is not easy to make projections for several years into the future.

Fourth, changes in taxlaws, can affect limited partnerships adversely. The Tax Reform Act of 1986 limited the attractiveness of limited partnerships severely.

III Comparative Analyses of Selected Mortgage Instruments

CHAPTER

32 FIFTEEN-YEAR VERSUS THIRTY-YEAR FIXED RATE MORTGAGES

Many lending institutions today offer 15-year (midgets) and 30-year fixed-rate mortgages. Some lenders are also offering 10-year mortgages. This chapter compares the first two types of fixed-rate mortgages.

FACTORS TO CONSIDER

The comparative analysis takes into account the interest rate of the mortgages, the sizes of the monthly payments, the tax savings, the interest rate on savings, and the speed of amortization.

In a 15-year mortgage, the lender's funds are tied up for a shorter period of time, and the risks associated with changes in market interest rates are smaller. For this reason, interest rates on 15-year mortgages tend to be .25 percent to .50 percent lower than those on 30-year mortgages.

The number of points on a 15-year and 30-year mortgage are generally the same, but they may be different.

Given the same loan amount, the monthly payment of a 15-year mortgage is higher than that of a 30-year mortgage, even if there is a difference of .50 percent in the mortgage rates. At very high interest rates—such as 60 percent—this statement would not be true. The monthly payments would be approximately the same. However, such mortgage rates do not apply in today's markets. So, we can safely assume that the 30-year mortgage offers lower payments, although the difference diminishes as mortgage rates rise. And of course, the borrower pays more over the course of a 30-year mortgage for the same property.

The interest deduction generated by a 30-year mortgage is greater than the interest deduction generated by a 15-year mortgage. Thus, the 30-year mortgage generates greater tax savings. The higher the marginal tax rate of the borrower, the greater the tax savings will be.

The 30-year mortgage generates payment and tax savings that can be invested. The higher the interest rate on the savings, the more attractive the 30-year mortgage becomes.

The 15-year mortgage amortizes faster than the 30-year mortgage. In other words, the mortgage balance of a 15-year mortgage declines faster than that of the 30-year mortgage. As a result, the homeowner's equity builds up faster. So, if the homeowner sells the property before the loan is paid off, the pay-off balance of the 15-year mortgage will be lower. This is a major benefit of the 15-year mortgage.

To summarize the main points, the 30-year mortgages offers lower payments on an after-tax basis and the 15-year mortgages offer faster equity buildup. Without complete analysis, it is difficult to tell which mortgage is better for the borrower. Often, choosing the better mortgage length also depends on how long the borrower wishes to stay in the same house.

ANALYSIS

The following example will be used to show a procedure for evaluating 15-year and 30-year fixed-rate mortgages. The procedure takes into account all the factors that were discussed in the previous section.

Consider the data in Table 32–1.

Table 32–1 Comparing 15-Year and 30-Year Mortgages

Factor	*15-Year Mortgage*	*30-Year Mortgage*
Mortgage Rate (%)	8.25	8.75
Number of Points	3.75	2.75
Loan Amount	$100,000	$100,000
Marginal Tax Rate (%)	28	28
Interest Rate on Savings (%)	8.25	8.25

The results of the calculations are shown in Tables 32–2 through 32–5. The tables are self-explanatory.

The after-tax monthly interest rate on savings of 0.495 percent (1 – .28)(.0825)/12) is used as a discount rate in calculating the present values of the after-tax payment savings and the differences between the mortgage balances.

Column 15 of Table 32–5 shows the after-tax cumulative savings of the 30-year mortgage. Column 16 of that table shows the excess equity buildup associated with the 15-year mortgage. Since the benefit of the excess equity buildup of the 15-year mortgage exceeds the after-tax savings of the 30-year mortgage during the entire 15-year period, the 15-year mortgage would be better for the borrower.

TABLE 32–2 Comparing Interest Payments for 15-Year and 30-Year Mortgages

Month	*(1) Mortgage Payment 15-Year*	*(2) Mortgage Payment 30-Year*	*(3) = (1) – (2) Payment Difference*	*(4) Interest Paid 30-Year*	*(5) Interest Paid 15-Year*
1	970.14	786.70	183.44	729.17	687.50
2	970.14	786.70	183.44	728.75	685.56
3	970.14	786.70	183.44	728.32	683.60
4	970.14	786.70	183.44	727.90	681.63
5	970.14	786.70	183.44	727.47	679.65
6	970.14	786.70	183.44	727.04	677.65
7	970.14	786.70	183.44	726.60	675.64
8	970.14	786.70	183.44	726.17	673.61
9	970.14	786.70	183.44	725.72	671.58
10	970.14	786.70	183.44	725.28	669.52
11	970.14	786.70	183.44	724.83	667.46
12	970.14	786.70	183.44	724.38	665.38

TABLE 32-3 Determining the Present Value of After-Tax Savings

Month	*(6) = (4) − (5) Difference In Interest*	*(7) = (6) * .28 Tax Savings*	*(8) = (3) + (7) TATS*	*(9) PV of (8)*	*(10) PV of TATS (Cumulative)*
1	41.67	11.67	195.11	194.14	194.14
2	43.19	12.09	195.53	193.61	387.76
3	44.72	12.52	195.96	193.08	580.84
4	46.27	12.96	196.39	192.55	773.39
5	47.82	13.39	196.83	192.03	965.42
6	49.39	13.83	197.27	191.51	1156.93
7	50.96	14.27	197.71	190.99	1347.92
8	52.55	14.71	198.15	190.48	1538.40
9	54.15	15.16	198.60	189.97	1728.37
10	55.76	15.61	199.05	189.46	1917.83
11	57.37	16.06	199.50	188.96	2106.78
12	59.00	16.52	199.96	188.46	2295.24

(8) = TATS = Total after-tax savings
(9) = PV of (8) = Present value of the total after-tax savings
(10) = PV of TATS = Present value of the total after-tax savings

TABLE 32–4 Calculating the Present Value of the Difference in the Mortgage Balances for First 12 Months

Month	*(11) Mortgage Balance 30-Year*	*(12) Mortgage Balance 15-Year*	*(13) = (11) – (12) Difference*	*(14) Present Value of (13)*
1	99,942.47	99,717.36	225.11	224.00
2	99,884.52	99,432.78	451.74	447.30
3	99,826.14	99,146.24	679.91	669.91
4	99,767.34	98,857.72	909.61	891.82
5	99,708.11	98,567.24	1140.88	1113.05
6	99,648.44	98,274.74	1373.70	1333.60
7	99,588.34	97,980.24	1608.10	1553.47
8	99,527.81	97,683.72	1844.09	1772.66
9	99,466.83	97,385.16	2081.67	1991.19
10	99,405.41	97,084.54	2320.87	2209.05
11	99,343.53	96,781.86	2561.67	2426.24
12	99,281.21	96,477.09	2804.12	2642.79

TABLE 32–5 Finding the Present Value of the Difference in the Mortgage Balances over 15 Years

Year	*(15) Present Value of the Total After-Tax Savings of the 30-Year Mortgage (Cumulative)*	*(16) Present Value of the Difference in Mortgage Balances*
1	2295.24	2642.79
2	4518.83	5191.50
3	6676.20	7652.74
4	8772.52	10,032.85
5	10,812.68	12,337.79
6	12,801.30	14,573.19
7	14,742.78	16,744.45
8	16,641.31	18,856.62
9	18,500.85	20,914.52
10	20,325.17	22,922.71
11	22,117.86	24,885.52
12	23,882.33	26,807.08
13	25,621.83	28,691.28
14	27,339.47	30,541.85
15	29,038.19	32,362.34

CHAPTER

33 Refinancing Versus Keeping an Existing Mortgage

Many factors affect the decision to refinance a mortgage. Perhaps the most important reason people choose to refinance is a decline in mortgage rates. When mortgage rates decline sharply, homeowners rush to refinance. This was clearly demonstrated in the spring of 1986.

FACTORS TO CONSIDER

Although a declining interest rate is the main reason for refinancing a mortgage, there are also other factors that influence refinancing. These factors are closing costs, the holding period, the homeowner's marginal tax rate, the interest rate on savings, and the age of the existing loan. The term of the new loan may also affect the decision to refinance.

A simple example can be used to show the basic idea of refinancing. Suppose refinancing reduces the monthly payment by $100 and that closing costs amount to $2000. Ignoring taxes and the time value of money, the homeowner will be able to recover the closing costs in 20 months. The twentieth month is the crossover month or breakeven month. In other words, the payback period for refinancing is 20 months. If the homeowner expects to stay in the house for more than 20 months, he or she should refinance; otherwise, refinancing would not be advisable.

Although the example just given conveys the basic idea of

refinancing, the analysis ignores the time value of money and taxes. A more complete analysis should take these factors into account.

ANALYSIS

The main cost of refinancing a mortgage consists of closing costs and prepayment penalties. The main benefits of refinancing are lower monthly payments (after taxes) and lower pay-off balances.

The lower monthly payment results from a lower mortgage rate and, possibly, from a longer term of the new mortgage. The interest deduction associated with the new mortgage is lower than the interest deduction generated by the existing mortgage. For this reason, refinancing results in lower tax savings. The greater the marginal tax rate of the homeowner, the greater the sacrifice in tax savings due to refinancing will be. So the after-tax payment savings is the difference between the monthly payments less the tax savings lost because of refinancing.

To make the monthly after-tax payment savings comparable to closing costs, the savings are discounted to the present using the after-tax monthly interest rate on savings and cumulated from year to year.

Refinancing also gives the homeowner faster equity buildup. The pay-off balance of the new mortgage declines faster than that of the existing mortgage. The present value of the differences in pay-off balances are added to the cumulative after-tax payment savings to get the total benefits of refinancing. The benefits of refinancing are then compared with the closing costs and prepayment penalty to determine whether or not refinancing will benefit the homeowner.

The data shown in Table 33-1 will be used to show the applica-

Table 33-1 Refinancing Data for an Existing Mortgage Balance of $99,228.21*

Existing Mortgage		*New Mortgage*	
Original loan amount ($)	= 100,000	Loan Amount ($)	= 99,228.21
Interest rate (%)	= 12	Interest Rate (%)	= 10
Term (years)	= 30	Term (years)	= 30
Remaining term (months)	= 336	No. of points	= 2
Prepayment penalty	= 0	Other closing costs	= 950
Current balance ($)	= 99,228.21		

*The marginal tax rate = 28 percent and the interest rate on savings = 9.25 percent.

tion of a procedure for evaluating mortgage refinancing for a property that has a $99,228.21 mortgage balance.

Tables 33–2 through 33–5 show the results of the calculations. The tables are self-explanatory.

The total closing costs are $2934.56 (points = $1984.56 plus other closing costs of $950). The total benefits of refinancing are shown in column 16 of Table 33–5. The benefits exceed the costs from the second year on. The breakeven month is the twenty-second month.

TABLE 33–2 Comparing Payments of Existing and New Loans

Month	*(1) Monthly Payment (Old Loan)*	*(2) Monthly Payment (New Loan)*	*(3) = (1) – (2) Payment Difference*	*(4) Interest (Old Loan)*	*(5) Interest (New Loan)*
1	1028.61	870.80	157.81	992.28	826.90
2	1028.61	870.80	157.81	991.92	826.54
3	1028.61	870.80	157.81	991.55	826.17
4	1028.61	870.80	157.81	991.18	825.80
5	1028.61	870.80	157.81	990.81	825.42
6	1028.61	870.80	157.81	990.43	825.04
7	1028.61	870.80	157.81	990.05	824.66
8	1028.61	870.80	157.81	989.66	824.28
9	1028.61	870.80	157.81	989.27	823.89
10	1028.61	870.80	157.81	988.88	823.50
11	1028.61	870.80	157.81	988.48	823.10
12	1028.61	870.80	157.81	988.08	822.71

TABLE 33-3 Determining the Present Value of the Savings in Payments

Month	(6) = (4) − (5) − K Interest Difference	(7) = (6) • T Tax Savings of Old Loan	(8) = (3) − (7) Payment Difference (After-Tax)	(9) Present Value of (8) @ .555%
1	159.87	44.76	113.05	112.43
2	159.87	44.76	113.05	111.81
3	159.87	44.76	113.05	111.19
4	159.87	44.76	113.05	110.57
5	159.87	44.76	113.05	109.96
6	159.87	44.76	113.05	109.36
7	159.87	44.76	113.05	108.75
8	159.87	44.76	113.05	108.15
9	159.87	44.76	113.05	107.56
10	159.87	44.76	113.05	106.96
11	159.87	44.76	113.05	106.37
12	159.86	44.76	113.05	105.79

K = Amortized points = $4.512678
T = Marginal tax rate = 28%

TABLE 33-4 Calculating the Present Value of the Difference Between Payments

Month	(10) Balance Old Loan	(11) Balance New Loan Minus TS*	(12) = (10) − (11) Difference Between Balances	(13) Present Value of (12) @ .555%
1	99,191.88	98,630.18	561.70	558.60
2	99,155.18	98,587.46	567.73	561.48
3	99,118.12	98,544.37	573.75	564.30
4	99,080.69	98,500.91	579.78	567.09
5	99,042.88	98,457.06	585.82	569.93
6	99,004.69	98,412.84	591.85	572.52
7	98,966.12	98,368.25	597.88	575.15
8	98,927.18	98,323.28	603.90	577.74
9	98,887.83	98,277.90	609.93	580.29
10	98,848.09	98,232.14	615.95	582.79
11	98,807.96	98,185.99	621.98	585.24
12	98,767.43	98,139.44	627.99	587.64

*TS = Tax savings resulting from the writeoff of the unamortized points.

TABLE 33-5 Finding the Present Value of Cumulative Payment Difference and Differences in Balances

Year	(14) Present Value of After-Tax Payment Difference	(15) Present Value of After-Tax Payment Difference (Cumulative)	(16) = (13) + (15) Present Value of After-Tax Payment Difference (Cum.) & Present Value of Difference in Balances
1	1308.90	1308.90	1896.54
2	1224.96	2533.86	3146.47
3	1146.73	3680.59	4310.85
4	1073.86	4754.45	5394.72
5	1006.04	5760.49	6402.77
6	942.98	6703.47	7339.36
7	884.40	7587.86	8208.54
8	830.05	8417.92	9014.11
9	779.70	9197.61	9759.54
10	733.12	9930.74	10,448.10
11	690.13	10,620.87	11,082.81
12	650.53	11,271.40	11,666.46
13	614.15	11,885.54	12,201.61
14	580.84	12,466.38	12,690.63
15	550.45	13,016.84	13,135.71
16	522.86	13,539.70	13,538.83
17	497.95	14,037.65	13,901.83
18	475.60	14,513.25	14,226.36
19	455.74	14,968.99	14,513.93
20	438.26	15,407.24	14,765.90
21	423.09	15,830.33	14,983.46
22	410.17	16,240.51	15,167.70
23	399.45	16,639.95	15,319.55
24	390.87	17,030.82	15,439.83
25	384.40	17,415.22	15,529.24
26	380.01	17,795.23	15,588.32
27	377.67	18,172.90	15,617.56
28	377.38	18,550.27	15,617.28

CHAPTER

34 Biweekly Versus Monthly Payment Mortgages

Although most residential mortgages involve monthly payments, some lenders offer biweekly payment mortgage (BPM) plans. The biweekly payment is equal to 50 percent of the monthly payment mortgage (MPM) and there are 26 biweekly payments a year. As a result, the sum of the biweekly payments in any given year will be 13 times the monthly payment (26 * (monthly payment/2)), regardless of the size of the monthly payment and the corresponding biweekly payment. In other words, the total payments of a BPM in any given year will exceed the total payments of an MPM by an amount equal to the monthly payment of the MPM.

Because of the extra payment that results each year and the effect of compounding, the term of the mortgage and the total undiscounted interest cost of the mortgagte are reduced. The effective term of the biweekly mortgage is calculated as follows:

$$N = -\frac{\ln\,[1 - L(i/26)/M]}{26 * \ln\,(1 + i/26)} \tag{34-1}$$

where: N = term of the biweekly payment mortgage, in years
L = the loan amount
M = the biweekly payment
i = the annual interest rate
ln = natural logarithm

This formula is derived in an appendix at the end of this chapter.

FACTORS TO CONSIDER

The reduction in the term of the BPM depends on the level of the mortgage rate. The higher the rate, the greater the reduction in the term of the mortgage will tend to be. See Table 34–1.

On the surface, the BPM seems better than the MPM for the borrower. The BPM cuts the term of the mortgage substantially and the total interest cost (undiscounted) is reduced considerably. However, it is not always the better choice.

First, the BPM may not work well for a homeowner who is paid monthly. Second, when income taxes and the time value of money are taken into account, the MPM could be more attractive to the borrower in the high income tax bracket, expecially, if interest rates on savings are high. The interest rate on savings is used as the appropriate rate of discount.

The Effect of Income Taxes

The interest on a mortgage loan is tax deductible. The benefit of the deductibility of the interest can be realized throughout the year by claiming an appropriate number of exemptions. The resulting increase in take-home pay can be invested right away or used to reduce interest-bearing debt.

TABLE 34–1. The Effect of Biweekly Mortgage Payments on Mortgage Terms for Different Interest Rates

(1) Interest Rate (%)	*(2) Monthly Payment*	*(3) = .5(2) Biweekly Payment*	*(4) Term BPM*
8	476.95	238.47	22.84
10	570.42	285.21	20.96
12	668.60	334.30	19.02
14	770.17	385.08	17.16
16	874.09	437.05	15.47

BPM = Biweekly Payment Mortgage
Loan Amount = $65,500
Term of the Monthly Payment Mortgage = 30 years

Although an individual may be paid monthly, weekly, or even daily, for purposes of this analysis, the assumption is that the homeowner is paid biweekly and that he or she claims additional exemptions to benefit from the interest deductions throughout the year. The calculations of the tax savings is explained in steps 1 through 3 of the next section.

ANALYSIS

Briefly, the procedure involves calculating the present values of the total costs of the two mortgage plans and selecting the payment plan with the lower total cost. More specifically, the following steps are followed:

1. For both the monthly payment plan and the biweekly payment plan, the annual interest payments are calculated for each year during the life of the mortgage.
2. Assuming that a homebuyer is paid biweekly, the annual interest payments are divided by 26.
3. The biweekly interest payments from step 2 are multiplied by the homebuyer's marginal tax rate to get the biweekly tax savings.
4. The biweekly tax savings are discounted to the present using an appropriate discount rate and cumulated on an annual basis. The appropriate discount rate is the after-tax interest rate that the home buyer can earn on his or her savings.
5. The mortgage payments are discounted to the present and cumulated on an annual basis.
6. The present values of the annual, cumulative tax savings are subtracted from the present values of the annual, cumulative payments to get the annual, cumulative after-tax mortgage payments.
7. The payoff balances at the end of each year are discounted to the present.
8. The present values of the payoff balances at the end of each year are added to the annual, after-tax cumulative mortgage payments to get the present value of the total cost of the mortgage.
9. In any given year, the mortgage with the smaller present value of the total cost is better for the borrower.

EXAMPLE: Consider a homebuyer in the 33 percent tax bracket who wishes to borrow $65,000 at 12 percent per year for 30 years. The monthly payment for this loan is \$668.60. If the lender allows it, the borrower could pay \$334.30 (half the monthly amount) biweekly and pay off the loan fully in 19.02 years.

To perform a comparative analysis of the two payment plans, the nine-step procedure described earlier was applied. The calculations were performed for 19 years, since the biweekly payment mortgage will be paid off in 19 years.

The results are summarized in Table 34–2. The pattern that emerged from the analysis suggests that the biweekly payment plan is better suited to borrowers with low marginal tax rates and low opportunity discount rates and that at high income tax brackets and high opportunity discount rates, the monthly payment plan is better than the biweekly payment plan.

When the discount rate (before-tax) is equal to the mortgage rate, the MPM seems to be better, regardless of the marginal tax rate levels (0 percent to 33 percent).

APPENDIX: DERIVATION OF THE TERM OF THE BIWEEKLY PAYMENT PLAN

The monthly payment (M1) of the monthly payment plan is calculated using equation (2).

TABLE 34–2. Preferred Mortgage Payment Plan for Different Marginal Tax Rates and After-Tax Discount Rates.

Marginal Tax Rate (%)	*After-tax Discount Rates (%)*		
	6	*8*	*10*
0	B	B	B
15	B	B	B,M (1)
28	B	B,M (2)	M
33	B	B,M (3)	M

Loan Amount = \$65,000
Term of M = 30 years
Mortgage Rate = 12%
M = Monthly Payment Mortgage
B = Biweekly Payment Mortgage
1. For years 1–3, M is preferred to B. For years 4 and after, B is preferred to M.
2. For years 1–2, M is preferred to B. For years 3 and after, B is preferred to M.
3. For years 1–14, M is preferred to B. For years 15 and after, B is preferred to M.

(2) $$M1 = \frac{L(i/12)}{[1 - (1 + i/12)^{-12N1}]}$$

where: L = loan amount
i = annual interest rate
N1 = life of the loan, in years

The biweekly payment (M) is, simply, half the monthly payment (= .5 * M1) and assumes biweekly compounding. As a result, equation (3) should hold. Solving equation (3) for the term of the biweekly payment mortgage (N) yields equation (1) in the text.

(3) $$M = \frac{L(i/26)}{[1 - (1 + i/26)^{-26N}]}$$

CHAPTER

35 Lower Interest Rate Versus More Points

Even with 15-year or 30-year fixed-rate mortgages, lenders may offer two or more options. A borrower may be able to buy down the interest rate on the mortgage by paying more points.

Consider the example in Table 35–1, which lists terms for two types of 30-year fixed-rate mortgages.

Which of these mortgages is better for the borrower? The answer depends on a number of factors. The next section will discuss these factors, and the question is then answered in the last section.

FACTORS TO CONSIDER

The crux of which type of 30-year fixed-rate mortgage is best for a particular homebuyer depends on the marginal tax rate of the borrower, the after-tax interest rate on savings, and the amount of cash the borrower has at hand.

Buyers with little cash may have no choice but to take the option with fewer points. On the other hand, if the purchase is the result of job relocation and the buyer's employer pays the points, the mortgage with the lower interest rate but greater number of points is naturally better.

For people who pay points themselves and have enough cash for points, the major determinants are their marginal tax rate and the after-tax interest rate on savings. The after-tax interest rate on savings is used to discount future values to the present.

ANALYSIS

First, note that a *point* is always 1 percent of the loan amount. Second, discount points for an initial mortgage with respect to the

Table 35–1 Terms for 30-Year Fixed-Rate Mortgages

Mortgage	*Note Rate (%)*	*Points*
First Mortgage	10.25	1
Alternative Mortgage	10.00	2

purchase of a principal residence are deductible in the year of purchase, if they are paid by the buyer.

EXAMPLE: Assuming a loan of $100,000 with a term of 30 years, the alternative mortgage (with a lower mortgage rate and 2 points) would cost the buyer $1000 more (before taxes) at closing than would the first mortgage, but it would also save the buyer $18.53 (before taxes) each month, as shown in Table 35–2.

Ignoring income taxes and the time value of money, the borrower could recover the extra cost (1 point, equal to $1000) in about 54 months (1000/18.53) or about 4.5 years. Assuming a marginal tax rate of 28 percent and a discount rate of 9.25 percent (before taxes), a similar result is obtained. The results are show in Tables 35–3 to 35–6.

The after-tax additional cost of the alternative mortgage at closing is $720, but it generates after-tax payment savings (Column 6 of Table 35–2) and produces faster equity buildup or lower payoff balances (Column 10 of Table 35–3). Column 15 of Table 35–4 shows the present values of the extra benefits of the alternative mortgage. The extra benefits exceed the extra cost ($720) from year 5 on.

Table 35–2 Comparing Savings from Lower Points with Savings from Lower Loan Interest Rate

Mortgage	*Note Rate (%)*	*Number of Points*	*Points Before Taxes*	*Points After Taxes*	*Monthly Payment*
First	10.25	1	$1000	$720	$896.10
Alternative	10.00	2	2000	1440	877.57
Difference	0.25	−1	−1000	−720	18.53

Now, going back to the question that was posed in the first section, the answer is, the type of mortgage that saves the borrower most depends on the holding period. If the borrower does not plan to move or refinance in the next five years, he or she should use the alternative mortgage; otherwise, the first mortgage should be used.

TABLE 35-3 Calculating Difference in Interest Paid Each Month

Month	*(1) Payment Difference*	*(2) Interest First Mortgage*	*(3) Interest Alternative Mortgage*	*(4) = (2) − (3) Difference in Interest*
1	18.53	854.17	833.33	20.83
2	18.53	853.81	832.96	20.84
3	18.53	853.45	832.59	20.85
4	18.53	853.08	832.22	20.86
5	18.53	852.72	831.84	20.88
6	18.53	852.34	831.46	20.89
7	18.53	851.97	831.07	20.90
8	18.53	851.59	830.69	20.91
9	18.53	851.21	830.30	20.92
10	18.53	850.83	829.90	20.93
11	18.53	850.44	829.51	20.94
12	18.53	850.05	829.10	20.95

TABLE 35–4 Finding the Present Value of the After-Tax Difference in Payments

Month	(5) = (4) * .28 Tax Savings	(6) = (1) − (5) After-Tax Payment Difference	(7) Present Value of (6) @ 6.660001%
1	5.83	12.70	12.63
2	5.84	12.69	12.55
3	5.84	12.69	12.48
4	5.84	12.69	12.41
5	5.85	12.68	12.34
6	5.85	12.68	12.27
7	5.85	12.68	12.20
8	5.85	12.67	12.13
9	5.86	12.67	12.06
10	5.86	12.67	11.99
11	5.86	12.67	11.92
12	5.87	12.66	11.85

TABLE 35–5 Determining the Present Value of the Difference Between Balances

Month	(8) Balance First Mortgage	(9) Balance Alternative Mortgage	(10) = (8) − (9) Difference Between Balances	(11) Present Value of (10) @ 6.66001%
1	99,958.06	99,955.76	2.30	2.29
2	99,915.77	99,911.15	4.62	4.57
3	99,873.11	99,866.18	6.94	6.82
4	99,830.09	99,820.81	9.28	9.08
5	99,786.71	99,775.08	11.63	11.31
6	99,742.94	99,728.97	13.98	13.52
7	99,698.81	99,682.47	16.34	15.72
8	99,654.31	99,635.58	18.73	17.92
9	99,609.41	99,588.30	21.12	20.09
10	99,564.14	99,540.62	23.52	22.25
11	99,518.49	99,492.56	25.93	24.40
12	99,472.44	99,444.09	28.35	26.53

TABLE 35-6

Year	(12)* PV of ATDP	(13)† PV of ATDP (Cumulative)	(14)‡ PV of DMB	(15) = (13) + (14)§ PV of ATDP + PV of DMB
1	146.80	146.80	26.53	173.33
2	136.98	283.79	50.99	334.78
3	127.82	411.61	73.45	485.06
4	119.27	530.88	93.94	624.83
5	111.30	642.18	112.56	754.75
6	103.87	746.06	129.37	875.43
7	96.96	843.01	144.40	987.41
8	90.52	933.53	157.67	1091.21
9	84.53	1018.06	169.24	1187.30
10	78.97	1097.04	179.10	1276.13
11	73.82	1170.85	187.29	1358.14
12	69.04	1239.89	193.80	1433.69

*PV of ATDP = Present value of after-tax difference in payments

†PV of aTDP = Present value of the after-tax difference in the payments (cumulative) @ 6.660001%

‡PV of DMB = Present value of the difference in the mortgage balances @ 6.660001%

§Total after-tax benefits from the mortgage with the lower interest rate but more points

IV Security of a Mortgage Loan

CHAPTER 36 QUALIFYING THE BORROWER: Residential Properties

In order to get a mortgage loan, a borrower has to meet the criteria used by the lender. The criteria used by a lender are not the same for all residential loans. In many cases, the criteria reflect the requirements of those who insure or guarantee mortgages or those who buy mortgages. In some cases, they reflect the primary lender's requirements, particularly if the lender plans to keep the loans in its portfolio.

This chapter covers the Fannie Mae/Freddie Mac underwriting guidelines for conventional loans and the underwriting guidelines for FHA and VA loans.

UNDERWRITING GUIDELINES—CONVENTIONAL LOANS

Fannie Mae and Freddie Mac buy loans from primary lenders if the loans meet their own requirements. For this reason, primary lenders who wish to sell their loans to Fannie Mae or Freddie Mac will qualify applicants using the Fannie Mae/Freddie Mac guidelines.

The Guidelines

The guidelines help the underwriters in evaluating the applicant's ability and willingness to repay the loan and the extent of his or her resources. The underwriters examine the nature and stability of the applicant's income and employment, assets and liabilities, and credit history. They also use income ratios.

As far as income is concerned, the underwriters consider primary and secondary sources of income. In other words, they count base income from regular employment and other incomes, such as overtime income, part-time income, dividends and interest, bonuses, pensions, and welfare assistance as long as they have been fairly regular in the last two years and there is reasonable expectation that they will continue in the future. They may even consider child support and alimony payments.

In general, stable employment is favored, but job changes associated with growth in the same line of work are positive. Education also strengthens the case for the applicant.

Other favorable points are liquid assets that are large enough to cover the downpayment, closing costs and moving expenses, accumulation of net worth, and evidence of responsible debt management.

Income, employment, and deposits are verified and credit reports are obtained. Self-employed applicants have to submit financial statements and copies of federal income tax returns for the preceding two years.

To simplify the underwriting function, two income ratios are used:

1. The ratio of monthly housing expense to gross monthly income should not exceed 25 percent. If the borrower has large net worth, makes a large downpayment, and has good credit, a ratio of up to 28 percent may be acceptable. The monthly housing expenses include debt service (principal and interest), taxes, hazard insurance and, if applicable, private mortgage insurance and homeowner's association dues.
2. The ratio of monthly housing expenses and other debt payments to gross monthly income should not exceed 33 percent to 36 percent. Other debt payments include installment payments that are expected to last more than 10 months, child support, and alimony payments.

It should be pointed out at this point that:

1. The Equal Credit Opportunity Act (ECOA) prohibits discrimination in the area of credit on the basis of race, color, religion, national origin, sex, marital status, and age. Also, the fact that a person's income consists of welfare assistance payments is not a basis for denying credit.

2. The Fair Credit Reporting Act (FCRA) requires lenders to state the reason for denying credit. If the adverse action is based on a credit report, the name and address of the credit bureau has to be given to the applicant. The applicant can examine the summary report free of charge within a certain period of time after the adverse decision. The applicant can also challenge the report.
3. The Real Estate Settlement Procedures Act (RESPA) requires lenders to give the applicant a copy of the "Settlement Costs" booklet prepared by the Department of Housing and Urban Development (HUD) and good faith estimates of settlement costs at the time of application. The good faith estimates can be mailed to the applicant within three days of the application date.

Illustration

The example given here shows the calculation of the income ratios presented in the previous section. The applicant is assumed to have good credit history, 20 percent downpayment, and fairly large net worth.

The balance in the applicant's credit card account is $1600, and the monthly payment is assumed to be 10 percent.

As you can see the ratios are below the limits of 28 percent and 36 percent.

Principal and interest	$1028.61
+ Taxes	250.00
+ Insurance	40.00
= Monthly housing expenses (MHE)	$1318.61
/ Monthly gross income (MGI)	$4883.74
= MHE/MGI ratio	*0.27*
MHE	$1318.61
+ Car loan payment	248.85
+ Credit card loan payment	160.00
= Total debt payments (TDP)	$1727.46
/ MGI	$4883.74
= TDP/MGI ratio	*0.35*

UNDERWRITING GUIDELINES—FHA LOANS

Although there are similarities between conventional and FHA underwriting guidelines, FHA guidelines are different.

The Guidelines

FHA rates loan applicants on the basis of the following four criteria:

1. Credit characteristics. The applicant should have a good credit history.
2. Adequacy of effective income. The adequacy of effective income is determined by comparing total housing expense (THE) and total fixed payment (TFP) with net effective income (NEI). The THE/NEI ratio should not exceed 38 percent and the TFP/NEI ratio should not be greater than 53 percent.

   NEI is determined from the total monthly income (TMI) less federal income taxes withheld, and TMI consists of the base pay and other earnings that are expected to continue in the future.

   THE is the sum of principal and interest, hazard insurance, taxes, maintenance and common expenses, and utilities. TFP, in turn, is the sum of THE, state and local taxes, social security taxes, child support, and alimony and debt payments that are expected to be made for the next 12 months or more.

   If an applicant does not meet this requirement, FHA may use the balance for family support method used by VA to qualify her/him.
3. Stability of effective income. The income of the applicant has to be from regular employment or from sources that are expected to continue.
4. Adequacy of available assets. The applicant should have liquid assets that are large enough to cover the downpayment and closing costs.

Here again, income employment and deposits are verified and credit reports are obtained.

Illustration

In this example also, the applicant is assumed to have good credit history and sufficient cash assets for the downpayment and closing costs. The ratios do not indicate a problem.

Total monthly income	$3800
– Federal taxes	650
= Net effective income	*$3150*

	Principal and interest	$600
+	Hazard insurance	30
+	Taxes	200
+	Maintenance expenses	100
+	Heat and utilities	110
=	Total housing expense (THE)	$1040
+	State and local taxes	95
+	Social security taxes	270
+	Auto loan payment	220
=	Total fixed payment (TFP)	$1625
/	Net effective income (NEI)	3150
=	TFP/NEI ratio	0.516
	THE/NEI ratio	1040/3150 = 0.33

UNDERWRITING GUIDELINES—VA LOANS

VA uses two methods for qualifying applicants. The methods are discussed in the next section.

The Guidelines

The applicant (veteran) should have good credit history and liquid assets that are large enough to cover closing costs. In addition, the VA calculates the balance for family support and income ratios to determine the adequacy of the applicant's income. Income is presumed to be adequate if the balance for family support exceeds the appropriate minimum residual income and the ratio of the total monthly payments to the monthly gross income is not more than 41 percent.

The balance for family support is calculated as follows:

Monthly gross income
− Federal taxes
= Net effective income
− Principal and interest
− Hazard insurance
− Taxes
− Maintenance expenses
− Heat and utilities
− State and local taxes
− Social security taxes
− Auto loan payment

- − Other debt payments that are expected to continue for 6 months or more
- = Balance for family support
- − Minimum residual income
- = Excess residual income (ERI)
- / Minimum residual income (MRI)
- = ERI/MRI ratio

The minimum residual income (MRI) represents a minimum consumption budget that a family needs to cover necessities. It depends on family size and geographical region. The VA prepares the estimated MRIs.

The excess residual income (ERI) represents a margin of safety for the applicant. The greater the excess, the better. If the ratio of ERI to MRI exceeds 20 percent, the applicant's income is presumed to be adequate even if the applicant does not pass the second test.

The second test involves the calculation of the ratio of total monthly payments to monthly gross income. The ratio should be 41 percent or less. The total monthly payments are calculated as follows:

- Principal and interest
- \+ Hazard insurance
- \+ Taxes
- \+ State and local taxes
- \+ Auto loan payment
- \+ Other payments that are expected to continue for 6 months or more
- = Total monthly payments (TMP)
- / Monthly gross income (MGI)
- = TMP/MGI ratio

Illustration

The example that was used in the FHA case is also used here. The Minimum Residual Income is assumed to be 627. The applicant passes both tests.

Monthly gross income	$3800
− Federal taxes	650
= Net effective income	$3150
− Principal and interest	600
− Hazard insurance	30

− Taxes	200
− Maintenance expenses	100
− Heat and utilities	110
− State and local taxes	95
− Social security taxes	270
− Auto loan payment	220
− Other debt payments	0
= Balance for family support	$1525
− Minimum residual income	627
= Excess residual income (ERI)	$ 898
/ Minimum residual income (MRI)	627
= ERI/MRI ratio	1.43
Principal and interest	$ 600
+ Hazard insurance	30
+ Taxes	200
+ State and local taxes	95
+ Auto loan payment	220
+ Other qualifying payments	0
= Total monthly payments (TMP)	$1145
/ Monthly gross income (MGI)	3800
= TMP/MGI ratio	0.30

CHAPTER

37 APPRAISING THE PROPERTY

A fundamental principle in secured lending is that the value of the property pledged as collateral should be greater than the loan amount. There are maximum loan-to-value (L/V) ratios for different types of real properties. For example, for conventional loans, the maximum L/V ratio is 80 percent without private mortgage insurance (PMI) and 95 percent with PMI. For income properties, it may be 70 percent or less.

In practice, the purchase price and the appraised value are, often, not the same. So, for purposes of L/V ratio, the lower of the price or the appraised value is used.

There are three major methods of appraising real estate. They are the market data approach, the cost approach, and the income approach.

THE MARKET DATA APPROACH

The market data approach is most useful for appraising residential properties such as single-family homes, townhouses, condominium units, and other properties for which market data is readily available.

Description

In the market data approach, the appraiser identifies properties in the same neighborhood that are similar to the subject property and compares the subject property to the comparable properties on the basis of lot size, number of rooms, number of bathrooms, etc. Positive or negative adjustments are made for differences in the features to arrive at an estimated value of the subject property.

How It Works

The property that is being appraised is called the *subject property* and the other properties with which the subject property is compared are called *comparable properties.* These comparable properties should be in the same neighborhood or area served by the same school district. The comparables should have been sold recently and they should be similar to the subject property. The closer the comparable properties to the subject property, the greater the similarity between the comparable and subject properties and the more recent the time of sale, the greater the accuracy of the appraised value will tend to be.

Generally, three comparable properties are used but more can be used too. Sometimes, it may be difficult to find three comparable properties that were actually sold and they may use properties that are listed for sale. However, prices at which properties are listed are not the same as actual market prices.

In performing the comparisons, the appraiser takes into account the location of the property, the site/view, the date of sale, sales or financing concessions, and the particular features of the properties.

To the extent that all the properties are in the same neighborhood, it is not necessary to make an adjustment for neighborhood. However, if a comparable property is located in a neighborhood where prices are, generally, higher, the price of the comparable property should be adjusted downward. Even if the properties are in the same neighborhood, adjustments may be needed for differences in site/view.

If the comparable property was sold six months ago and prices in the area have been increasing at an average annual rate of 12 percent, the price of the comparable property has to be adjusted upward by 6 percent.

Financing concessions can result in higher prices. When a borrower assumes a low-interest mortgage or when the seller finances the purchase at a rate lower than the going market rate, the purchaser would be willing to pay a higher price for it. In such cases, a downward adjustment is in order. A transaction between related parties may also require adjustment. The price could be lower than the price in an arms-length transaction.

Finally, adjustments are made for differences in the features of the properties. The FHCMC/FNMA Appraisal Report lists design/appeal, quality of construction, age, condition, gross living area, basement, energy-efficient items, garage, air conditioning, pools, and porches. For example, if the subject property has more bathrooms than the comparable property, the price of the comparable property is adjusted upward.

The adjustments are rather subjective, and different appraisers can make different adjustments. As you can see, appraising is an art. With experience, however, the adjustments would be more accurate.

To minimize the effect of subjective adjustments, some appraisers use statistical techniques to establish the appraised value. Price is regressed on various factors such as age of the property, number of bedrooms, number of bathrooms, and lot size.

The multiple regression model is estimated using market data. Suppose the following equation is estimated using data from 50 homes sold in an area in the last six months:

$$P = 10{,}000 + 5X1 + 6000X2 + 750X3 - 200X4 + 3500X5$$

where: P = estimated price of the property
X1 = lot size
X2 = number of rooms
X3 = number of cars the garage can hold
X4 = age of the property
X5 = 1, if the house has air conditioning
= 0, if the house does not have air conditioning

As an example, assume that a property sits on 2000 square feet of land and has 11 rooms, a two-car garage, central air, and that the house is 10 years old. The indicated value of the property is $89,000, calculated as follows:

$$P = 10{,}000 + 5(2000) + 6000(11) + 750(2) - 200(10) + 3500(1)$$
$$= 89{,}000$$

Advantages of the Market Data Approach

The main advantage of the approach is that it can generate fairly accurate indications of value when good comparables exist. It uses current market data. Furthermore, if good comparables exist, the data on the comparables can be obtained fairly easily.

Disadvantages of the Market Data Approach

The market data approach would not work well if comparables cannot be obtained. For properties that are not sold frequently, other approaches have to be used.

THE COST APPROACH

For some buildings, it is difficult to find market data on comparable properties. Examples are church and school buildings and bowling alleys. For these and other similar buildings, the cost approach is better. The cost approach can be used even for properties for which comparables exist but it would not be as reliable as the market data approach, unless the properties are new. For fairly new buildings, the cost approach is appropriate.

Description

In the cost approach, the indicated value is the cost of reproducing or replacing the property less accrued depreciation plus the value of land. Reproduction cost means the cost of replicating the building using the same materials. If reproducing the property is not possible, the cost of a functionally equivalent building is used. This is called the *replacement cost.*

How the Cost Method Works

The cost method involves the estimation of reproduction or replacement costs, reducing the costs by accrued depreciation and then adding the estimated value of land to the result.

The first step is to estimate the total reproduction or replacement costs. There are three methods of estimating the reproduction or replacement cost—the quantity survey method, the unit-in-place method, and the comparative unit method. Inthe quantity survey method, the reproduction or replacement cost is estimated by adding up the costs of labor and materials that would be needed to reproduce or replace the property. Other items, such as insurance, are also included. While this method would be the most accurate, it is also the most costly of the three methods to use.

In the unit-in-place method, the total costs are based on costs of major components as installed. Examples of major components are foundations, plumbing, and roofing.

Finally, in the comparative unit method, replacement costs are based on unit costs of comparable buildings. Costs of nonstandard items, such as fireplaces or built-in ovens, are also included. Cost indexes are used to update the unit costs.

Cost data may be obtained from American Appraisal Associates, Marshall and Swift Publication Company, F.W. Dodge Corporation, and Robert Snow Means Co.

The next step is to estimate accrued depreciation. There are three types of depreciation—physical deterioration, functional obsolescence, and economic obsolescence. ***Physical deterioration*** refers to wear and tear, ***functional obsolescence*** refers to decline in value due to outdated designs or other features, and ***economic obsolescence*** refers to decline in value due to factors that adversely affect the neighborhood. Increased noise and pollution could lower property values.

Physical deterioration and functional obsolescence may be curable or incurable. Those items that can be repaired are called curable and those that cannot be repaired at a cost that is smaller than the value added to the property by repairing the item are called incurable.

Estimating accrued depreciation is not easy. The simplest—although not the most satisfactory—way of estimating depreciation is to use the straight line method. Accrued depreciation is calculated as the product of the replacement cost and the ratio of the effective age of the building to the estimated life of the building. The major problems in this method are estimating the effective age and the economic life of the building.

The land value is estimated using the market data approach, assuming that it is not improved.

Given all the estimates, the indicated value is:

Replacement (reproduction) cost	$150,000
− Accrued depreciation	20,000
+ Land value	30,000
= Indicated Value	$160,000

Advantages of the Cost Method

The cost method is the only way of estimating cost when there are no comparables for nonincome-producing properties. It is also useful when the comparables are not close to the subject property.

Disadvantages of the Cost Method

The cost method is not likely to produce fairly accurate indications of value when the building is relatively old. There are difficulties in estimating costs and depreciation.

THE INCOME APPROACH

The income method is best suited for the evaluation of income-producing properties, but it can also be used to evaluate nonincome residential properties. The indicated value depends on the income generated by the property.

Description

In its simplest form, the income method involves the estimation of the project's net operating income for a typical year and capitalizing the income using an appropriate discount rate. In a more complete analysis, the net operating incomes for all the years during the holding period and the net proceeds from sales (reversion) would be discounted to the present to get the indicated value.

How It Works

The first step is to estimate the net operating income (NOI). The second step is to estimate the capitalization rate. The capitalization rate, or simply the cap rate, is a measure of the investor's required yield. The third step is to divide the NOI by the cap rate to get the indicated value (capitalized value).

Net Operating Income

NOI is calculated as follows:

  Potential gross income
− Vacancy costs
= Effective gross income
− Operating expenses
= Net operating income

The operating expenses include taxes, repair and maintenance, management fees, telephone, insurance, legal and accounting fees, trash removal, and other costs. As an example, consider an apartment building with 100 units, each renting for $500 per month. The vacancy cost is assumed to be 5 percent or $30,000 per year. If operating expenses amounted to $270,000 per year, the annual NOI would be $300,000.

The Capitalization Rate

There are four ways of estimating the cap rate—the market extraction method, the band of investment method, the summation method, and the Ellwood method.

The Market Extraction Method The market extraction method is the easiest way of estimating the cap rate, if the data is readily available. The cap rate is simply NOI divided by the sales price. Data from comparable income properties that were sold recently is used to calculate the cap rate. If available, three or four comparables should be used.

The example shown in Table 37-1 shows the application of the market extraction method. The cap rate would be somewhere between 10 percent and 11 percent. If the third property bears the closest resemblance to the subject property, a cap rate of 10.5 percent should be used.

The Band of Investment Method In the band of investment method, the cap rate is the weighted average of the equity dividend rate and the mortgage constant, where the weights are the equity/value ratio and the loan/value ratio respectively.

The *equity dividend rate,* also called the *cash-on-cash return,* is the cash flow before taxes divided by the investor's equity in the property. The *cash flow before taxes* is NOI less the expected annual debt service (principal and interest). The *mortgage constant* is the annual debt service divided by the loan amount.

If there is also a junior or second mortgage, the cap rate is the weighted average of the equity dividend rate and the mortgage constants of the two mortgages.

Table 37-1 Market Extraction Method Applied to Three Comparable Properties

	Comparable 1	*Comparable 2*	*Comparable 3*
NOI	10	12	9
Sales price (SP)	100	109	86
NOI/SP	0.1	0.11	0.105

The example in Table 37-2 shows the application of this method.

The Summation Method The cap rate is an investor's required rate of return. This rate consists of the rate of return an investor would earn on a risk-free investment (such as the Treasury bill rate) a risk premium, an illiquidity premium and management premium.

The example in Table 37-3 shows the application of the summation method.

The Ellwood Method The Ellwood method is the most complicated of the four methods. It also assumes a multiperiod analysis. The Ellwood formula for the cap rate is:

$$r = i1(L/V1) + (1 - L/V1)i2 + [1 - (V2/V1) - (L/V1)(F1/F2)]/F3$$

where: r = cap rate
i1 = Mortgage constant = (12 × monthly mortgage payment)/L
L = Loan amount
V1 = Current value of the property
i2 = Equity dividend rate
V2 = Value of the property at the end of the holding period
F1 = Future value of a monthly deposit of $1 at the end of the holding period at a rate equal to the mortgage rate

$$= \frac{(1 + i3/12)^{12m} - 1,}{i3/12}$$

where: i3 = mortgage rate
m = holding period in years

F2 = Future value of a monthly deposit of $1 at the end of the term of the mortgage at a rate equal to the mortgage rate

Table 37-2 Determining the Weighted Rate with the Band of Investment Method

(1) *Source of Funds*	*(2)* *Amount*	*(3)* *%*	*(4)* *Rate (%)*	*(5) = (3) * (4)* *Weighted Rate (%)*
Equity	$300,000	30	14	4.2
Mortgage	$700,000	70	12	8.4
	$1,000,000	100		Cap Rate *12.6*

Table 37-3 Determining the Cap Rate with the Summation Method

Component	*Rate (%)*
Risk-free rate	6
Risk premium	2
Illiquidity premium	1
Management premium	1
Cap rate	*10*

$$= \frac{(1 + i3/12)^{12n} - 1,}{i3/12}$$ where: n = term of the loan in years

F3 = Future value of an annual deposit of $1 at the end of the holding period at a rate equal to the equity dividend rate

$$= \frac{(1 + i2)^{m} - 1}{i2}$$

EXAMPLE: The value of a property at the end of a 5-year holding period is expected to be 1.6 times its current value. The current loan-to-value ratio is 70 percent. The loan is for 25 years at 12 percent interest. The equity dividend rate for comparable properties is 14 percent.

SOLUTION:

1. The monthly payment of a loan of $1 for 25 years at 12 percent is $0.0105.
2. The annual debt service is $0.126 (=0.0105 × 12).
3. The mortgage constant is $0.126 (=0.126/1).
4. $F1 = \frac{(1 + .12/12)^{12(5)} - 1}{.12/12} = 81.67$
5. $F2 = \frac{(1 + .12/12)^{12(25)} - 1}{.12/12} = 1878.8466$
6. $F3 = \frac{(1 + .14)^{5} - 1}{.14} = 6.6101$

$$r = 0.126(0.7) + (1 - 0.7)(.14)$$
$$+ [1 - 1.6 - 0.7(81.67/1878.8466)]/6.6101$$
$$= 0.0348$$

The cap rate is 10.49 percent. As you can see, the Ellwood method requires relatively involved calculations.

The Indicated Value

Once NOI and the cap rate are estimated, the indicated value is simply NOI/cap rate. As an example, suppose NOI = $300,000 and the cap rate is 10 percent:

$$\text{Indicated Value} = 300{,}000/0.10 = 3{,}000{,}000$$

The Rent Multiplier

The rent multiplier shows the property value supported by a dollar of rent. It is estimated by dividing the actual sales price by monthly rent for each property that is comparable to the subject property. The multiplier is then multiplied by the estimated monthly rent of the subject property to get its indicated value. Table 37-4 shows sample calculations.

Assuming that the similarity between property C and the subject property is the greatest and the estimated monthly rent of the subject property is 525, the indicated value would be about $60,375 (525 × 115).

The Gross Income Multiplier

The gross income multiplier is similar to the rent multiplier, but instead of monthly rent, annual potential gross income is used. The ratio of sales price to potential gross income is calculated for three or four comparable properties. A plausible multiplier is derived for the subject property from the multipliers of the comparables based on similarity and the multiplier is multiplied by the estimated potential

Table 37-4 Determining Value Using the Rent Multiplier

Property	*Sales Price*	*Monthly Rent*	*Sales Price/ Monthly Rent*
A	50,000	500	100.00
B	65,000	550	118.18
C	60,000	520	115.38

gross income of the subject property to establish its indicated value.

Advantages of the Income Approach

The main advantage of the income approach is that it establishes value using the future income from the property. A capital asset has value because it generates future income and the income approach makes use of that.

Disadvantages of the Income Approach

The income approach is not appropriate for properties that do not generate future income. Even for income-producing properties, there are difficulties estimating the net operating income and the cap rate, especially when the appraisal involves a multiperiod analysis.

Correlation of Values

Hopefully, the market data method, the cost method, and the income method produce close estimates of the subject property's value. If there are substantial differences among the values of the three methods, the appraiser will arrive at an appropriate value by giving more weight to the value generated by the most appropriate method for evaluating the property in question. Averaging the values is, generally, not appropriate unless all methods are believed to be equally appropriate for the evaluation of the property.

CHAPTER

38 Financial Analysis of Income-Producing Properties

In evaluating a loan, particularly a recourse loan (a loan for which the borrower is personally responsible), the lender evaluates not only the property but also the ability and willingness of the borrower to repay the loan. For this reason, the borrower has to submit financial statements.

On the basis of the financial statements and information from other sources, the lender can determine the profitability, liquidity, and debt position of the borrowing firm. The lender can also evaluate the utilization of assets.

Profitability is determined by computing the profit margin (net income/sales), the operating profit margin (operating profit/sales), rate of return on equity (net income/equity), and rate of return on assets (net income/total assets).

Liquidity is determined by calculating the current ratio (current assets/current liabilities), and the quick ratio [(current assets − inventory)/current liabilities].

Debt position is measured by calculating the ratio of total liabilities to total assets, long-term debt to total assets, or long-term debt to equity.

Finally, utilization of assets can be evaluated by dividing sales by different assets, such as accounts receivable, inventory, and fixed assets.

For a more meaningful interpretation of ratios, industry averages or historical values of the ratios are used.

As far as willingness to pay is concerned, the lender can get information from firms like Dun and Bradstreet, Inc. and other organizations that provide credit information.

For nonrecourse loans, however, the focus of the analysis is on the property itself. So, the rest of the chapter deals with the main financial criteria used in underwriting income-producing property loans.

UNDERWRITING CRITERIA

There are no uniform criteria for underwriting income-producing property loans. The criteria vary from lender to lender and from property to property. Nonetheless, the main ratios used for this purpose are presented in this section and illustrated in the next section.

$$\text{(38-1)} \qquad \text{Debt Coverage Ratio} = \frac{\text{Net Operating Income}}{\text{Annual Debt Service}}$$

This ratio represents the amount of net income available to service a dollar of principal and interest. The higher the ratio, the better. Lenders specify minimum debt-coverage ratios for different types of income properties. The minimum ratios may be 1.1, 1.2, 1.3, and so on.

$$\text{(38-2)} \qquad \text{Operating Expense Ratio} = \frac{\text{Operating Expenses}}{\text{Effective Gross Income}}$$

This ratio represents the proportion of effective gross income that is used to cover operating expenses. This ratio may be compared with ratios of similar properties or the lender may specify the maximum value that is acceptable. For example, loans may be accepted only if the operating expense ratio is not more than 89 percent, 85 percent, and so on.

$$\text{(38-3)} \qquad \text{Breakeven Ratio} = \frac{\text{Debt Service} + \text{Operating Expenses}}{\text{Effective Gross Income}}$$

This ratio shows the amount of principal, interest, and operating expenses per dollar of effective gross income. For example, if it is 90 percent, it implies a safety margin of 10 percent. The safety margin indicates that effective gross income can decline by up to 10 percent and the income will still be large enough to cover debt service and operating expenses. The smaller the breakeven ratio or the higher the safety margin, the better.

(38–4) $$\text{Return on Assets} = \frac{\text{Net Operating Income}}{\text{Total Assets}}$$

This ratio shows the income per dollar of total investment (equity plus debt). The higher the ratio, the better.

(38–5) $$\text{Return on Equity} = \frac{\text{Net Operating Income}}{\text{Equity}}$$

This ratio shows the income per dollar of investment by the owners. The higher the ratio, the better.

(38–6) Cash Flow = Net Operating Income − Debt Service

The higher the cash flow, the better.

(38–7) Equity Dividend Rate = Cash Flow/Equity

This ratio measures the cash flow per dollar of equity. The higher it is, the better.

(38–8) Loan-to-Value Ratio = Loan Amount/Appraised Value

Lenders specify the maximum acceptable ratios for different types of properties.

(38–9) $$\text{Interest Coverage} = \frac{\text{Net Operating Income}}{\text{Interest Expense}}$$

This ratio shows the amount of net operating income available to cover interest expense. The higher the ratio the better.

Illustration

Consider the following data pertaining to an apartment building:

Potential gross income (400 units with monthly rent of $650)	=	$3,120,000
Vacancy cost (5% of potential gross income)	=	156,000
Operating expenses	=	1,964,000
Capitalization rate	=	12%
Proposed loan amount	=	5,000,000
Proposed interest rate	=	10%
Term of the proposed loan	=	25 years

The lender's parameters are:

Debt-coverage ratio	=	1.25 minimum
Breakeven ratio	=	85% maximum
Loan-to-value ratio	=	70% minimum

As the following calculations show, the proposed loan amount of $5 million meets all the lender's minimum requirements. In fact, the loan-to-value ratio and debt-coverage ratio would allow loan amounts of $5,833,333 and $8 million, respectively but these amounts would cause the breakeven ratio to exceed the lender's maximum level of 85 percent.

	Potential gross income	=	$3,120,000
−	Vacancy costs	=	156,000
=	Effective gross income (EGI)	=	2,964,000
−	Operating expenses (OE)	−	1,964,000
=	Net operating income (NOI)	=	1,000,000
/	Cap rate	/	.12
=	Indicated value (IV)	=	8,333,333

Debt service (DS) = Loan amount × Loan constant

$= 5{,}000{,}000 \times 0.110168$*

$= 550{,}840$

Debt-coverage ratio = NOI/DS = 1,000,000/550,840 = 1.82

Breakeven ratio = (DS + OE)/EGI

$$= \frac{550{,}840 + 1{,}964{,}000}{2{,}964{,}000} = 0.848$$

L/V ratio = L/IV = 5,000,000/8,333,333 = 0.6

Cash flow = NOI − DS = 1,000,000 − 550,840 = 449,160

Equity dividend rate = Cash flow/Equity

= 449,160/3,333,333 = 0.1347

Rate of return on equity = NOI/Equity

= 1,000,000/3,333,333

= 0.3

Rate of return on assets = NOI/Total assets

= 1,000,000/8,333,333

= 0.12

---

*$.10/[1-(1+.1)^{-25}] = 0.110168$

CHAPTER

39 NOTES, MORTGAGES, AND DEEDS OF TRUST

A mortgage loan requires a note and a mortgage or a note and deed of trust. In some states, the first combination is used; in others, the second combination is used. This chapter discusses notes, mortgages, and deeds of trust.

NOTES

A mortgage note is a legal document for transferring funds from the lender (mortgagee) to the borrower (mortgagor). It represents a promise to pay on the part of the borrower. It is the main evidence of debt. The note contains the interest rate, the loan amount, the term of the loan, and the scheduled monthly payments. For adjustable rate mortgages, it also explains the determination of the interest rate and the monthly payments.

Furthermore, it covers late payment charges, defaults, and the personal obligations of all persons who sign the note, including guarantors. However, since promises to pay are not enough, the note is secured by either a mortgage or a deed of trust.

MORTGAGE

A mortgage is not a promise to pay. It is a legal document that allows the lender to force the sale of property and recover his or her funds when the borrower defaults. The borrower pledges the property as collateral for the loan. For this reason, the property is explicitly identified or described in the mortgage.

As an example of a mortgage, the FNMA/FHCMC uniform mortgage for Illinois, shown in Appendix X, contains uniform and nonuniform covenants. The uniform covenants apply to all states and the nonuniform covenants apply to specific states.

Mortgage Covenants or Clauses

The mortgage lists a number of covenants. The covenants include the borrower's obligation to pay principal, interest, taxes, insurance, any prepayment and late charges; not to destroy or damage the property; and the rights of the lender to inspect the property, to receive condemnation proceeds and to accelerate payments in the event of the sale of the property. Acceleration or due on sale clause means the entire balance of the loan is due and payable immediately. This situation may arise when the property is sold or when there is a breach of contract.

The mortgage may also contain receiver, estoppel, and warrant of title and satisfaction of mortgage clauses. The receiver clause allows the appointment of a receiver by a court to collect rents and pay expenses on a foreclosed property until the property is sold. This clause applies, mainly, to income- producing properties.

The estoppel clause is used primarily with the assignment of a mortgage. The lender can assign the mortgage to another party. In such a situation, the mortgagor is required to confirm the mortgage balance.

In the warrant of title clause, the borrower states that he or she is the owner of the property and that he or she will defend the title against any claims, except the encumbrances of record.

The satisfaction of mortgage clause releases the mortgage. After the loan is fully paid off, the lender sends the borrower a signed statement confirming the full payment of the loan. When the satisfaction of the mortgage or release of mortgage is recorded at the county recorder's office, the lien on the property is removed.

DEEDS OF TRUST

A deed of trust is similar to a mortgage. It is used to secure a mortgage note. The clauses or covenants of the deed of trust and the mortgage are about the same. The main difference is that in a deed of trust, there are three parties—the trustor (borrower), the beneficiary (lender), and the trustee. In a mortgage, there are only two parties—the borrower and the lender.

The trustee holds title to the property in behalf of the lender. When the loan is paid off, the title is transferred to the borrower. If the borrower defaults, the trustee sells the property and uses the proceeds to pay off the loan. A trustee sale is explained further under foreclosures.

CHAPTER

40 DEFAULTS AND FORECLOSURES

Failure to perform obligations as required by the mortgage constitutes default by the borrower. If the borrower does not make the payments within a specified number of days (usually 30 days) after the due date, the borrower is in default. Also, failure to pay taxes, buy hazard insurance, or damaging the property may constitute default.

The lender notifies the borrower to cure the default within a specified number of days. If the borrower fails to cure the default, the lender may initiate foreclosure proceedings to force the sale of the house and recover his or her funds.

DEFAULT AND ACCELERATION

The main reason for default is nonpayment of principal and interest. After the due date, there is usually a grace period during which the borrower pays the monthly payment with a late payment charge. After the grace period, the lender may remind the borrower to tender the arrears or decide to accelerate the debt. With acceleration, the entire debt would be due and payable immediately.

The mere delay of the payments does not, automatically, result in acceleration. First, the mortgage should have an acceleration clause. Second, the lender should notify the borrower that the debt has been accelerated. Once the lender accelerates the debt, the lender can reject payment of arrears to bring the account up to date. The lender can also impose new conditions like higher interest rate for accepting the borrower's tender of arrears. Before, the acceleration of the debt, the lender would be obligated to accept all back payments of principal, interest, and other payments.

TYPES OF FORECLOSURES

What happens after acceleration depends on the type of foreclosure. There are four types of foreclosures: strict foreclosure, writ of entry, judicial sale, and power of sale.

Strict Foreclosure

In a strict foreclosure, a court orders the borrower to pay the amount due within a defined period of time. If the borrower fails to make the payment within the specified period of time, the title to the property is transferred to the lender.

Writ of Entry

In a writ of entry, the lender notifies the borrower of foreclosure and takes possession of the property. Foreclosure by entry and strict foreclosure are not widely used. The most widely used types are judicial sale and power of sale.

Judicial Sale

In a judicial sale, the lender notifies the borrower that the entire debt is due and payable immediately. If the borrower fails to make the payment, the lender orders a title search, notifies all concerned parties, and files a complaint of default with a court. At the same time, a *lis pendens* is filed with the county recorder's office. The *lis pendens* notifies the public that a law suit is pending. If the lender proves default, the court issues a foreclosure judgment and orders the sale of the property at a public auction.

If the borrower has a statutory right to redeem the property, the buyer of the property is given a certificate of sale. If the borrower is unable to buy back the property during the redemption period, the buyer receives a sheriff's deed.

The proceeds from the sale are first used to pay the lender for the balance, including legal costs. Then other (junior) creditors are paid. Any remaining funds are given to the borrower.

Sometimes, the price at which the property is sold may be lower than the mortgage balance. In this case, the court may award the lender a deficiency judgment. The borrower would be required to make up the difference out of pocket.

If the property cannot be sold at the minimum auction price, the auction price may be reduced, or the lender may get title to the property.

Power of Sale

The power of sale is, usually, used with a trust deed. A clause in the deed of trust allows the trustee to sell the property without going to court. First, the borrower is given a notice of default and the notice is recorded. If the borrower does not pay all the debt within a given period of time, the trustee issues a notice of sale, advertises it, and sells the property in a public sale. The trustee sale through a power of sale clause is faster than a judicial sale.

REDEMPTION RIGHTS

Even after the debt has been accelerated, the borrower has the right to redeem the property by paying the amount due. The borrower has an equitable right of redemption and, possibly, a statutory right of redemption.

In an equitable right of redemption, the borrower has the right to redeem the property at any time before the foreclosure sale takes place. With the cooperation of the lender, the borrower may be able to sell the property before the foreclosure sale. This right exists in all states.

In some states, the borrower may have another chance to redeem the property within a specified period after the date of the foreclosure sale. This right is called the *statutory right of redemption.* In this case, the public sale of the property by the sheriff is not a final sale. The sale becomes final if the borrower fails to redeem the property within the statutory redemption period.

DEED IN LIEU OF FORECLOSURE

As an alternative to foreclosure, the borrower may be able to give a deed to the lender. The lender takes title subject to all the liens on the property.

CHAPTER

41 Private Mortgage Insurance, Title Insurance, and Hazard Insurance

Private mortgage insurance (PMI), title insurance (TI), and hazard insurance (HI) reduce the risks of real estate loans. TI and HI also reduce the risks of homeownership for the buyer/borrower.

PRIVATE MORTGAGE INSURANCE

A previous chapter pointed out that a mortgage loan is normally smaller than the smaller of the appraised value or price of the property. In other words, the loan-to-value ratio (LTV) is less than one. The higher the LTV, the greater the risk to the lender. So, when the LTV exceeds 80 percent, the lender requires PMI.

PMI shifts the risk associated with higher LTV from the lender to the mortgage insurance company.

Description

In PMI, the mortgage insurance company insures a portion of the loan amount. The cost of the insurance is paid by the borrower.

How It Works

If the LTV exceeds 80 percent, the lender sends the application for PMI to a mortgage insurance company that the lender works with.

The application package includes a credit report, verifications of employment and deposit, appraisal report, purchase agreement, and other materials required by the mortgage insurance company. The company evaluates the application using its own criteria. Generally, PMI companies prefer low debt ratios, borrowers with their own money for downpayment, and borrowers who buy properties to be occupied by themselves.

If the borrower and the property meet the mortgage insurance company's requirements, the PMI company agrees to insure a portion of the loan amount. The coverage or proportion insured may vary from 10 percent to 35 percent.

The cost of the PMI (the premium) varies from company to company. Even within the same company, the premium depends on the coverage, the LTV ratio, and the type of mortgage to be obtained. Depending on these factors and the pattern of payments, a PMI company may have quite a few premium plans. As an example, the premium for a fixed-rate mortgage with a LTV of 91 percent through 95 percent and a 25 percent coverage may be 1 percent of the loan amount in the first year and 0.34 percent every year thereafter. For a LTV of 81 percent through 85 percent and 20 percent coverage, the first year premium may be 0.30 percent and renewal premiums may be 0.29 percent each year.

The first year premium plus, possibly, two months' premiums are collected at closing. The renewal premiums are paid monthly as part of the regular monthly payment. The monthly renewal premium (amount) is simply the renewal premium (a percent) times the loan amount divided by 12.

The premiums may decline after 10 years. Moreover, the lender may at his or her option, cancel PMI when the LTV ratio falls below 80 percent.

As long as the PMI company is strong, PMI reduces the lender's risk. It is a substitute for a downpayment, although PMI does not increase the borrower's equity in the property. Suppose, for example, that the price of the property is $100,000 and the loan amount is $95,000. With 25 percent coverage, PMI reduces the lender's risk exposure to $71,250 [= 100,000 − 5000 − (95,000 × .25)].

If the borrower defaults, the lender's claim may be settled in one of two ways. The PMI company may pay the lender's entire claim (balance, legal fees, taxes, and so on), take title to the property and sell it; or it may simply pay a claim based on the coverage.

Advantages of PMI

PMI enables people with little money for downpayments to purchase homes. PMI is also good for lenders. It enables them to expand their loan activities to buyers who otherwise would not qualify. PMI applications are also processed relatively quickly.

Disadvantages of PMI

On the negative side, unless loans are underwritten carefully, PMI companies can face major losses and when PMI companies suffer major financial losses, PMI is less dependable.

TITLE INSURANCE

Title insurance is another device that lenders require to protect their loans. Title insurance can also protect the interests of the buyer of the property.

Description

Title insurance is a policy in which the title company agrees to protect the insured against losses or damages resulting from defects in a title that were not, specifically, excluded by the policy.

How It Works

Typically, the buyer of the property buys title insurance policy for the lender. This is called the *mortgagee's title policy.* The seller of the property also buys title insurance policy for the buyer. This policy is called the *owner's title policy.* The mortgagee's title policy protects the lender and the owner's title policy protects the buyer. These policies are separate policies and the face amounts are different. The face amount of the mortgagee's policy is equal to the loan amount, while that of the owner's policy is equal to the purchase price of the property.

The premium of a title insurance policy is a one-time premium paid at closing. The owner's policy protects the buyer for as long as the buyer owns the property, the owner's successors and heirs, but not new buyers. If the property is sold, the new buyer will not be protected by the seller's policy. However, if the seller's policy was purchased recently, a new policy can be issued at a discount, because the amount of search required will be smaller. The more recent the issue date of the seller's policy, the greater the discount.

A substantial discount also applies when both the mortgagee's policy and the owner's policy are issued simultaneously, because two policies are issued on the basis of one title search. The premiums vary from company to company.

The mortgagee's policy insures that the mortgage is the first lien on the property. It also insures a marketable title, that is, if a well-informed party is not willing to buy the property because of a title defect, the title company will cover the loss resulting from the non-marketability of the title.

The title company will also protect the owner of the property from any claims that were not excluded by the policy. It will defend the owner in court at its own expense, and if the owner suffers losses as a result of the claims, the title company will cover the losses up to the face value of the policy.

Exclusions

The title policy insures against defects that exist as of the date of the policy, not after, because the title search is made up to the date of the policy. Even then, the title company does not insure the owner against all defects. Some title defects are specifically excluded. Examples of exceptions are taxes that are not shown in public records, changes in government laws, eminent domain, defects that were known to the insured but not to the title company at the date of policy, and future defects.

Covered Defects

The title company covers claims arising from defects that are shown in the public records, such as liens, mortgages and easements, and hidden defects. *Hidden defects* are defects that are not shown in the public records and examples of hidden defects are claims arising from forged signatures, misrepresentation of marital status, incompetence of the seller of the property (due, for example, to minority or senility), rights of undisclosed heirs, and errors made by the title company in doing the title search.

The title insurance policy has two schedules: A and B. Schedule A names the insured and shows the legal description of the property. Schedule B lists the exceptions.

An Abstract of Title

An abstract of title with a legal opinion is sometimes used in place of title insurance. The abstract of title shows the chain of title and all the documents that affect the title. It is examined by an attorney to determine whether the title is good.

However, the abstract is not as good as title insurance. There is no insurance protection. Moreover, it is time-consuming to prepare.

A Warranty Deed

A warranty deed by the seller also provides some protection. The seller warrants that the title is good and that he or she will forever defend any claims against the title. The warranty is good for claims arising from existing or future defects. Because of this, the warranty deeds seems to offer greater protection than a title insurance policy.

However, a buyer has to consider two potential problems with warranty deeds. First, the seller may move to an unknown place and become difficult to find. Second, even if the seller is found, he or she may not have the financial capacity to honor the warranties, especially if the seller is an individual. A financially strong title insurance company would be in a better position to provide protection against claims.

HAZARD INSURANCE

Hazard insurance is another device that protects the interests of the lender and the owner. Hazard insurance is required by the lender, but even if the lender did not require it, it would be prudent for an owner to buy hazard insurance or a broad homeowner's insurance policy.

Description

Hazard insurance provides protection to the insured from losses or damages arising from a broad list of risks or perils. Examples of covered perils would be fire and storm. The cost of the insurance is borne by the property owner.

How It Works

The buyer must buy hazard insurance before closing. The buyer can choose the insurance company from which to purchase the policy.

The lender requires that the lender and his or her successors or assignees be designated as beneficiaries.

In addition to requiring the purchase of hazard insurance before closing, the lender usually collects two months of insurance premiums at closing. This amount is held in escrow. The regular monthly payments also include insurance premiums that are placed in escrow. The monthly insurance premium is, simply, the annual premium divided by 12. The lender uses the accumulated amount in escrow to renew the insurance policy for the borrower.

Forms of the Homeowner's Insurance Policy

There are different forms of homeowner's insurance policies. HO–1 or the basic form covers 10 perils or risks. HO–2 is broader than HO–1. It covers more risks. HO–3 is even broader than HO–2. HO–5 offers the broadest coverage. It covers all risks on buildings and personal property. There are also policies for renters (HO–4) and condominium owners (HO–6).

Coverage

Homeowner's insurance policies provide two types of coverage: property coverage and liability coverage. The property coverage insures dwellings, accompanying structures, and unscheduled personal property against perils. It also covers living expenses.

Liability coverage provides protection from claims arising from negligence of the owner. It also includes medical payments to others.

Coinsurance

Coinsurance is a clause that requires the insured to buy a policy with a face amount equal to a specified percentage of the replacement cost in order to get the full benefit of insurance. For example, suppose a property is insured on a replacement cost basis and its estimated replacement cost is $200,000. With coinsurance of 80 percent, the face amount of the policy should be $160,000. Now, assume the garage is damaged and that it would cost $8000 to repair it. The insurance company pays the entire $8000.

However, if the face amount of the policy is only 60 percent of the replacement cost ($120,000), the insurance company would pay only $6,000 ($= .6/.8 \times 8000$).

CHAPTER

42 TITLE CLOSING

The signing of a purchase agreement or sales contract represents the formal beginning of the process of purchasing real estate. The *purchase agreement* contains the names of the parties, the legal description of the property, and the terms and conditions under which the purchase will be completed. For example, the purchase contract may require the seller to deliver a warranty deed and a marketable title. The contract may also state that the agreement is contingent on the buyer obtaining a loan within a specified period of time.

When all the items that are required for the completion of the purchase are ready, there is a title closing. The closing date usually is three to four weeks from the date of the signing of the purchase agreement, but may be more.

Description

Basically, a *title closing* is a meeting in which the seller signs the deed and delivers it to the buyer. The buyer signs the mortgage note and mortgage or deed of trust, and the proceeds of the loan, together with the downpayment, are paid to the seller. All closing costs are also paid at closing.

HOW IT WORKS

The actual closing does not take much time if all the items needed for the closing are done before the actual closing. On the buyer's side, the items include credit reports, appraisal reports, verifications of employment and deposit, survey, hazard insurance, PMI (if the loan-to-value ratio exceeds 80 percent) and mortgagee's title insurance policy.

On the seller's side, a deed and a bill of sale have to be prepared, the owner's title insurance policy has to be obtained, and a letter to tenants advising them to send rents to the new owner should be prepared. The seller should also show proof of payment of taxes and utility bills and should be prepared to give the keys to the new buyer at closing. If the building is new, the seller should obtain a certificate of occupancy from the city. The certificate shows that the building is ready for occupancy.

The uniform settlement statement form has to be prepared before closing. This form shows the settlement charges and the net amount to be paid by the borrower and the net amount that will be received by the seller. The settlement charges that are paid by the buyer include the loan origination fee, discount points, appraisal fee, credit report fee, prepaid interest, closing fee, title insurance premium, document preparation fee, survey fee, recording fees, and—where an assumption is involved—possibly an assumption fee. Furthermore, the buyer may have to deposit tax and insurance reserves with the lender.

Typical expenses on the seller's side include title insurance charges, deed preparation fee, and broker's commission.

Because some items (such as rent) are paid in advance and some expenses (like taxes) in some counties are paid in arrears, prorations have to be made. The items that are, typically, prorated are property taxes, rents or rental properties, utility bills, mortgage interest, and an insurance premium if the buyer assumes the seller's mortgage and insurance policies.

Although the buyer is entitled to good faith estimate of settlement costs at the time of loan application, these costs are only estimates. The actual closing costs may not be ready until a day or so before closing. The buyer receives a copy of the closing statement at closing.

Other documents that the buyer receives at closing include the truth-in-lending statement and copies of the mortgage note and the mortgage. The deed and title insurance policy may be received at a later date.

After closing, the deed and mortgage have to be recorded at the county recorder's office. They provide constructive notice to the world of the change in the title to the property and the new lien on the property.

CLOSING IN ESCROW

Sometimes, titles are closed in escrow. This arrangement is especially convenient in land contract cases. A third party, called the *escrow agent,* is selected. The escrow agent may be an attorney, a bank, or a broker.

The escrow agent holds the downpayment from the buyer, the deed to the property, the title, and hazard insurance policies until all required payments by the buyer are completed, at which time the deed is given to the buyer.

CLOSING A PERMANENT LOAN ON AN INCOME PROPERTY

As in the case of residential properties, the actual closing of a permanent loan should not take much time if all the items needed for closing have been prepared.

The objective is to get the loan from the permanent lender and, for new properties, pay off the construction loan. In order to get the permanent loan, the construction lender and developer/builder have to meet the permanent lender's requirements. The requirements are spelled out in the loan commitment.

The items that are typically needed to close a permanent loan include proof of completion (such as certificates of occupancy or certification by an engineer), financial statements from the borrower, proof of payment of taxes, survey after the completion of the construction project, permits or approvals from government units, hazard insurance policy, title insurance policy, subordination agreement for ground leases, assignment of leases, and the articles of incorporation for corporations or partnership agreements for partnerships.

V Interest Rates and Financial Futures

CHAPTER 43 INTERESTRATES

The interest rate of a real estate loan, like any other type of loan, affects the size of the borrower's periodic payment. When interest rates increase, fewer people are able to qualify for mortgage loans, and the quantity of mortgage credit demanded declines. This also tends to force a decline in the demand for real properties.

Moreover, higher interest rates reduce the values of mortgages. Investors who own mortgages suffer capital losses when interest rates rise and experience gains when interest rates decline.

The growing securitization of mortgages has made mortgage rates more sensitive to changes in the bond markets and other developments in the economy. This chapter explains interest rates and their determinants.

THE DETERMINATION OF INTEREST RATES

Interest is the price of credit. It is determined by the interaction between the supply of credit and the demand for credit. When the supply of credit exceeds the demand for credit, the excess supply of credit exerts a downward pressure on the interest rate and it falls. When the demand for credit exceeds its supply, the excess demand forces the interest rate up. When demand equals supply, the interest rate remains stable and is called the *equilibrium interest rate.* The equilibrium interest rate changes only when the demand for credit changes, the supply of credit changes, or both change. This theory of interest rate determination is called the *loanable funds theory.*

SOURCES AND USES OF CREDIT

The sources of credit in the economy are households and businesses. Household saving—called *personal saving*—is, simply, the portion of disposable income that is not consumed, while *business saving* consists of undistributed corporate profits (retained earnings) and capital consumption allowances (depreciation allowances). The government could also be a source of credit if its revenues exceeded its expenditures. The Federal Reserve System (FRS) or central bank also has the ability to increase the supply of credit in the economy. Finally, inflows of foreign capital increase the supply of credit.

Most of the credit is channeled to ultimate users through financial intermediaries—banks, savings and loans, mutual savings banks, credit unions, insurance companies, pension funds, and finance companies. This process is called *financial intermediation* (*indirect finance*). When the credit flows directly to the ultimate users, it is called *direct finance*.

The ultimate users of credit are also households, businesses, and the government. Households borrow money to buy real estate and consumer durables (automobiles, furniture, appliances, and so on). Businesses borrow money to finance expenditures on plant and equipment and inventory. Finally, the government borrows money to finance budget deficits.

DETERMINANTS OF INTEREST RATES

If household saving or business saving or both increase, the supply of credit increases and—given the same level of demand—the interest rate declines. The interest rate also declines if the FRS increases the supply of money and credit. The FRS can increase the supply of credit by buying securities (such as Treasury bills) from the public, lowering the legal reserve requirements against bank deposits, and cutting the discount rate. The purchase of securities by the FRS (called *open market operations*) injects new money into the banking system. The banks use the money to make loans (bank credit).

A reduction in the legal reserve requirement enables banks to have more money for lending purposes. They keep lower reserves against deposits.

Finally, a cut in the discount rate encourages bank borrowing and credit expansion. This instrument has weaker effect on credit expansion, but it has a psychological effect. A cut indicates a liberal credit policy by the government. The discount rate is the interest rate that the FRS charges on loans to banks.

Interest rates fall if personal and business savings decline and the FRS reduces the supply of credit by selling securities (open market operations), raising legal reserve requirements against bank deposits, or raising the discount rate.

Changes in the demand for credit also affect the interest rate. The interest rate increases if there is an increase in household demand for mortgage and consumer credit, if businesses demand more commercial credit, or if the government borrows more money to finance a widening budget deficit.

INTEREST RATES AND INFLATION

Inflation is the sustained increase in the general price level as measured by the consumer price index or a price index based on the gross national product (GNP). As prices increase, the purchasing power of the dollar decreases. The dollar becomes worth less in terms of goods and services.

With inflation, the purchasing value of loans declines. To protect the decline in the purchasing value of their loans, lenders sometimes include an inflation premium to the interest rate at which loans are made, that is, in the nominal interest rate. The inflation premium compensates the lender for price increases.

Consider a one-year loan of $100. The interest rate is 3 percent and there are no risks, taxes, or inflation. At the end of the year, the amount will be $103, the principal amount plus the interest of $3. If we assume a 3 percent expected inflation and a nominal interest rate of 3 percent, the nominal amount at the end of the year will still be $103, but its real value will be $100 ($103/1.03). The real value is the nominal value divided by 1 plus the inflation rate.

The real or inflation-adjusted interest in the previous example is 0 percent (3 percent − 3 percent). It is the nominal interest rate minus the inflation rate. If the lender wishes to protect the real value of the loan and still earn 3 percent after adjusting for inflation, the lending rate should be roughly 6 percent (3 percent + 3 percent). The expected inflation rate is added to the interest rate in the absence of inflation (real rate).

The actual inflation rate may turn out to be different from the expected rate. If the actual exceeds the expected inflation rate, the lender will experience a loss in the real value of the loan. If the expected exceeds the actual inflation rate, the lender will realize a gain. Since forecasts of inflation or expectations of future inflation change from time to time, lenders react by changing interest rates whenever expectations of future inflation change. For example, people may expect higher inflation if there are unexpected increases in money supply or GNP and this, in turn, leads to higher interest rates as lenders do not wish to sustain losses in the real values of their loans.

MORTGAGE RATES

For simplicity of exposition, the previous sections assumed that there was only one interest rate in the economy. However, in the actual world, there are many interest rates in effect concurrently. There are different rates on deposits, commercial loans, mortgage loans, and consumer loans. Even in the mortgage markets, several different interest rates apply, depending on the lending institution, the type of property, the length of the loan, and the type of mortgage.

The principles discussed earlier still apply. Instead of a single market, we can think of a number of financial markets in which the interest rate on a particular type of credit is determined by the supply of and demand for that particular credit. This framework explains the existence of different mortgage rates.

A number of specific factors that create differences in mortgage rates can also be mentioned. Examples of such factors would be differences in risk, marketability, taxation, and administrative costs. Riskier loans require higher rates. For example, land development loans and construction loans have relatively high rates. Second mortgages have higher rates than first mortgages. Thirty-year fixed-rate mortgages, generally, have higher rates than 15-year fixed-rate mortgages, because there are more risks and uncertainties with the longer term. Also, initial rates on adjustable-rate mortgages are lower than rates on fixed-rate mortgages.

Marketability also affects mortgage rates. Rates on conforming loans are lower than loans on nonconforming loans. *Nonconforming loans* are large loans that exceed the limits for loans that can be purchased by Fannie Mae and Freddie Mac. Thus, they are more difficult to sell in the secondary mortgage markets.

Taxation also affects mortgage rates. State and local governments issue tax-exempt bonds to raise funds for financing home purchases by individuals. Since the interest on the bonds is not subject to federal income taxes, the rates on the bonds are relatively low and the mortgage rates are also low relative to rates on conventional mortgages.

Administrative costs may also affect mortgage rates. More efficient lenders may be able to charge lower rates on mortgage loans.

The overall level of mortgage rates depends on the supply of and demand for mortgage credit. The main sources of mortgage credit are savings and loans, banks, mutual savings banks, credit unions, insurance companies, pension funds, state and local governments, the federal government, federally sponsored credit agencies (Fannie Mae and Freddie Mac), and individuals. The main uses of mortgage credit are the financing of single-family and multifamily residences, commercial properties, and farm properties. Changes in the supply of and demand for mortgage credit result in changes in mortgage rates.

It must be pointed out that the financial markets are not compartmentalized. Changes in one market have a bearing on another. As mentioned earlier, the securitization of mortgages has made the mortgage market more sensitive to changes in the other capital markets, particularly the bond markets. Also, keep in mind that interest rates, in general, depend on the overall relationship between the supply of and the demand for credit in the economy. For this reason, interest rates move up or down together.

CHAPTER

44 FINANCIAL FUTURES

In the 1970s, the level and volatility of interest rates in the economy started to increase. As a result, savings and loans were squeezed financially. Their assets were primarily long-term assets with fixed rates (mortgages), but their deposits were short-term. As rates on deposits increased, their profits declined.

A number of strategies were devised to reduce their exposure to interest rate risk. First, the use of adjustable-rate mortgages and short-term consumer loans effectively reduced the duration of S&L assets. Second, lengthening of liabilities and interest rate swaps helped S&Ls during the high interest rate 1970s. In an interest rate swap, a savings and loan pays another firm's interest on long-term liabilities, and the other firm pays interest on the S&L's short-term liabilities (deposits). Interest rate swaps help in duration (maturity) matching. Third, financial futures were used to reduce exposure to interest rate risk. This third strategy is the subject of this chapter.

DESCRIPTION

A *financial future* is a contract to deliver or take at a specified time in the future a specific amount of a specific financial asset at a specified price and place. The financial asset may be Treasury securities (bills, notes, and bonds), bank certificates of deposit, foreign currencies or Ginnie Maes.The contracts are standardized with respect to quantity (size), delivery month, and price changes.

The futures contracts are traded in organized exchanges. The oldest and largest futures exchange is the Chicago Board of Trade, but there are over 10 other futures exchanges.

A trader's futures contract to deliver or take financial assets are actually contracts with the clearinghouse that guarantees the delivery or acceptance of the underlying assets. However, as a safety measure, the trader is required to post an initial margin. This is a good faith deposit and is a small fraction of the futures contract. There is also a maintenance margin. This margin is lower than the initial margin, and if the balance in the account falls to a level lower than the maintenance margin, the trader is required to make an additional deposit.

Each account is "marked to market" daily. A loss reduces the account balance; a profit increases it. Large losses could trigger margin maintenance calls.

The underlying securities of futures contracts—Treasury securities, CDs, and so on—can be bought and sold in the cash market at cash or spot prices. The spot prices are for the immediate delivery of the assets. The futures prices are for the future delivery of assets. The difference between the cash price and futures price of an asset is called the *basis*.

The futures markets are used by speculators to make profits and by hedgers to reduce risks. This chapter deals with hedging only.

When a trader hedges a current (existing) position in the cash market, it is called a *cash hedge;* when the trader hedges an expected or anticipated position in the cash market, it is called an *anticipatory hedge*.

To protect the cash value of a portfolio of assets in the cash market, a trader sells futures contracts. This is called a *short hedge*. To protect himself or herself from increases in the cost of a position, the trader buys futures contracts; this is called a *long hedge*. Thus, selling is a short position and buying is a long position.

A *perfect hedge* (a no risk position) exists when the basis remains the same. If the basis increases, there is a net gain from a short hedge and a net loss from a long hedge. The opposite holds if the basis decreases. So, the key to hedging is the reduction of basis risk. For a perfect hedge, the basis should stay the same.

A major factor in reducing basis risk is the selection of the hedging vehicle. If the underlying asset of a futures contract is the same as the asset in the cash market that has to be hedged, the basis risk will be low. This is called a *direct* or *straight hedge*. For example, a portfolio of GNMA securities may be protected using GNMA futures.

Sometimes, it is difficult to find a futures contract with an underlying asset that is the same as the asset in the cash market to be hedged. Even if the instruments are the same, the instruments may differ with respect to quantity, coupon rate, and risk level. Moreover, the delivery month of the futures contract may not match the trader's hedging horizon. In this case, it would be a *cross hedge*, not a direct hedge. The price of the instrument in the cash market should be highly correlated with the futures price. As an example of a cross hedge, futures contracts on Treasury bonds may be used to hedge mortgage portfolios.

Although a futures contract is for the future delivery of a specific asset, traders need not take delivery of the assets. They can get out of the contract by reversing their trades. The seller of a futures contract can cancel the sale by buying a futures contract with the same underlying asset and the same delivery month.

HOW FINANCIAL FUTURES ARE USED

In order to use futures to reduce exposure to interest rate risks, the hedger has to:

1. Determine the dollar amount of the position in the cash market that has to be hedged.
2. Select an appropriate futures contract to minimize basis risk. A direct hedge would be ideal.
3. Determine the number of contracts that would be needed to hedge the position.
4. Buy or sell futures contracts.
5. Reverse the trade at the end of the hedging horizon. Although a hedger can accept or make delivery, it is, generally, more convenient to make a reversing trade to cancel the original futures contract.

EXAMPLE: Consider a savings and loan association with $5 million of Ginnie Mae pass-throughs in its portfolio. The savings and loan is concerned that interest rates will rise over the next few months and cause a decline in the value of its pass-throughs.

The savings and loan uses financial futures to hedge its existing position. The steps that were outlined above are followed. First, the amount to be hedged is $50 million.

Second, a GNMA futures contract is used. There are two types of GNMA futures contracts—the GNMA CDR and CD GNMA futures contracts. The GNMA Collateralized Deposit Receipt (CDR) was the first financial futures contract to be introduced. It was introduced by the Chicago Board of Trade in 1975. This contract requires the delivery of certificates backed by GNMA 8 percent certificates with a principal balance of $100,000. The receipt can be used to redeem the equivalent of GNMA 8 percent certificates with a $100,000 balance from a depository such as a bank. It can also be sold or held for interest income.

In 1978, a second GNMA futures contract was introduced—the Certificate Delivery GNMA futures contract. This contract requires the delivery of the actual GNMA certificates.

In each case, the par value (trading unit) of a contract is $100,000 and the coupon rate is 8 percent. The prices are quoted as percent of par. For example, a quote of 90–16 means 90 16/32 percent of the par value. For purposes of this example, the GNMA CDR futures contract is used.

Third, the number of futures contracts to be bought is determined by dividing the amount to be hedged by the par value of the futures contract. In this case it is 50 (=5,000,000/100,000). For a cross hedge, this amount would be adjusted by other factors that are not discussed here.

Fourth, the savings and loan sells 50 September GNMA CDR futures contracts in March at a price of 90–00. Meanwhile, the spot price of a GNMA certificate in the cash market in March is 95–16.

Fifth, the savings and loan association (S&L) reverses its trade in June by buying 50 September GNMA CDR futures contracts at 85–00. The price of GNMA certificate in the cash market in June is assumed to be 90–16.

The results of the hedge are summarized in Table 44–1.

Table 44–1 Hedging Pass-Throughs

Cash Market	*Futures Market*
March	
S & L wants to protect value of $5mn. GNMA portfolio at 95–16 (value = $4,775,000)	S & L sells 50 Sept. GNMA futures contracts at 90–00 (value = $4,500,000)
June	
Price of GNMA certificate declines to 90–16 (value $4,525,000)	S & L buys 50 Sept. GNMA futures contracts at 85–00 (value $4,250,000)

Loss in cash market = $250,000
Gain in futures market = $250,000

As the table indicates, the losses in the cash market were fully offset by gains in the futures market. This perfect hedge was possible because the basis remained the same. It was 5–16 (95–16 less 90–00) in March and 5–16 in June (90–16 less 85–00). The basis remained the same because, this was a direct hedge. However, a perfect hedge may be difficult to attain. There may be gains or losses from the hedge.

VI Appendixes

APPENDIX

1 MATHEMATICS OF FINANCE: A Review

A complete understanding of real estate finance requires knowledge of financial mathematics. This appendix reviews mathematical concepts and formulas that will be useful throughout the chapters of this book. Specifically, the appendix covers compounding and discounting concepts and the calculations of the various elements of the present value of an ordinary annuity formula.

THE FUTURE VALUE OF A PRESENT SUM

Two future value formulas are presented here. The first assumes annual compounding. The second may be used with any finite frequency of compounding.

Annual Compounding

The future value of a present sum can be easily calculated if the annual interest rate and the period of time are known. The formula for calculating the future value is given by Equation 1-1.

$$A_n = A_o(1 + i)^n \tag{1-1}$$

Where: A_n = Amount n years from now
A_o = Present amount
i = annual interest rate
n = number of years

EXAMPLE: Suppose an investor deposits $100,000 at a bank and the annual interest rate is 10 percent. What is the amount 2 years from now? The answer is $121,000. This is calculated as follows:

$$A_2 = \$100{,}000(1 + .10)^2$$
$$= \$100{,}000(1.21)$$
$$= \$121{,}000$$

Other Finite Frequencies of Compounding

Equation 1-1 assumes that interest is compounded once a year. If interest is compounded more than once a year but less than continually, Equation 1-1 has to be adjusted. For example, if interest is compounded monthly (12 times a year), the annual interest rate has to be divided by 12 to get the monthly interest rate. In addition, the number of years has to be multiplied by 12 to get the number of months. In general, the annual interest rate has to be divided by the number (frequency) of compounding and the number of years has to be multiplied by the frequency of compounding.

After these adjustments, the future value formula will look like Equation 1-2.

(1-2) $$A_n = A_0(1 + i/c)^{cn}$$

Where: c = frequency of compounding

EXAMPLE: Suppose an investor deposits $200,000 at a financial institution. The annual interest rate is 12 percent and interest is compounded monthly. The amount 2 years from now will be $253,946.93. This is calculated as follows:

$$A_2 = \$200{,}000(1 + .12/12)^{12(2)}$$
$$= \$200{,}000(1.27)$$
$$= \$253{,}946.93$$

The reader should note that Equation 1-1 is a subcase of Equation 1-2. When c = 1, Equation 1-2 reduces to Equation 1-1.

PRESENT VALUE OF FUTURE SUMS

Two cases will be identified here, also. In the first case a single lump-sum payment is expected at some point in the future. In the second case, a series of payments is expected over a defined period of time.

Single Payment

The calculation of the present value of a future sum involves a process known as *discounting,* which is, simply, the reverse of compounding. The future value, the interest rate, and the period are known, and the present amount has to be determined.This can be done by solving Equation 1-2 for the present sum (A_o). The resulting present value formula is given by Equation 1-3. This formula applies for any frequency of compounding, other than continuous.

$$A_o = A_n[1/(1 + i/c)^{cn}] \qquad (1\text{-}3)$$

Where: $1/(1 + i/c)^{cn}$ = discount factor

EXAMPLE: A borrower promises to pay a lender $500,000 at the end of 2 years. The annual interest rate is 12 percent and interest is compounded monthly. What is the maximum amount that the lender should lend the borrower? In other words, what is the present value of $500,000? The answer is $393,783.06. This is calculated as follows:

$$A_o = \$500{,}000/(1 + .12/12)^{12(2)}$$
$$= \$500{,}000/1.27$$
$$= \$393{,}783.06$$

The discount factor portion of Equation 1-3 can be used to construct a table of present value factors, which can be multiplied by the future sum to get the PV of the future sum. Table 1 shows the calculations.

The present value of $500,000 for the factors in the table can be

TABLE 1 Calculations of Present Value Factors

	i(%)		
Period	*10%*	*12%*	*14%*
1	.9917	.9901	.9885
2	.9835	.9803	.9771
.	.	.	.
.	.	.	.
.	.	.	.
24	.8194	.7876	.7570

calculated by multiplying $500,000 by the discount factor of 0.7876 from the table to get $393,800. The small difference is due to the fact that the discount factors are carried to only four decimal places.

Series of Payments

If a series of payments is expected in the future, the present value of the payments is determined by calculating the present value of each expected payment and then adding the present values of all the payments. A slightly modified version of Equation 1–3 is used to calculate the present value of each expected payment. The resulting present value formula is given by Equation 1–4.

$$(1\text{–}4) \qquad A_o = \frac{P_1}{(1 + i/q)^1} + \frac{P_2}{(1 + i/q)^2} + \cdots + \frac{P_k}{(1 + i/q)^k}$$

Where: P = expected periodic payments
q = number of expected payments per year
k = total number of expected payments
= q * n
n = number of years

EXAMPLE: A borrower promises to pay a lender $600 every 6 months for 2 years. The annual interest rate is 10 percent. How much will the lender lend the borrower today? The answer is $2,127.57. This amount is calculated as follows:

$$A_o = \$600/(1 + .10/2)^1 + \$600/(1 + .10/2)^2 + \$600/(1 + .10/2)^3 + \$600/(1 + .10/2)^4$$

$$= \$571.43 + \$544.22 + \$518.30 + \$493.62$$

$$= \$2{,}127.57$$

If the number of payments is large, say 360, Equation 1–4 can be cumbersome. Fortunately, if the expected payments are the same ($P_1 = P_2 = \ldots = P_k$), Equation 1–4 can be reduced to Equation 1–5. Equation 1–5 is derived later in this appendix.

$$(1\text{–}5) \qquad A_o = P[\{1 - (1 + i/q)^{-qn}\}/i/q]$$

Equation 1–5 is called the *present value of a simple ordinary annuity formula.* It is an annuity formula because equal payments are expected at equal intervals. It is ordinary because the payments are expected at the end of each period, rather than at the beginning of each period. Finally, it is a simple annuity formula because the frequency of compounding is equal to the number of expected payments per year (q). The expression within the square brackets is the present value of a simple ordinary annuity of $1. It is the present value of a stream of payments of $1 per period for qn periods.

EXAMPLE: X promises to pay a lender $600 every month for 5 years. The annual interest rate is 12 percent. What is the present value of the expected payments? The answer is $26,973.02. This amount is calculated as follows:

$$A_o = \$600[\{1 - (1 + .12/12)^{-12(5)}\}/.12/12]$$

$$= \$600[\{1 - .55\}/.01] = \$600(44.96)$$

$$= \$26{,}973.02$$

The expression within the square brackets of Equation 1-5 can be used to construct the present value of an annuity table. Table 2 shows the calculations.

For the previous example, the present value of the monthly stream of $600 at 12 percent per year for 5 years would simply be $600 times 44.955 from the table or $26,973.

The previous example showed the calculation of the present value of a stream of future payments. However, if the values of all the variables in Equation 1-5, but one are known, the value of the unknown can be determined. In the following sections, the calculations of the periodic payment, the number of periods, and the interest rate are illustrated.

TABLE 2 Calculations of Present Value Factors

	i(%)		
Period	*10%*	*12%*	*14%*
1	.9917	.9901	.9885
2	1.9753	1.9704	1.9655
.	.	.	.
.	.	.	.
.	.	.	.
60	47.0654	44.9550	42.9770

The Calculation of the Periodic Payment

If the present value, the annual interest rate, the number of payments per year and the number of years are known, Equation 1–5 can be solved for the periodic payment. When Equation 1–5 is rewritten, it looks like Equation 1–6.

(1–6) $$P = A_0(i/q)/[\{1 - (1 + i/q)^{-qn}\}]$$

EXAMPLE: A home buyer borrowed \$80,000 at 12 percent for 15 years. What is the monthly payment? The answer is \$960.13. This amount is calculated as follows:

$$P = \$80{,}000(.12/12)/[\{1 - (1 + .12/12)^{-12(15)}\}]$$
$$= \$80{,}000.01/[(1 - .1668)] = \$80{,}000(.012)$$
$$= \$960.13$$

The Calculation of the Number of Payments

To calculate the number of payments, Equation 1–5 has to be solved for qn. The resulting formula is given in Equation 1–7.

(1–7) $$k = qn = \{-\ln [1 - A_o * (i/q)/P]\}/\ln (1 + i/q)$$

Where: k = total number of payments
ln = natural logarithm

EXAMPLE: The monthly payment of a \$50,000 loan is \$2353.67. The annual interest rate is 12 percent. How many payments will be needed to pay off the loan? The answer is 24 monthly payments. This amount is calculated as follows:

$$k = \frac{-\ln [1 - (\$50{,}000 * ((.12/12)/\$2{,}353.67))]}{\ln (1 + .12/12)}$$

$$= \frac{-\ln [1 - (\$50{,}000 * 0.000004249)]}{\ln (1.01)}$$

$$= -\ln (.787565802)/\ln (1.01)$$

$$= 0.238808354/0.009950331$$

$$= 24$$

Very often, the number of periods is not an exact integer. It will have a fractional part. In such cases, a partial payment will be required at the end of the period. The amount of the last payment is calculated using Equation 1-8.

$$(1\text{-}8) \qquad LP = [A_o - P * \{(1 - (1 + i/q)^{-t})/i/q\}] * (1 + i/q)^{t+1}$$

Where: LP = last payment
T = the number of payments minus the fractional part

EXAMPLE: The monthly payment of a $10,000 loan is $400. The annual interest rate is 12 percent. How many payments will be needed to pay off the loan fully? What is the last payment? The answers are 28.91 monthly payments and $364.88. They are calculated as follows:

$$k = \frac{-\ln[1 - (\$10{,}000 * ((.12/12)/\$400))]}{\ln(1 + .12/12)} = 28.91$$

$$LP = [\$10{,}000 - \$400 * \{(1 - (1 + .12/12)^{-28})/.12/12\}] * (1 + .12/12)^{28+1}$$
$$= (\$10{,}000 - \$9{,}726.5773) * 1.3345$$
$$= \$364.88$$

Calculating the Interest Rate: The Trail and Error Method

The calculation of the interest rate in Equation 1-5 is, by far, the most difficult of the calculations that have been illustrated so far. It requires the use of the trial and error method. This means trying different values for the interest rate until the value that equates the two sides of Equation 1-5 is identified. One can start the process by using some plausible value for i, such as 10 percent, and calculating the value on the right side of the equation. If the resulting value is greater that A_o, a higher value such as 20 percent is used. If at 20 percent, the value of the expression on the right hand side (RHSV) turns out to be smaller than A_o, the interest rate will be somewhere between 10 percent and 20 percent. Different values between 10 percent and 20 percent would be tried until a value that equates the two sides is identified.

EXAMPLE: The monthly payment of a 30-year, $100,000 loan is $1264.444. What is the annual interest rate? The answer is 15 percent. The interest rate is calculated as follows:

First trial: 12 percent is arbitrarily selected for i. At 12 percent,

RHSV = \$122,927.1354. This is greater than \$100,000.

$$\text{RHSV} = \$1{,}264.444[(1 - (1 + .12/12)^{-12(30)})/(.12/12)] = \$122{,}927.1354$$

Second trial: Since the right side value is greater than \$100,000, a higher interest rate value should be used. A value of 18 percent is, arbitrarily, selected. At 18 percent, RHSV = \$83,899.96. This is smaller than \$100,000.

Third trial: Now, we know that the interest rate should be between 12 percent and 18 percent. We will try 15 percent. At this rate, the two sides are equal. The annual interest rate on the loan is 15 percent.

As you can see, the trial and error method can be very cumbersome. A large number of trials may be needed to identify the correct interest rate. A more systematic way of determining the interest rate is the Newton-Raphson Method.

Calculating the Interest Rate: The Newton-Raphson Method

The Newton-Raphson method is more systematic than the trial and error method described in the previous section, but it is still cumbersome and time-consuming. It involves a series of iterations. Equations 1–9 and 1–10 are used repeatedly until a stable value of the periodic interest rate is obtained. For a detailed explanation of the Newton-Raphson method, see Appendix 2.

$$(1\text{-}9) \qquad R(r_t) = \frac{1 - (1 + r_t)^{-k} - (A_o/P) * r_t}{k(1 + r_t)^{-k-1} - [1 - (1 + r_t)^{-k}]/r_t}$$

$$r_{t+1} = r_t - R(r_t)$$

Where: r_t = the periodic interest rate in iteration t
= i/q in iteration t
k = number of periods

FIRST ITERATION: An initial value of 1 percent is arbitrarily assigned to r. Thus, $r_o = .01$.

$$R(.01) = \frac{1 - (1 + .01)^{-360} - (\$100{,}000/\$1{,}264.444) * .01}{360(1 + .01)^{-360-1} - [1 - (1 + .01)^{-360}]/.01}$$

$$= \frac{.972183311 - .790861438}{9.91485952 - 97.2183311} = \frac{.181321873}{-87.30347158}$$

$$= -.002076915$$

$$r_1 = r_0 + R(r_0) = .01 + 0.002076915 = 0.012076915$$

SECOND ITERATION: $r_1 = 0.012076915$

R(0.012076915)

$$= \frac{1 - (1.012076915)^{-360} - (100{,}000/1264.444) * 0.012076915}{360(1.012076915)^{-361} - [1 - (1.012076915)^{-360}]/.012076915}$$

$$= \frac{.986721984 - .955116636}{4.723045958 - 81.70314886} = \frac{0.031605348}{-76.9801029}$$

$$= -0.000410565$$

$$r_2 = r_1 - R(r_1) = 0.012076915 + 0.000410565 = 0.01248748$$

THIRD ITERATION: $r_2 = 0.01248748$

R(0.01248748)

$$= \frac{1 - (1.01248748)^{-360} - (100{,}000/1264.444) * .01248748}{360(1.01248748)^{-361} - [1 - (1 + 0.01248748)^{-360}]/.01248748}$$

$$= \frac{.988525816 - .987586639}{4.079760398 - 79.16135329} = \frac{0.000939177}{-75.08159289}$$

$$= -0.000012509$$

$$r_3 = r_2 - R(r_2) = 0.01248748 + 0.000012509 = 0.012499989$$

FOURTH ITERATION: $r_3 = 0.012499989$

R(0.012499989)

$$= \frac{1 - (1.012499989)^{-360} - (100{,}000/1264.444) * 0.012499989}{360(1.012499989)^{-361} - [1 - (1 + .012499989)^{-360}]/.012499989}$$

$$= \frac{.988576735 - .988575927}{4.061605074 - 79.0862084} = \frac{.000000808}{-75.02460332}$$

$$= -0.000000011$$

$$r_4 = r_3 - R(r_3) = 0.012499989 + 0.000000011 = 0.0125$$

The value of the monthly interest rate has converged at 0.0125. If the iteration is continued, the monthly interest rate will still be 0.0125. The annual interest rate is, simply, 12 * 0.0125 or 15 percent.

The interest rate that equates the present sum (A_o) to the discounted present value of the stream of future payments is also called the internal rate of return.

Calculating the Interest Rate for a Variable Payment Stream

The method illustrated above is used when level future periodic payments are expected. If the future periodic payments are expected to vary from one period to another, different formulas are used to perform the iterations. Specifically, Equations 1-11, 1-12, and 1-13 are used repeatedly until a stable value of the periodic interest rate is obtained. This procedure is more general than the procedure described earlier. It can even be used to determine the interest rate of a level-payment annuity but it is more cumbersome.

(1-11)

$$NPV(r) = \frac{-A0}{(1 + r)^0} + \frac{P1}{(1 + r)^1} + \frac{P2}{(1 + r)^2} + \cdots + \frac{Pk}{(1 + r)^k}$$

(1-12)

$$NPV'(r) = -\left[\frac{P1}{(1 + r)^{(1+1)}} + 2 * \frac{P2}{(1 + r)^{(2+1)}} + \cdots + K * \frac{Pk}{(1 + r)^{(k+1)}}\right]$$

(1-13) $$r_{t+1} = r_t - \frac{NPV(r_t)}{NPV'(r_t)}$$

Where: $NPV'(r)$ = first derivative of the net present value function = $dNPV(r)/dr$

r_t = periodic interest rate (= i/q) in round t or iteration t

k = total number of payment periods = qn

DERIVATION OF THE FORMULA FOR THE PERIODIC PAYMENT OF A SIMPLE ANNUITY

The loan amount is equal to the sum of the present value of the monthly payments:

(1–14) $$A_o = \frac{P}{(1 + r)^1} + \frac{P}{(1 + r)^2} + \cdots + \frac{P}{(1 + r)^k}$$

Where: A_o = loan amount = present sum
P = periodic payment
r = periodic interest rate = i/q
q = number of periods in a year
n = number of years
k = total number of periods

Multiplying Equation 1–14 by (1 + r), we get:

(1–15) $$A + Ar = P + \frac{P}{(1 + r)} + \frac{P}{(1 + r)^2} + \cdots + \frac{P}{(1 + r)^{k-1}}$$

Subtracting Equation 1–14 from Equation 1–15 and dividing both sides of the result by r, we get:

(1–16) $A = (P/r)\,[1 - (1 + r)^{-k}]$, the same as Equation 1-5.

APPENDIX

2 THE NEWTON-RAPHSON METHOD

In installment loans in which the loan amount, the periodic payment, and the term of the loan are given, the calculation of the interest rate can be rather cumbersome. For the simplest case in which there is only one payment, the net present value equation can be solved for the interest rate directly. When there are two periodic payments, the interest rate can be determined using the quadratic formula. When the number of periodic payments exceeds 2, however, the interest rate can be determined only through the trial and error method. This method is very tedious and time-consuming. However, the Newton-Raphson method makes the process easier. If a solution exists, this method can generally generate the interest rate after a few iterations.

An installment loan may be looked at from the position of the lender or the borrower. From the lender's position, a loan involves a payment (negative cash flow) in the current period and receipts (positive cash flows) in all subsequent periods. Consider a simple two-period loan in which the loan amount is $5000 and the periodic payment is $2958.490565. Table 1 shows that the net present value (NPV) of the cash flows switches from a positive value of $918.98 at 0 percent interest rate to a negative value of $480.08 at an interest rate of 20 percent. As the interest rate increases, the NPV declines to zero and then turns negative. The rate at which the NPV is zero is the yield to the lender or the internal rate of return. In this example, the lender's yield or interest rate is 12 percent. Figure 1 shows the NPV function.

The Newton-Raphson method can be used to determine the lender's yield. The process is started by assuming an initial interest rate

TABLE 1 Cash Flows and NPVs—Lender's Position

	YEAR 0	YEAR 1	YEAR 2
Cash Flow	−5000	2958.490565	2958.490565
Interest Rate (%)	0	12	20
NPV	916.98	0	−480.08

of i(1) and determining the NPV at i(1) and the slope of the NPV function at i(1). This process leads to i(2), which, in turn, is used as the value of i for the second round of iterations and so on until i = 12 percent.

At i(1), the slope of the NPV function equals:

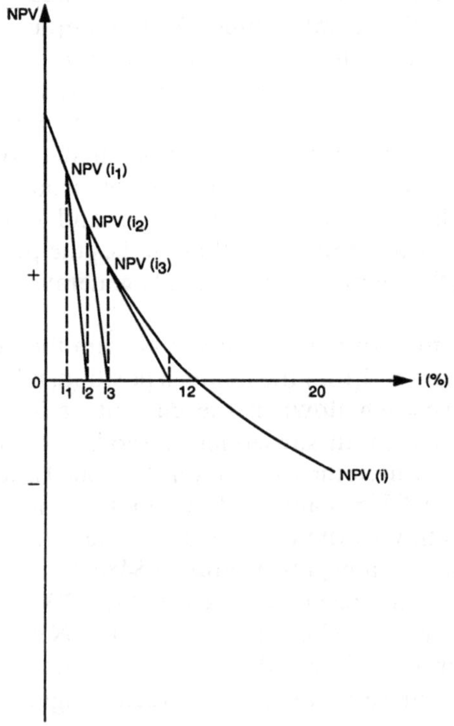

FIGURE 1. NPV AS A FUNCTION OF THE INTEREST RATE: LENDER'S POSITION

$$NPV'(i_t) = \frac{NPV(i_1)}{(i_2 - i_1)}$$

$$(i_2 - i_1) = \frac{NPV(i_1)}{NPV'(i_1)}$$

$$i_2 = i_1 + \frac{NPV(i_1)}{NPV'(i_1)} = \text{2nd round value of i}$$

At i_2:

$$NPV'(i_2) = \frac{NPV(i_2)}{(i_3 - i_2)}$$

$$(i_3 - i_2) = \frac{NPV(i_2)}{NPV'(i_2)}$$

$$i_3 = i_2 + \frac{NPV(i_2)}{NPV'(i_2)} = \text{3rd round value of i}$$

In general,

$$i_{q+1} = i_q + \frac{NPV(i_q)}{NPV'(i_q)}$$

The loan may also be looked at from the position of the borrower. From the borrower's position, a loan involves a positive cash flow in the current period and negative cash flow in all subsequent periods. Table 2 shows the loan from the borrower's side. The graph of the NPV function is shown in Figure 2.

In this case also, the process is started by assuming that the initial interest rate is i_1:

At i_1:

$$NPV'(i_1) = \frac{NPV(i_1)}{(i_1 - i_2)}$$

$$(i_1 - i_2) = \frac{NPV(i_1)}{NPV'(i_1)}$$

$$i_2 = i_1 - \frac{NPV(i_1)}{NPV'(i_1)} = \text{round 2 value}$$

Table 2 Cash Flows and NPVs: Borrower's Position

	YEAR 0	*YEAR 1*	*YEAR 2*
Cash Flow	5000	−2958.490565	−2958.490565
Interest Rate (%)	0	12	20
NPV	−916.98	0	480.08

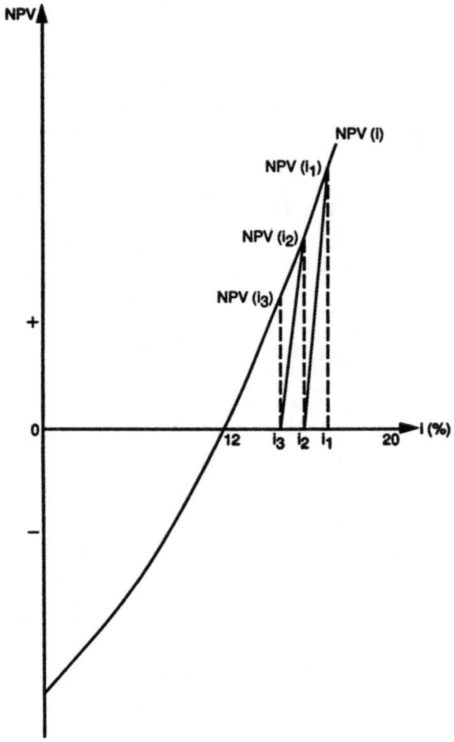

FIGURE 2. NPV AS A FUNCTION OF THE INTEREST RATE: BORROWER'S POSITION

At i_2:

$$NPV'(i_2) = \frac{NPV(i_2)}{(i_2 - i_3)}$$

$$(i_2 - i_3) = \frac{NPV(i_2)}{NPV'(i_2)}$$

$$i_3 = i_2 - \frac{NPV(i_2)}{NPV'(i_2)} = \text{round 3 value}$$

In general,

$$i_{q+1} = i_q - \frac{NPV(i_q)}{NPV'(i_q)}$$

This is the approach used in the text but you can see that both approaches lead to the same result. This method can be used in the determination of the interest rate of a loan even if the number of payments is large, like 365.

Assuming that the loan amount (present sum) is denoted by A, the number of payments by k, the monthly payment by P and the monthly interest rate by r, the loan amount is equal to the sum of the present values of the monthly payments as follows:

$$A = \frac{P}{r}[1 - (1 + r)^{-k}]$$

$$A * r = P * [1 - (1 + r)^{-k}]$$

$$NPV(r) = P * [1 - (1 + r)^{-k}] - A * r$$

$$NPV(r) = 1 - (1 + r)^{-k} - (A/P) * r$$

$$NPV'(r) = \frac{d(NPV(r))}{dr} = k(1 + r)^{-k-1} - (A/P)$$

$$= k(1 + r)^{-k-1} - \frac{P}{r * P}[1 - (1 + r)^{-k}]$$

$$= k(1 + r)^{-k-1} - \frac{[1 - (1 + r)^{-k}]}{r}$$

$$R(r) = NPV(r)/NPV'(r)$$

(2-1) $$R(i_t) = \frac{1 - (1 + r_t)^{-k} - (A/P) * r}{k(1 + r)^{-k-1} - \frac{[1 - (1 + r)^{-k}]}{r_t}}$$

(2-2) $$r_{t+1} = r_t - R(r_t)$$

Where: r_t = value of r in round t
A = loan amount = present sum A can also represent the loan amount less the finance charge

APPENDIX

3 FINANCIAL LEVERAGE

The purchase of real estate may be financed with equity funds, debt funds (other peoples' money), or both. If the property is financed fully with equity funds, it is 100 percent equity financing. If it is fully financed with debt funds, it is 100 percent debt financing. These are extreme cases. Generally, the purchase of real estate involves a combination of equity financing and debt financing.

The purpose of this chapter is to define financial leverage, explain how it works and discuss its advantages and disadvantages.

DESCRIPTION

Financial leverage refers to the use of debt or credit to finance the purchase of real estate. If the debt or credit constitutes a large fraction—say 90 percent—of the purchase price of the property, the purchase is highly leveraged; if the debt is only a small fraction of the price—say 10 percent—financial leverage is small. Positive financial leverage exists if financial leverage increases the rate of return on equity relative to the free and clear rate of return on investment, that is, relative to the rate of return on a 100 percent equity investment. If financial leverage results in a rate of return on equity that is lower than the free and clear rate of return on equity it is called *negative financial leverage.* For positive leverage to exist, the borrowing rate has to be smaller than the rate of return on the investment. If an investor can borrow money at 10 percent and earn 20 percent, the investor will make a profit, not only on his or her investment, but also on the borrowed funds.

HOW IT WORKS

The concept of financial leverage and how it works can be explained using a simple example. Consider a real property with a price of

$100,000. Within a week, the price of the property can rise to $120,000 or fall to $80,000. The investor has the option of making an all-cash purchase or putting down 50 percent of the price and financing the other 50 percent. If the property is sold for $120,000, the gross gain, ignoring interest and other expenses, will be $20,000. The free and clear rate of return is 20 percent, and the rate of return on equity (ROE) of the leveraged investment would be 40 percent ($20,000/ $50,000). This is positive financial leverage.

If the property is sold at $80,000, the free and clear rate of return would be −20 percent, and the ROE of the leveraged investment would be −40 percent. This is negative financial leverage. In both cases, the ROE on the leveraged investment is 2 times the ROE of the all-cash investment. This is because the leverage factor, which is the reciprocal of the initial equity/price ratio, is 2. If there had been 80 percent debt financing (loan/price ratio of .8), the leverage factor would be 5 $[=(1/(1-.8))]$ and the ROE on the leverage investment would be plus or minus 5 times the ROE on the unleveraged investment.

Although this example conveys the basic idea of financial leverage, it is highly simplistic. A realistic analysis of financial leverage should take into account appreciation or deterioration of the property value, increases or decreases in incomes and expenses, tax factors, and the holding period. All these factors influence the way financial leverage affects the ROE.

Consider the following data:

Current Price of a 20-unit Property	= $700,000.00
Land	= 150,000.00
Improvements	= 550,000.00
Annual Straight Line depreciation over a 27½ year period = 550,000/27.5	= 20,000.00
Loan data:	
30-year, 9.5%, $525,000 fixed-rate loan with:	
Annual debt service (principal and interest)	= 53,382.31
Loan balance at the end of year 1	= 521,492.92
Loan balance at the end of year 2	= 517,652.19
Marginal tax rate of investor	= 34%
Annual Rent per unit	= 6,000.00
Selling Expenses as % of selling price of the property	= 4%
Holding period, in years	= 1

Given the data listed, what is the effect of financial leverage on the internal rate of return (IRR) on a real estate investment? First we will compare an all-equity (no-debt) investment with an investment with 75 percent debt financing and then show the effect on the IRR of changing the holding period, the appreciation rate of the property value, and the marginal tax rate.

Table 1 shows the after-tax cash flows from operations for the two financing alternatives. Table 2 shows the after-tax cash flows resulting from the sale of the property (reversion). Table 3 summarizes the cash flows and shows the IRRs. For this example, debt financing has resulted in a higher IRR, and the investor should use debt.

The Effect of Changing the Holding Period

In the previous example, the property was sold at the end of the first year. In this section, we assume that the property will be sold at the end of the second year. The property value, the rent per unit, the vacancy costs, and operating expenses are assumed to increase by 5 percent. The results of the analysis are summarized in Table 4.

The quadratic formula applies only for 2-period investments. The general form of the quadratic equation is:

$$ax^2 + bx + c = 0 \tag{3-1}$$

Table 1 Comparative Cash Flows from Operations for an All-Equity Investment and an Investment with 75% Debt Financing

ITEM	*NO DEBT*	*75% DEBT*
1. Potential gross income (20 * 6000)	$120,000	$120,000.00
− Vacancy costs (5% of (1))	6,000	6,000.00
2. = Effective gross income	114,000	114,000.00
− Operating expenses (28.33% of (1))	34,000	34,000.00
3. = Net operating income	80,000	80,000.00
− Depreciation allowance	20,000	20,000.00
− Interest expense	0	49,875.00
4. = Taxable income	60,000	10,125.00
* Marginal tax rate	.34	.34
5. = Income tax	20,400	3,442.50
6. Debt service	0	53,382.31
7. Cash flow after taxes [(3) − (5) − (6)]	59,600	23,175.19

Table 2 After-Tax Reversion—Comparative Cash Flows at Sale

ITEM		NO DEBT	75% DEBT
1.	Selling price (700,000 * 1.05)	$735,000.00	$735,000.00
	− Selling expenses (735,000 * .04)	29,400.00	29,400.00
2.	= Amount realized	705,600.00	705,600.00
3.	Purchase price	700,000.00	700,000.00
	− Depreciation	20,000.00	20,000.00
4.	= Adjusted basis	680,000.00	680,000.00
5.	Gain = (2) − (4)	25,600.00	25,600.00
	* Tax rate on gain	.34	.34
6.	= Tax on gain	8,704.00	8,704.00
7.	Mortgage balance	0	521,492.69
8.	After-tax cash flow from Sale = (2) − (6) − (7)	696,896	175,403.31

Table 3 Cash Flows and IRRs

YEAR	NO DEBT	75% DEBT
0	−700,000	−175,000.00
1	756,496[1]	198,578.50[2]
IRR	8.07%[3]	13%[3]

[1] After-tax cash flow from operations	= $ 59,600.00
+ After-tax cash reversion at year-end	= 696,896.00
= Total	= 756,496.00
[2] After-tax cash flow from operations	= 23,175.19
+ After-tax cash reversion at year end	= 175,403.31
= Total	= 198,578.50

[3]Cash flow in Year 1 divided by cash flow in Year 0 minus 1, ignoring the minus signs.

Table 4 Comparative Cash Flows and IRRs for a Holding Period of 2 Years

	CASH FLOWS	
YEAR	*NO DEBT*	*75% DEBT*
0	−700,000.00	−175,000.00
1	59,600.00	23,175.19
2	775,620.80[1]	221,430.52[1]
IRR	9.61%[2]	19.3%[2]

[1]Sum of the after-tax cash flow from operations and the after-tax cash reversion.
[2]The IRR can be calculated using the quadratic formula or the Newton-Raphson method explained in Appendix 2. In this case, the quadratic formula is easier.

The roots of the equation can be determined by the quadratic formula:

$$x_i = \frac{-b +/- \sqrt{b^2 - 4ac}}{2a} \tag{3-2}$$

Now, consider the no-debt case. The present value of the income stream should be equal to the purchase price of the property. See Equation 3-3.

$$700{,}000 = \frac{59{,}600}{(1 + i)} + \frac{775{,}620.80}{(1 + i)^2} \tag{3-3}$$

Subtracting 700,000 from both sides, and letting

$$x = \frac{1}{(1 + i)},$$

$$775{,}620.8x^2 + 59{,}600x - 700{,}000 = 0 \tag{3-4}$$

The value of i which equates the present value of the income stream to 700,000 or the value of i which satisfies Equation 3-4 is the internal rate of return.

Equation 3-4 can be solved using the quadratic formula Equation 3-2. To simplify calculations, divide each term of Equation 3-4 by 100. The resulting values of the parameters are $a = 7756.208$, $b = 596$, and $c = -7000$. Plugging these values into Equation 3-2, we get:

$$x_1 = \frac{-596 + \sqrt{596^2 - 4(7756.208)(-7000)}}{2(7756.208)}$$

$$= 0.912357283$$

Using this value of x, we can solve for i as follows:

$$0.912357283 = \frac{1}{(1 + i)}$$

$$i = 0.0961 \text{ or } 9.61\%.$$

$$x_2 = \frac{-596 - \sqrt{596^2 - 4(7756.208)(-7000)}}{2(7756.208)}$$

$$= -0.989198957$$

Because the second root of x is negative, we disregard it. The internal rate of return is 9.61 percent.

As you can see from Tables 3 and 4, the IRR of the no-debt investment increased by 19 percent (from 8.07 percent to 9.61 percent) and the IRR of the 75 percent debt financed investment increased by 48 percent (from 13 percent to 19.3 percent). So the positive effect of financial leverage increased with the increase in the length of the holding period.

The Effect of Changing the Marginal Tax Rate

Now suppose there is a tax cut. What will the effect be of the tax cut on the IRRs of the two investments? Using the original values of the variables but a marginal tax rate of 25 percent, we perform a similar analysis. The internal rate of return of the no-debt investment increased from 8.07 percent to 9 percent (a 12 percent increase) and that of the 75 percent debt financed investment increased from 13 percent to 15 percent (a 15 percent increase). The IRRs are higher in both cases. However, in this case, the relative attractiveness of debt financing is smaller.

The Effect of Changing The Appreciation Rate of the Property Value

Rapid increases in property values can also make financial leverage very attractive. In fact, many investors count on appreciation to more than offset negative after-tax cash flows from operations during the holding period.

Using the values of the original example but an appreciation rate of 10 percent (instead of 5 percent), we found that the IRR of the no-debt investment increased by 36 percent (from 8.07 percent to 11 percent) and that of the leveraged investment (75 percent debt) increased by 100 percent (from 13 percent to 26 percent).

The Effect of Changes in Mortgage Rates

Lower mortgage rates result in lower interest costs and a higher IRR. On the other hand, higher mortgage rates result in higher interest costs and lower IRR.

ADVANTAGES OF FINANCIAL LEVERAGE

There are two major advantages of financial leverage. First, financial leverage allows investors to purchase properties with values that are larger than the values of properties that could be purchased without leverage. Without debt financing, investors would not be able to buy multimillion dollar properties, and many individuals would not be able to buy homes.

Second, financial leverage increases the rate of return on equity. The increase in the rate of return on equity tends to increase as the holding period of the property increases, the value of the property appreciates, and mortgage rates decline. For properties with taxable incomes from operations and reversion, a tax cut also tends to increase the rate of return on equity. For properties that have no taxable incomes from operations, however, a tax increase may increase the internal rate of return by increasing the tax savings that result from interest and depreciation deductions.

DISADVANTAGES OF FINANCIAL LEVERAGE

Although the chapter focused on the benefits of financial leverage, financial leverage is not without drawbacks. First, if the conditions that were identified in this chapter were reversed, financial leverage would have produced larger declines in the rates of return on equity. Specifically, the declines in the rates of return corresponding to the debt financed investment would be larger than the declines of the rates of return corresponding to the all cash investment if the property value declined, the holding period became shorter and mortgage rates rose. As the simple example at the beginning of the chapter showed, financial leverage can magnify gains, but it can also magnify losses.

Second, as the proportion of debt increases, the risk exposure of the investor increases. With larger debt, larger interest and principal payments have to be made, whether the investor earns profits or not. This situation increases the probability of failure.

APPENDIX

4 FIXED-RATE MORTGAGE PROGRAM—Sample Run

```
***********************************************************

    THIS PROGRAM WILL CALCULATE THE MONTHLY MORTGAGE PAYMENT, THE
    MORTGAGE BALANCE AT ANY POINT DURING THE LIFE OF THE LOAN, AND
    THE ANNUAL PERCENTAGE RATE (APR). THE PROGRAM WILL ALSO CON-
    STRUCT AN AMORTIZATION SCHEDULE. FINALLY, IT WILL DETERMINE THE
    AMOUNT YOU CAN BORROW, GIVEN THE MONTHLY PAYMENT, THE TERM OF
    THE LOAN, AND THE ANNUAL INTEREST RATE.

***********************************************************

ENTER THE LOAN AMOUNT ? 100000

ENTER THE ANNUAL INTEREST RATE IN PERCENT? 12

ENTER THE TERM OF THE LOAN IN YEARS? 30

YOUR MONTHLY PAYMENT IS $1028.613

WOULD YOU LIKE TO SEE THE AMORTIZATION SCHEDULE? (Y OR N)? Y

FOR HOW MANY MONTHS?
? 12
```

AMORTIZATION SCHEDULE

MONTH	MONTHLY PAYMENT	INTEREST PAID	PRINCIPAL PAID	MORTGAGE BALANCE
1	1028.61	1000.00	28.61	99971.39
2	1028.61	999.71	28.90	99942.49
3	1028.61	999.42	29.19	99913.31
4	1028.61	999.13	29.48	99883.83

```
     5      1028.61      998.84      29.77      99854.06
     6      1028.61      998.54      30.07      99823.99
     7      1028.61      998.24      30.37      99793.61
     8      1028.61      997.94      30.68      99762.93
     9      1028.61      997.63      30.98      99731.94
    10      1028.61      997.32      31.29      99700.65
    11      1028.61      997.01      31.61      99669.04
    12      1028.61      996.69      31.92      99637.12

TOTAL PAYMENTS = $ 12343.35

TOTAL INTEREST PAID = $ 11980.47

THE LOAN BALANCE DECLINED BY $ 362.8786

WOULD YOU LIKE TO SEE ANOTHER AMORTIZATION SCHEDULE? (Y OR N)? N

WOULD YOU LIKE TO CALCULATE A MORTGAGE BALANCE? (Y OR N)? Y

AT THE END OF HOW MANY MONTHS? 180

THE MORTGAGE BALANCE AT THE END OF 180 MONTHS IS $ 85705.71

WOULD YOU LIKE TO CALCULATE ANOTHER MORTGAGE BALANCE? (Y OR N)? N

WOULD YOU LIKE TO CALCULATE THE ANNUAL PERCENTAGE RATE? (Y OR N)? Y

ENTER THE FINANCE CHARGES? 3000

 . . . WORKING . . .

THE ANNUAL PERCENTAGE RATE IS 12.4119 %

WOULD YOU LIKE TO CALCULATE ANOTHER APR? (Y OR N)? N

WOULD YOU LIKE TO DETERMINE HOW MUCH MONEY YOU CAN BORROW? (Y OR N)
? Y

WHAT IS THE DESIRED MONTHLY PAYMENT?
? 1200

GIVEN A MONTHLY PAYMENT OF $ 1200, AN ANNUAL INTEREST RATE OF 12 PERCENT
AND A TERM OF 30 YEARS, THE AMOUNT YOU CAN BORROW IS $ 116662

WOULD YOU LIKE TO CALCULATE ANOTHER LOAN AMOUNT (Y OR N)
? N

WOULD YOU LIKE TO SEE THE INTEREST FOR ANY PARTICULAR MONTH?
ENTER Y OR N
? Y
```

```
FOR WHICH MONTH? ENTER THE MONTH NUMBER.
? 180

THE INTEREST FOR MONTH 180 IS $ 858.751

WOULD YOU LIKE TO SEE THE INTEREST FOR ANOTHER MONTH? Y OR N
? N

WOULD YOU LIKE TO SEE THE PRINCIPAL PAID FOR ANY PARTICULAR
MONTH? Y OR N
? Y
FOR WHICH MONTH?
? 180

THE PRINCIPAL PAID FOR MONTH 180 IS $ 169.8616

WOULD YOU LIKE TO SEE THE PRINCIPAL PAID FOR ANOTHER MONTH? Y OR N
? N

WOULD YOU LIKE TO START AGAIN? Y OR N
? N

IT WAS A PLEASURE WORKING WITH YOU . COME AGAIN.
Ok
```

APPENDIX

5 FIXED-RATE MORTGAGE PROGRAM

```
250 PRINT "A FIXED RATE MORTGAGE PROGRAM - LISTING"
260 PRINT
262 PRINT "* * * * * * * * * * * * * * * * * * * * * * * * * * * * * * * * *"
263 PRINT
270 PRINT " THIS PROGRAM WILL CALCULATE THE MONTHLY MORTGAGE PAYMENT,"
280 PRINT " THE MORTGAGE BALANCE AT ANY POINT DURING THE LIFE OF THE"
290 PRINT " LOAN, AND THE ANNUAL PERCENTAGE RATE (APR). THE PROGRAM"
300 PRINT " WILL ALSO CONSTRUCT AN AMORTIZATION SCHEDULE. FINALLY,"
302 PRINT " IT WILL DETERMINE THE AMOUNT YOU CAN BORROW, GIVEN THE"
304 PRINT " MONTHLY PAYMENT, THE TERM OF THE LOAN, AND THE ANNUAL"
306 PRINT " INTEREST RATE."
310 PRINT
380 PRINT "* * * * * * * * * * * * * * * * * * * * * * * * * * * * * * * * *"
390 PRINT
400 PRINT "ENTER THE LOAN AMOUNT ";
410 INPUT A
420 PRINT
430 PRINT "ENTER THE ANNUAL INTEREST RATE IN PERCENT";
440 INPUT I
450 I=I/100
460 PRINT
470 PRINT "ENTER THE TERM OF THE LOAN IN YEARS";
480 INPUT N
485 N1=12*N
490 PRINT
500 M=(A*(I/12))/(1-((1+(I/12))^(-12*N)))
510 PRINT
```

```
520 PRINT
530 PRINT
540 PRINT "YOUR MONTHLY PAYMENT IS $";M
545 GOTO 760
550 PRINT
560 PRINT "WOULD YOU LIKE TO SEE THE AMORTIZATION SCHEDULE? (Y OR N)";
570 INPUT B$
580 IF B$="Y" THEN 854
590 PRINT
600 PRINT "WOULD YOU LIKE TO CALCULATE A MORTGAGE BALANCE? (Y OR N)";
610 INPUT G$
620 IF G$="Y" THEN 1200
625 PRINT
630 PRINT "WOULD YOU LIKE TO CALCULATE THE ANNUAL PERCENTAGE RATE? (Y OR N)";
640 INPUT F$
650 IF F$="Y" THEN 1400
655 PRINT
670 PRINT
680 PRINT "WOULD YOU LIKE TO DETERMINE HOW MUCH MONEY YOU CAN BORROW? (Y OR N)"
690 INPUT W$
700 IF W$="Y" THEN 1700
710 PRINT
720 GOTO 1820
760 DIM B(480), I(480), P(480)
765 PRINT
770 B(0)=0
780 B(0)=A
810 FOR T=1 TO N1
820 I(T)=B(T-1)*(I/12)
830 P(T)=M-I(T)
840 B(T)=B(T-1)-P(T)
850 NEXT T
852 GOTO 550
854 PRINT
855 PRINT "FOR HOW MANY MONTHS?"
856 INPUT V
860 D=E=F=0
870 FOR T=1 TO V
880 D=D+I(T)
890 E=E+P(T)
900 NEXT T
910 PRINT
```

```
920 PRINT "                    AMORTIZATION SCHEDULE "
930 PRINT
940 PRINT "      MONTH  MONTHLY    INTEREST    PRINCIPAL   MORTGAGE"
950 PRINT "             PAYMENT      PAID         PAID      BALANCE"
960 PRINT "____________________________________________________________"
970 PRINT
980 FOR T=1 TO V
990 PRINT USING " ###      ####.##      #######.##     #########.##  ##########.##";
T ,M,I(T),P(T),B(T)
1000 NEXT T
1010 PRINT
1020 PRINT
1030 F=V*M
1040 PRINT "TOTAL PAYMENTS = $";F
1050 PRINT
1060 PRINT "TOTAL INTEREST PAID = $";D
1070 PRINT
1080 PRINT "THE LOAN BALANCE DECLINED BY $";E
1085 PRINT
1090 PRINT "WOULD YOU LIKE TO SEE ANOTHER AMORTIZATION SCHEDULE? (Y OR N)";
1100 INPUT E$
1110 IF E$="Y" THEN 770
1120 GOTO 590
1200 PRINT
1210 PRINT "AT THE END OF HOW MANY MONTHS?";
1220 INPUT K
1232 B=(M/(I/12))*(1-((1+(I/12))^(K-(12*N))))
1240 PRINT
1241 PRINT
1250 PRINT " THE MORTGAGE BALANCE AT THE END OF "K" MONTHS IS $";B
1260 PRINT
1270 PRINT "WOULD YOU LIKE TO CALCULATE ANOTHER MORTGAGE BALANCE? (Y OR N)";
1280 INPUT H$
1290 IF H$="Y" THEN 1200
1300 GOTO 625
1400 PRINT
1410 PRINT "ENTER THE FINANCE CHARGES";
1420 INPUT FC
1421 P=N
1422 P=12*N
1430 PRINT
1440 PRINT
```

```
1450 PRINT ". . . WORKING . . ."
1460 R=.01
1465 L=0
1467 R1=0
1469 S1=0
1470 S2=0
1471 S3=0
1480 S1=S2=S3=0
1490 L=A-FC
1500 FOR J=1 TO P
1510 S1=1-(1+R)^(-J)-(L/M)*R
1520 S2=(J*(1+R)^(-J-1))-((1/R)*(1-(1+R)^(-J)))
1530 NEXT J
1540 S3=S1/S2
1550 R1=R
1560 R=R1-S3
1570 R2=R-R1
1580 IF R2<1E-11 THEN 1600
1590 GOTO 1480
1600 R=1200*R
1610 R=(INT((R+.00005)*10000))/10000
1620 PRINT
1630 PRINT
1640 PRINT
1650 PRINT "THE ANNUAL PERCENTAGE RATE IS ";R"%"
1660 PRINT
1670 PRINT "WOULD YOU LIKE TO CALCULATE ANOTHER APR? (Y OR N)";
1680 INPUT Q$
1690 IF Q$="Y" THEN 1400
1695 GOTO 670
1700 PRINT
1710 PRINT
1720 PRINT "WHAT IS THE DESIRED MONTHLY PAYMENT?"
1730 INPUT M1
1740 A1=(M1/(I/12))*(1-((1+(I/12))^(-12*N)))
1750 PRINT
1760 PRINT
1770 PRINT "GIVEN A MONTHLY PAYMENT OF $"M1", AN ANNUAL INTEREST RATE OF "100*I
1775 PRINT "PERCENT AND A TERM OF "N" YEARS, THE AMOUNT YOU CAN BORROW IS $"A1
1780 PRINT
1790 PRINT "WOULD YOU LIKE TO CALCULATE ANOTHER LOAN AMOUNT? (Y OR N)"
1800 INPUT U$
```

```
1810 IF U$="Y" THEN 1710
1820 PRINT
1830 PRINT "WOULD YOU LIKE TO SEE THE INTEREST FOR ANY PARTICULAR MONTH? "
1835 PRINT "ENTER Y OR N"
1840 INPUT C$
1850 IF C$="N" THEN 2010
1860 PRINT
1870 PRINT "FOR WHICH MONTH? ENTER THE MONTH NUMBER."
1880 INPUT N9
1890 PRINT
1900 PRINT "THE INTEREST FOR MONTH "N9" IS $"I(N9)
1910 PRINT
1920 PRINT "WOULD YOU LIKE TO SEE THE INTEREST FOR ANOTHER MONTH? Y OR N"
1930 INPUT D$
1940 IF D$="N" THEN 2010
1950 PRINT
1960 PRINT "FOR WHICH MONTH?"
1970 INPUT N9
1980 PRINT
1990 PRINT "THE INTEREST FOR MONTH "N9" IS $"I(N9)
2000 GOTO 1910
2010 PRINT
2020 PRINT "WOULD YOU LIKE TO SEE THE PRINCIPAL PAID FOR ANY PARTICULAR"
2030 PRINT "MONTH? Y OR N"
2040 INPUT E$
2050 IF E$="N" THEN 2190
2060 PRINT "FOR WHICH MONTH"
2070 INPUT N8
2080 PRINT
2090 PRINT "THE PRINCIPAL PAID FOR MONTH "N8" IS $"P(N8)
2100 PRINT
2110 PRINT "WOULD YOU LIKE TO SEE THE PRINCIPAL PAID FOR ANOTHER MONTH? Y OR N"
2120 INPUT F$
2130 IF F$="N" THEN 2190
2140 PRINT "FOR WHICH MONTH?"
2150 INPUT N7
2160 PRINT
2170 PRINT "THE PRINCIPAL PAID FOR MONTH "N7" IS $"P(N7)
2180 GOTO 2100
2190 PRINT
2200 PRINT "WOULD YOU LIKE TO START AGAIN? Y OR N"
2210 INPUT G$
```

```
2220 IF G$="N" THEN 2250
2230 ERASE B,I,P
2240 GOTO 390
2250 PRINT
2270 END
```

APPENDIX

6 An Adjustable-Rate Mortgage Program—Sample Run

```
THIS PROGRAM WILL SHOW YOU THE RELEVANT CALCULATIONS FOR THE ADJUSTABLE-
RATE MORTGAGE. IT ALLOWS ANNUAL (OR OTHER PERIOD) AND LIFETIME INTEREST
RATE CAPS, MARGINS, AN INDEX RATE OF YOUR CHOICE, PAYMENT CAPS, NEGATIVE
AMORTIZATION, AND VARIOUS COMBINATIONS OF THESE FEATURES.

ENTER THE LOAN AMOUNT
? 100000

ENTER THE INITIAL ANNUAL INTEREST RATE IN PERCENT
? 9

ENTER THE TERM OF THE LOAN IN YEARS
? 30

ENTER THE ADJUSTMENT PERIOD IN YEARS
? 1

ENTER THE MARGIN IN PERCENT
? 2.5

ENTER THE CURRENT INDEX RATE IN PERCENT
? 8

 . . . WORKING . . .

YOUR MONTHLY PAYMENT IS $ 804.6211

WOULD YOU LIKE TO SEE THE AMORTIZATION SCHEDULE? (Y OR N)
? Y
```

FOR HOW MANY MONTHS?
? 5

AMORTIZATION SCHEDULE

MONTH	MONTHLY PAYMENT	INTEREST PAID	PRINCIPAL PAID	MORTGAGE BALANCE
1	804.62	750.00	54.62	99945.38
2	804.62	749.59	55.03	99890.34
3	804.62	749.18	55.44	99834.90
4	804.62	748.76	55.86	99779.04
5	804.62	748.34	56.28	99722.76

WOULD YOU LIKE TO CALCULATE THE MONTHLY PAYMENTS FOR SUBSEQUENT PERIODS? (Y OR N)
?Y

FOR HOW MANY PERIODS?
? 8

ENTER THE ANNUAL (PERIODIC) INTEREST RATE CAP IN PERCENT
ENTER 0(ZERO), IF NONE.
? 2

ENTER THE LIFETIME INTEREST RATE CAP IN PERCENT. ENTER 0 (ZERO)
IF NONE.
? 5

ENTER THE PAYMENT CAP IN PERCENT. ENTER 0 (ZERO), IF NONE.
? 0

ENTER THE INTEREST RATE FLOOR IN PERCENT. ENTER 0 (ZERO), IF NONE.
? 8.5

ENTER THE INDEX RATE FOR PERIOD 1 IN PERCENT.
? 8

ENTER THE INDEX RATE FOR PERIOD 2 IN PERCENT.
? 10

ENTER THE INDEX RATE FOR PERIOD 3 IN PERCENT.
? 12

ENTER THE INDEX RATE FOR PERIOD 4 IN PERCENT.
? 14

ENTER THE INDEX RATE FOR PERIOD 5 IN PERCENT.
? 8

ENTER THE INDEX RATE FOR PERIOD 6 IN PERCENT.
? 6

ENTER THE INDEX RATE FOR PERIOD 7 IN PERCENT.
? 4

ENTER THE INDEX RATE FOR PERIOD 8 IN PERCENT.
? 2

WOULD YOU LIKE TO SEE THE RESULTS? (Y OR N)
? Y

ADJUSTMENT PERIOD	INDEX RATE (%)	INDEX RATE + MARGIN (%)	OLD NOTE RATE - PERIODIC CAP (%)
0	8.000	10.500	9.000
1	8.000	10.500	7.000
2	10.000	12.500	8.500
3	12.000	14.500	10.500
4	14.000	16.500	12.000
5	8.000	10.500	12.000
6	6.000	8.500	10.000
7	4.000	6.500	8.000
8	2.000	4.500	6.500

. . . MORE RESULTS? (Y OR N)
? Y

ADJUSTMENT PERIOD	OLD NOTE RATE + PERIODIC CAP (%)	NEW NOTE RATE (%)	MORTGAGE BALANCE	MONTHLY PAYMENT
0	9.000	9.000	100000.00	804.62
1	11.000	10.500	99316.81	913.06
2	12.500	12.500	98762.18	1061.41
3	14.500	14.000	98347.30	1174.79
4	16.000	14.000	97996.49	1174.79
5	16.000	12.000	97593.30	1027.88
6	14.000	10.000	96934.53	889.27
7	12.000	8.500	95910.69	792.31
8	10.500	8.500	94501.36	792.31

WOULD YOU LIKE TO SEE THE AMORTIZATION SCHEDULE? (Y OR N)
? Y
FOR HOW MANY MONTHS?
? 25

AMORTIZATION SCHEDULE

MONTH	MONTHLY PAYMENT	INTEREST PAID	PRINCIPAL PAID	MORTGAGE BALANCE
1	804.62	750.00	54.62	99945.38
2	804.62	749.59	55.03	99890.34
3	804.62	749.18	55.44	99834.90
4	804.62	748.76	55.86	99779.04
5	804.62	748.34	56.28	99722.76
6	804.62	747.92	56.70	99666.06
7	804.62	747.50	57.13	99608.93
8	804.62	747.07	57.55	99551.38
9	804.62	746.64	57.99	99493.39
10	804.62	746.20	58.42	99434.97
11	804.62	745.76	58.86	99376.11
12	804.62	745.32	59.30	99316.81
13	913.06	869.02	44.04	99272.78
14	913.06	868.64	44.42	99228.35
15	913.06	868.25	44.81	99183.54
16	913.06	867.86	45.20	99138.34
17	913.06	867.46	45.60	99092.74
18	913.06	867.06	46.00	99046.74
19	913.06	866.66	46.40	99000.33
20	913.06	866.25	46.81	98953.52
21	913.06	865.84	47.22	98906.31
22	913.06	865.43	47.63	98858.68
23	913.06	865.01	48.05	98810.62
24	913.06	864.59	48.47	98762.16
25	1061.41	1028.77	32.64	98729.52

WOULD YOU LIKE TO START AGAIN? (Y OR N)
? N

APPENDIX

7 An Adjustable-Rate Mortgage Program

```
58 PRINT
60 PRINT " AN ADJUSTABLE RATE MORTGAGE PROGRAM"
62 PRINT
84 PRINT
86 PRINT "THIS PROGRAM WILL SHOW YOU THE RELEVANT CALCULATIONS FOR "
88 PRINT "THE ADJUSTABLE-RATE MORTGAGE. IT ALLOWS ANNUAL (OR OTHER"
90 PRINT "PERIOD) AND LIFETIME INTEREST RATE CAPS, MARGINS, AN INDEX"
92 PRINT "RATE OF YOUR CHOICE, PAYMENT CAPS, NEGATIVE AMORTIZATION,"
94 PRINT "AND VARIOUS COMBINATIONS OF THESE FEATURES."
96 PRINT
100 PRINT
110 DIM A(481),B(481),C(481),D(481),E(481),F(481),G(481),H(481),
I(481),K(481),L(481),M(481),N(481),P(481)
120 PRINT "ENTER THE LOAN AMOUNT"
130 INPUT L
140 PRINT
150 PRINT "ENTER THE INITIAL ANNUAL INTEREST RATE IN PERCENT"
160 INPUT I1
170 I=I1/100
180 PRINT
190 PRINT "ENTER THE TERM OF THE LOAN IN YEARS"
200 INPUT N1
210 N=12*N1
220 PRINT
230 PRINT "ENTER THE ADJUSTMENT PERIOD IN YEARS"
240 INPUT N2
250 N3=12*N2
260 PRINT
```

```
270 PRINT "ENTER THE MARGIN IN PERCENT"
280 INPUT D
290 D=D/100
300 PRINT
310 PRINT "ENTER THE CURRENT INDEX RATE IN PERCENT"
320 INPUT D1
325 D1=D1/100
330 D(0)=D1
332 I(0)=D(0)+D
333 PRINT
340 PRINT
350 PRINT
360 PRINT ". . . WORKING . . ."
370 PRINT
380 PRINT
390 M=L*(I/12)/(1-((1+(I/12))^(-N)))
400 A(0)=L
410 FOR J=1 TO 60
420 B(J)=A(J-1)*(I/12)
430 C(J)=M-B(J)
440 A(J)=A(J-1)-C(J)
450 NEXT J
460 PRINT
470 PRINT "YOUR MONTHLY PAYMENT IS $"M
480 PRINT
490 PRINT "WOULD YOU LIKE TO SEE THE AMORTIZATION SCHEDULE? (Y OR N)"
500 INPUT B$
510 IF B$="N" THEN 610
520 PRINT
530 PRINT "FOR HOW MANY MONTHS"
540 INPUT N5
550 PRINT
552 PRINT "                    AMORTIZATION SCHEDULE "
554 PRINT
556 PRINT "MONTH      MONTHLY     INTEREST    PRINCIPAL    MORTGAGE"
557 PRINT "           PAYMENT       PAID        PAID       BALANCE"
558 PRINT "________________________________________________________"
560 PRINT
580 FOR J=1 TO N5
590 PRINT USING " ###      ###.##      #######.##    #########.##   ##########.##";
J,M,B(J),C(J),A(J)
600 NEXT J
```

```
610 PRINT
620 PRINT "WOULD YOU LIKE TO CALCULATE THE MONTHLY PAYMENTS FOR SUBSEQUENT"
630 PRINT "PERIODS? (Y OR N)"
640 INPUT C$
650 IF C$="N" THEN 1780
660 PRINT
670 PRINT "FOR HOW MANY PERIODS?"
680 INPUT N4
690 PRINT
700 PRINT "ENTER THE ANNUAL (PERIODIC) INTEREST RATE CAP IN PERCENT"
710 PRINT "ENTER 0(ZERO), IF NONE."
720 INPUT C2
730 C=C2/100
740 PRINT
750 PRINT "ENTER THE LIFETIME INTEREST RATE CAP IN PERCENT. ENTER 0 (ZERO)"
760 PRINT "IF NONE."
770 INPUT C1
780 C1=C1/100
790 PRINT
800 PRINT "ENTER THE PAYMENT CAP IN PERCENT. ENTER 0 (ZERO), IF NONE."
810 INPUT P1
820 P=P1/100
830 PRINT
840 PRINT "ENTER THE INTEREST RATE FLOOR IN PERCENT. ENTER 0 (ZERO), IF NONE."
850 INPUT I5
860 I5=I5/100
865 L(0)=I
870 H(0)=I
880 I(0)=D(0)+D
890 G(0)=I
900 F(0)=L
910 F(1)=A(12*N2)
915 P(0)=F(1)
920 M(0)=M
925 Q=0
930 I4=I+C1
940 PRINT
950 FOR J=1 TO N4
960 PRINT "ENTER THE INDEX RATE FOR PERIOD "J" IN PERCENT."
970 INPUT D(J)
975 D(J)=D(J)/100
980 IF C=0 THEN 1010
```

```
990 H(J)=I+C
1000 L(J)=I-C
1010 I(J)=D(J)+D
1020 IF C=0 THEN 1050
1030 IF I(J)>H(J) THEN 1070
1040 IF I(J)<L(J) THEN 1090
1050 I=I(J)
1060 GOTO 1110
1070 I=H(J)
1080 GOTO 1120
1090 I=L(J)
1100 GOTO 1130
1110 PRINT
1120 PRINT
1130 GOTO 1150
1140 I=I(J)
1150 IF C1=0 THEN 1165
1160 IF I>I4 THEN 1280
1165 IF C=0 THEN 1190
1170 IF I(J)>H(J) THEN 1210
1180 IF I(J)<L(J) THEN 1230
1190 I=I(J)
1200 GOTO 1250
1210 I=H(J)
1220 GOTO 1260
1230 I=L(J)
1240 GOTO 1270
1250 PRINT
1260 PRINT
1270 GOTO 1300
1280 I=I4
1290 GOTO 1435
1300 IF I5=0 THEN 1315
1310 IF I<I5 THEN 1425
1315 IF C=0 THEN 1340
1320 IF I(J)>H(J) THEN 1360
1330 IF I(J)<L(J) THEN 1380
1340 I=I(J)
1350 GOTO 1400
1360 I=H(J)
1370 GOTO 1410
1380 I=L(J)
```

```
1390 GOTO 1420
1400 PRINT
1410 PRINT
1420 GOTO 1445
1425 I=I5
1430 GOTO 1440
1435 PRINT
1440 PRINT
1445 G(J)=I
1450 N6=(12*(N1-(J*N2)))
1460 M(J)=F(J)*(I/12)/(1-((1+(I/12))^(-N6)))
1470 N7=(((J+1)*N3)-N)
1472 IF P1=0 THEN 1480
1474 IF M(J)>(M(J-1)*(1+P)) THEN 1500
1480 F(J+1)=(M(J)/(I/12))*(1-((1+(I/12))^(N7)))
1490 GOTO 1570
1500 M(J)=(M(J-1)*(1+P))
1520 FOR T=1 TO N3
1530 Q=Q+1
1540 K(Q)=P(Q-1)*(I/12)
1550 N(Q)=M(J)-K(Q)
1560 P(Q)=P(Q-1)-N(Q)
1565 F(J+1)=P(Q)
1567 NEXT T
1570 PRINT
1571 NEXT J
1572 ERASE A,B,C
1573 DIM A(481),B(481),C(481)
1575 A(0)=L
1576 Q=0
1577 FOR T=0 TO N4
1578 FOR J=1 TO N3
1579 Q=Q+1
1580 B(Q)=A(Q-1)*(G(T)/12)
1581 C(Q)=M(T)-B(Q)
1582 A(Q)=A(Q-1)-C(Q)
1583 E(Q)=M(T)
1584 NEXT J
1585 NEXT T
1586 PRINT
1590 PRINT "WOULD YOU LIKE TO SEE THE RESULTS? (Y OR N)"
1600 INPUT E$
```

```
1610 IF E$="N" THEN 1782
1612 PRINT
1614 PRINT "ADJUSTMENT   INDEX      INDEX RATE +    OLD NOTE RATE -"
1615 PRINT "  PERIOD    RATE(%)     MARGIN (%)     PERIODIC CAP (%) "
1616 PRINT " ____________________________________________________________"
1618 PRINT
1670 FOR J=0 TO N4
1680 PRINT USING " ##      ##.###         ##.###             ##.###";
J,D(J)*100,I(J)*100,L(J)*100
1690 NEXT J
1700 PRINT
1710 PRINT ". . . MORE RESULTS? (Y OR N)"
1720 INPUT F$
1730 IF F$="N" THEN 1784
1732 PRINT
1736 PRINT "ADJUSTMENT  OLD NOTE RATE +  NEW NOTE  MORTGAGE   MONTHLY"
1737 PRINT "  PERIOD   PERIODIC CAP(%)  RATE (%)   BALANCE   PAYMENT"
1738 PRINT " ____________________________________________________________"
1740 PRINT
1750 FOR J=0 TO N4
1760 PRINT USING "##         ##.###         ##.###    #########.##   ####.##";
J,H(J)*100,G(J)*100,F(J),M(J)
1761 NEXT J
1762 PRINT
1763 PRINT "WOULD YOU LIKE TO SEE THE AMORTIZATION SCHEDULE? (Y OR N)"
1764 INPUT G$
1765 IF G$="N" THEN 1785
1766 PRINT "FOR HOW MANY MONTHS?"
1767 INPUT N9
1768 PRINT
1769 PRINT "                    AMORTIZATION SCHEDULE"
1770 PRINT
1771 PRINT "    MONTH   MONTHLY     INTEREST   PRINCIPAL   MORTGAGE"
1772 PRINT "            PAYMENT       PAID        PAID      BALANCE "
1773 PRINT " ____________________________________________________________"
1774 PRINT
1775 FOR J=1 TO N9
1776 PRINT USING "###       ####.##      ######.##     ########.##  #########.##";
J,E(J),B(J),C(J),A(J)
1777 NEXT J
1778 PRINT
1780 PRINT
```

```
1782 PRINT
1784 PRINT
1785 PRINT
1786 PRINT "WOULD YOU LIKE TO START AGAIN? (Y OR N)"
1788 INPUT H$
1790 IF H$="N" THEN 1800
1792 ERASE A,B,C,D,E,F,G,H,I,K,L,M,N,P
1794 GOTO 100
1800 PRINT
1820 END
```

APPENDIX

8 A Graduated-Payment Mortgage Program—Sample Run

```
*******************************************************************

    THIS PROGRAM WILL CALCULATE THE MONTHLY PAYMENTS OR THE ANNUAL
           PERCENTAGE RATE OF A GRADUATED-PAYMENT MORTGAGE.

                              MENU

                    1. THE MONTHLY PAYMENTS
                    2. THE ANNUAL PERCENTAGE RATE
                    3. EXIT

*******************************************************************

WHICH OPTION WOULD YOU LIKE TO USE? ENTER 1 OR 2 OR 3
? 1

ENTER THE LOAN AMOUNT
? 100000

ENTER THE ANNUAL INTEREST RATE IN PERCENT
? 10.75

ENTER THE TERM OF THE LOAN IN YEARS
? 30

ENTER THE GRADUATION PERIOD IN YEARS
? 5

ENTER THE ANNUAL RATE OF GRADUATION IN PERCENT
? 7.5
```

. . . WORKING . . .

WOULD YOU LIKE TO SEE THE MONTHLY PAYMENTS? (Y OR N)
? Y

YEAR	MONTHLY PAYMENT
1	712.77
2	766.23
3	823.70
4	885.48
5	951.89
6–30	1023.28

WOULD YOU LIKE TO SEE THE AMORTIZATION SCHEDULE? (Y OR N)
? Y

FOR HOW MANY MONTHS?
? 25

AMORTIZATION SCHEDULE

MONTH	MONTHLY PAYMENT	INTEREST PAID	PRINCIPAL PAID	MORTGAGE BALANCE
1	712.77	895.83	−183.06	100183.10
2	712.77	897.47	−184.70	100367.80
3	712.77	899.13	−186.35	100554.10
4	712.77	900.80	−188.02	100742.10
5	712.77	902.48	−189.71	100931.90
6	712.77	904.18	−191.41	101123.30
7	712.77	905.90	−193.12	101316.40
8	712.77	907.63	−194.85	101511.20
9	712.77	909.37	−196.60	101707.80
10	712.77	911.13	−198.36	101906.20
11	712.77	912.91	−200.14	102106.30
12	712.77	914.70	−201.93	102308.30
13	766.23	916.51	−150.28	102458.50
14	766.23	917.86	−151.63	102610.20
15	766.23	919.22	−152.98	102763.20
16	766.23	920.59	−154.36	102917.50
17	766.23	921.97	−155.74	103073.20
18	766.23	923.36	−157.13	103230.40
19	766.23	924.77	−158.54	103388.90
20	766.23	926.19	−159.96	103548.90
21	766.23	927.63	−161.39	103710.30

```
22          766.23       929.07       -162.84       103873.10
23          766.23       930.53       -164.30       104037.40
24          766.23       932.00       -165.77       104203.20
25          823.70       933.49       -109.79       104313.00

WOULD YOU LIKE TO CALCULATE ANOTHER SERIES OF MONTHLY PAYMENTS?
ENTER Y OR N
? N
```

APPENDIX

9 A Graduated-Payment Mortgage Program

```
58 PRINT
60 PRINT " A GRADUATED PAYMENT MORTGAGE PROGRAM"
62 PRINT
88 PRINT
90 PRINT " * * * * * * * * * * * * * * * * * * * * * * * * * * * * * * * * *"
91 PRINT
92 PRINT
93 PRINT "THIS PROGRAM WILL CALCULATE THE MONTHLY PAYMENTS OR THE ANNUAL"
94 PRINT "PERCENTAGE RATE OF A GRADUATED-PAYMENT MORTGAGE. "
95 PRINT
96 PRINT "                            MENU "
97 PRINT
98 PRINT "                    1. THE MONTHLY PAYMENTS"
99 PRINT "                    2. THE ANNUAL PERCENTAGE RATE "
100 PRINT "                   3. EXIT"
101 PRINT
102 PRINT
103 PRINT " * * * * * * * * * * * * * * * * * * * * * * * * * * * * * * * * *"
104 PRINT
105 PRINT "WHICH OPTION WOULD YOU LIKE TO USE? ENTER 1 OR 2 OR 3"
106 INPUT D
107 PRINT
108 IF D <> 1 THEN 460
110 PRINT
112 DIM A(481),B(481),C(481),D(481),E(481),F(481),M(481),P(481)
114 PRINT "ENTER THE LOAN AMOUNT"
120 INPUT A
130 PRINT
```

```
140 PRINT "ENTER THE ANNUAL INTEREST RATE IN PERCENT"
150 INPUT I
155 I=I/100
160 PRINT
170 PRINT "ENTER THE TERM OF THE LOAN IN YEARS"
180 INPUT N
190 PRINT
200 PRINT "ENTER THE GRADUATION PERIOD IN YEARS"
210 INPUT T
220 PRINT
230 PRINT "ENTER THE ANNUAL RATE OF GRADUATION IN PERCENT"
240 INPUT G
245 G=G/100
248 PRINT
250 PRINT
252 PRINT ". . . WORKING . . . "
254 PRINT
256 PRINT
260 R=(1+(I/12))
270 R1=R^12
280 G1=(1+G)
290 K=(G1/R1)-1
300 R2=(1-(R^-12))/(I/12)
310 R3=(((1+K)^T)-1)/K
320 R4=(1-(R^((-12)*(N-T))))/(I/12)
330 R5=(R^(12*T))
340 M1=A/((R2*R3)+((G1^T)*(R4/R5)))
342 D(1)=M1
343 Q=0
344 A(0)=A
345 FOR K=1 TO N
346 FOR J=1 TO 12
347 Q=Q+1
348 B(Q)=A(Q-1)*(I/12)
349 C(Q)=D(K)-B(Q)
350 A(Q)=A(Q-1)-C(Q)
351 E(Q)=D(K)
352 NEXT J
353 D(K+1)=D(K)*G1
354 NEXT K
360 FOR J=0 TO T
370 M(J+1)=M1*(G1^(J))
```

```
372 NEXT J
374 PRINT
375 PRINT "WOULD YOU LIKE TO SEE THE MONTHLY PAYMENTS? (Y OR N)"
376 INPUT H$
377 IF H$="N" THEN 425
378 PRINT
380 PRINT "              YEAR                          MONTHLY PAYMENT"
382 PRINT "____________________________________________________________"
383 PRINT
384 FOR J=1 TO T
386 PRINT USING "        ###                           ####.##";
J,M(J)
388 NEXT J
390 M(T+1)=(INT((M(T+1)+.005)*100))/100
392 PRINT "        "T+1"-"N"        "M(T+1)
400 PRINT
425 PRINT
426 PRINT "WOULD YOU LIKE TO SEE THE AMORTIZATION SCHEDULE? (Y OR N)"
427 INPUT D$
428 IF D$="N" THEN 450
429 PRINT
430 PRINT "FOR HOW MANY MONTHS?"
431 INPUT N5
432 PRINT
433 PRINT "                    AMORTIZATION SCHEDULE "
434 PRINT
435 PRINT  "  MONTH    MONTHLY    INTEREST    PRINCIPAL    MORTGAGE"
436 PRINT "             PAYMENT      PAID        PAID       BALANCE "
437 PRINT "____________________________________________________________"
442 PRINT
444 FOR J=1 TO N5
446 PRINT USING " ###     #####.##     #######.##     #########.##   ##########.##";
J,E(J),B(J),C(J),A(J)
448 NEXT J
450 PRINT
452 PRINT "WOULD YOU LIKE TO CALCULATE ANOTHER SERIES OF MONTHLY PAYMENTS?"
453 PRINT "ENTER Y OR N"
455 INPUT F$
456 IF F$="N" THEN 459
457 ERASE A,B,C,D,E,F,M,P
458 GOTO 110
459 GOTO 95
```

```
460 IF D <> 2 THEN 1030
470 PRINT
480 PRINT
500 Q=0
510 PRINT
520 PRINT "ENTER THE LOAN AMOUNT"
530 INPUT P(0)
540 P(0)=P(0)* -1
550 PRINT
560 PRINT
570 PRINT "ENTER THE NUMBER OF PAYMENT LEVELS"
580 INPUT N2
590 FOR I=1 TO N2
600 PRINT
610 PRINT "ENTER THE NUMBER OF PAYMENTS IN LEVEL "I
620 INPUT P1
630 PRINT "ENTER THE MONTHLY PAYMENT FOR LEVEL "I
640 INPUT M1
650 FOR J=1 TO P1
660 PRINT
670 Q=Q+1
680 P(Q) = M1
690 NEXT J
700 NEXT I
710 PRINT
720 PRINT
730 I=0
740 I1=0
750 I2=0
760 S1=0
770 S2=0
780 S3=0
790 S4=0
800 FOR J=0 TO Q
810 S1 = S1 + (P(J) / ((1 +I) ^J))
820 S2 = S2 + ((P(J) * J)/((1 + I) ^ (J + 1)))
830 NEXT J
840 S3=S2*(-1)
850 S4=S1/S3
860 I1=I
870 I=I1-S4
880 I2=I-I1
```

```
890 IF (I-I1) < 1E-10 THEN 910
900 GOTO 740
910 I=1200*I
920 I=(INT((I +.005)*100))/100
930 PRINT
931 PRINT
932 PRINT
933 PRINT " . . . WORKING . . ."
934 PRINT
935 PRINT
940 PRINT
950 PRINT "THE ANNUAL PERCENTAGE RATE IS "I
960 PRINT
970 PRINT "WOULD YOU LIKE TO CALCULATE ANOTHER APR? (Y OR N)"
980 INPUT K$
990 IF K$= "Y" THEN 480
1000 PRINT
1010 PRINT
1020 GOTO 96
1030 PRINT
1040 PRINT
1060 END
```

APPENDIX

10 A Growing Equity Mortgage Program—Sample Run

```
THIS PROGRAM WILL CALCULATE THE MONTHLY PAYMENTS, INTEREST PAYMENTS,
PRINCIPAL PAYMENTS, AND MORTGAGE BALANCES FOR THE GROWING EQUITY
MORTGAGE.

ENTER THE LOAN AMOUNT
? 100000

ENTER THE ANNUAL INTEREST RATE IN PERCENT
? 10

ENTER THE TERM OF THE LOAN IN YEARS
? 30

YOUR MONTHLY PAYMENT FOR THE FIRST YEAR IS $ 877.5722

ENTER THE ANNUAL GROWTH RATE OF YOUR MONTHLY PAYMENTS IN PERCENT
? 3

 . . . WORKING . . .

YOUR LOAN WILL BE PAID OFF FULLY IN MONTH 194

WOULD YOU LIKE TO SEE THE RESULTS? (Y OR N)
? Y
```

YEAR	MONTHLY PAYMENT
1	877.57
2	903.90
3	931.02

4	958.95
5	987.72
6	1017.35
7	1047.87
8	1079.30
9	1111.68
10	1145.03
11	1179.38
12	1214.76
13	1251.21
14	1288.74
15	1327.41
16	1367.23

WOULD YOU LIKE TO SEE THE AMORTIZATION SCHEDULE? (Y OR N)
? Y

FOR HOW MANY MONTHS?
? 25

AMORTIZATION SCHEDULE

MONTH	MONTHLY PAYMENT	INTEREST PAID	PRINCIPAL PAID	MORTGAGE BALANCE
1	877.57	833.33	44.24	99955.76
2	877.57	832.96	44.61	99911.15
3	877.57	832.59	44.98	99866.18
4	877.57	832.22	45.35	99820.81
5	877.57	831.84	45.73	99775.08
6	877.57	831.46	46.11	99728.97
7	877.57	831.07	46.50	99682.47
8	877.57	830.69	46.89	99635.58
9	877.57	830.30	47.28	99588.30
10	877.57	829.90	47.67	99540.62
11	877.57	829.51	48.07	99492.56
12	877.57	829.10	48.47	99444.09
13	903.90	828.70	75.20	99368.89
14	903.90	828.07	75.83	99293.06
15	903.90	827.44	76.46	99216.60
16	903.90	826.81	77.09	99139.51
17	903.90	826.16	77.74	99061.77
18	903.90	825.51	78.38	98983.38
19	903.90	824.86	79.04	98904.34

20	903.90	824.20	79.70	98824.65
21	903.90	823.54	80.36	98744.29
22	903.90	822.87	81.03	98663.26
23	903.90	822.19	81.71	98581.55
24	903.90	821.51	82.39	98499.16
25	931.02	820.83	110.19	98388.97

```
WOULD YOU LIKE TO START AGAIN? (Y OR N)
? N
```

APPENDIX

11 A Growing Equity Mortgage Program

```
76 PRINT
77 PRINT " A GROWING EQUITY MORTGAGE PROGRAM"
79 PRINT
80 PRINT "THIS PROGRAM WILL CALCULATE THE MONTHLY PAYMENTS, INTEREST "
82 PRINT "PAYMENTS, PRINCIPAL PAYMENTS, AND MORTGAGE BALANCES FOR THE"
84 PRINT "GROWING EQUITY MORTGAGE."
86 PRINT
100 PRINT
110 DIM A(481),B(481),C(481),D(481),I(481),M(481),P(481)
120 PRINT
130 PRINT "ENTER THE LOAN AMOUNT"
140 INPUT L
150 PRINT
160 PRINT "ENTER THE ANNUAL INTEREST RATE IN PERCENT"
170 INPUT I1
180 I=I1/100
190 PRINT
200 PRINT "ENTER THE TERM OF THE LOAN IN YEARS"
210 INPUT N1
220 N=12*N1
230 M=L*(I/12)/(1-((1+(I/12))^(-N)))
240 PRINT
250 PRINT "YOUR MONTHLY PAYMENT FOR THE FIRST YEAR IS $"M
260 PRINT
270 PRINT "ENTER THE ANNUAL GROWTH RATE OF YOUR MONTHLY PAYMENTS IN PERCENT"
271 INPUT G
272 G=G/100
273 PRINT
```

```
274 PRINT
275 PRINT
276 PRINT ". . . WORKING . . ."
277 PRINT
278 PRINT
279 PRINT
290 P(1)=M
300 I=I/12
305 Q=0
310 A(0)=L
320 FOR T=1 TO N1
330 FOR J=1 TO 12
340 Q=Q+1
350 B(Q)=A(Q-1)*I
360 C(Q)=P(T)-B(Q)
370 A(Q)=A(Q-1)-C(Q)
380 IF A(Q)<5 THEN 440
385 M(Q)=P(T)
390 NEXT J
400 P(T+1)=P(T)*(1+G)
410 NEXT T
420 PRINT
430 IF B(Q-1)<5 THEN 460
440 PRINT
450 PRINT "YOUR LOAN WILL BE PAID OFF FULLY IN MONTH "Q
452 PRINT
453 PRINT
455 PRINT "WOULD YOU LIKE TO SEE THE RESULTS? (Y OR N)"
456 INPUT B$
457 IF B$="N" THEN 570
458 Q1=Q
459 Q2=INT(Q1/12)
460 PRINT
462 PRINT "           YEAR           MONTHLY PAYMENT "
463 PRINT "__________________________________________"
464 PRINT
465 FOR J=1 TO Q2
466 PRINT USING "      ##             ######.##";
J,P(J)
467 NEXT J
470 PRINT
472 PRINT "WOULD YOU LIKE TO SEE THE AMORTIZATION SCHEDULE? (Y OR N)"
```

```
473 INPUT C$
474 IF C$="N" THEN 575
475 PRINT
500 PRINT
510 PRINT "FOR HOW MANY MONTHS?"
512 INPUT N4
514 PRINT
515 PRINT "                    AMORTIZATION SCHEDULE "
516 PRINT
517 PRINT "     MONTH    MONTHLY     INTEREST    PRINCIPAL   MORTGAGE "
519 PRINT "              PAYMENT       PAID        PAID      BALANCE "
520 PRINT "____________________________________________________________"
522 PRINT
540 FOR J=1 TO N4
550 PRINT USING " ###      ####.##       #######.##     #########.##   ##########.##";
J,M(J),B(J),C(J),A(J)
552 NEXT J
570 PRINT
575 PRINT
580 PRINT "WOULD YOU LIKE TO START AGAIN? (Y OR N)"
590 INPUT C$
600 IF C$="N" THEN 630
610 ERASE A,B,C,M
620 GOTO 100
630 PRINT
650 END
```

APPENDIX

12 Reverse Annuity Mortgage—Sample Run

```
THIS PROGRAM WILL CALCULATE THE MONTHLY ANNUITY, THE INTEREST OWED, AND
THE ACCUMULATION OF DEBT FOR A REVERSE ANNUITY MORTGAGE.

WHAT IS THE CURRENT VALUE OF YOUR HOME
? 142860

ENTER THE ANNUAL EXPECTED RATE OF APPRECIATION OF THE VALUE OF
YOUR HOME IN PERCENT
? 7

ENTER THE AMOUNT THAT THE LENDER IS WILLING TO LEND YOU
? 100000

ENTER THE ANNUAL INTEREST RATE IN PERCENT
? 12

ENTER THE TERM OF THE ANNUITY IN YEARS
? 10

GIVEN THE INFORMATION SUPPLIED, YOU CAN EXPECT TO RECEIVE $ 430.4057
FROM THE LENDER EVERY MONTH FOR 10 YEARS.

. . . WORKING . . .

WOULD YOU LIKE TO SEE THE RESULTS? (Y OR N)
? Y

FOR HOW MANY MONTHS?
? 5
```

ACCUMULATION OF DEBT SCHEDULE

(1) MONTH	(2) AMOUNT RECEIVED	(3) AMOUNT RECEIVED (CUMULATIVE)	(4) ACCRUED INTEREST (CUMULATIVE)	(5) = (3) + (4) LOAN BALANCE (ACCUM. DEBT)
1	430.41	430.41	4.30	434.71
2	430.41	860.81	12.96	873.77
3	430.41	1291.22	26.00	1317.21
4	430.41	1721.62	43.47	1765.10
5	430.41	2152.03	65.43	2217.46

. . . MORE? (Y OR N)
? Y

ACCUMULATION OF DEBT SCHEDULE

(1) YEAR	(2) AMOUNT RECEIVED	(3) AMOUNT RECEIVED (CUMULATIVE)	(4) ACCRUED INTEREST (CUMULATIVE)	(5) = (3) + (4) LOAN BALANCE (ACCUM. DEBT)
1	5164.87	5164.87	348.34	5513.21
2	5164.87	10329.74	1395.88	11725.62
3	5164.87	15494.61	3231.33	18725.93
4	5164.87	20659.47	5954.58	26614.05
5	5164.87	25824.34	9678.24	35502.59
6	5164.87	30989.21	14529.19	45518.40
7	5164.87	36154.08	20650.40	56804.48
8	5164.87	41318.95	28202.97	69521.91
9	5164.87	46483.82	37368.43	83852.25
10	5164.87	51648.68	48351.32	100000.00

AFTER 10 YEARS, THE APPRECIATED VALUE OF YOUR HOME WILL BE $ 281027.4

AFTER 10 YEARS, THE NET EQUITY IN THE HOUSE WILL BE $ 181027.4

WOULD YOU LIKE TO START AGAIN? (Y OR N)
? N

APPENDIX

13 A Reverse Annuity Mortgage Program

```
76 PRINT
78 PRINT " A REVERSE ANNUITY MORTGAGE PROGRAM"
80 PRINT
82 PRINT "THIS PROGRAM WILL CALCULATE THE MONTHLY ANNUITY, THE INTEREST OWED,"
84 PRINT "AND THE ACCUMULATION OF DEBT FOR A REVERSE ANNUITY MORTGAGE."
100 PRINT
105 DIM A(360),B(360),I(360),V(360)
110 PRINT "WHAT IS THE CURRENT VALUE OF YOUR HOME"
112 INPUT V
114 PRINT
116 PRINT "ENTER THE ANNUAL EXPECTED RATE OF APPRECIATION OF THE VALUE OF "
118 PRINT "YOUR HOME IN PERCENT"
120 INPUT R
130 PRINT
140 PRINT "ENTER THE AMOUNT THAT THE LENDER IS WILLING TO LEND YOU"
150 INPUT L
160 PRINT
170 PRINT "ENTER THE ANNUAL INTEREST RATE IN PERCENT"
180 INPUT I1
190 I=I1/1200
200 PRINT
210 PRINT "ENTER THE TERM OF THE ANNUITY IN YEARS"
220 INPUT N1
230 N=12*N1
240 M=(L*I)/((((1+I)^(N))-1)*(1+I))
250 PRINT
260 PRINT "GIVEN THE INFORMATION SUPPLIED, YOU CAN EXPECT TO RECEIVE $"M
270 PRINT "FROM THE LENDER EVERY MONTH FOR "N1" YEARS."
```

```
280 PRINT
300 PRINT
310 PRINT ". . . WORKING . . ."
320 PRINT
330 PRINT
350 FOR J=1 TO N
360 V(J)=(M/I)*((1+I)^(J)-1)*(1+I)
370 I(J)=V(J)-(J*M)
380 NEXT J
390 FOR J=1 TO N1
400 A(J)=V(12*J)
410 B(J)=V(12*J)-(12*J*M)
420 NEXT J
520 PRINT
530 PRINT "WOULD YOU LIKE TO SEE THE RESULTS? (Y OR N)"
540 INPUT C$
550 IF C$="N" THEN 705
552 PRINT
554 PRINT "FOR HOW MANY MONTHS?"
556 INPUT N2
558 PRINT
560 PRINT "                ACCUMULATION OF DEBT SCHEDULE "
562 PRINT
564 PRINT " (1)        (2)          (3)           (4)      (5) = (3) + (4)"
566 PRINT
568 PRINT "  MONTH   AMOUNT      AMOUNT       ACCRUED     LOAN BALANCE"
570 PRINT "          RECEIVED    RECEIVED     INTEREST    (ACCUM. DEBT)"
572 PRINT "                      (CUMULATIVE) (CUMULATIVE) "
573 PRINT
574 PRINT "______________________________________________________________"
575 PRINT
576 PRINT
600 FOR J=1 TO N2
610 PRINT USING "###  ######.##     #######.##      #######.##     #########.##";
J,M,J*M,I(J),V(J)
620 NEXT J
622 PRINT             " _______"
630 PRINT
640 PRINT ". . . MORE? (Y OR N)"
650 INPUT D$
660 IF D$="N" THEN 710
662 PRINT
```

```
663 PRINT "                  ACCUMULATION OF DEBT SCHEDULE"
664 PRINT
665 PRINT " (1)        (2)          (3)           (4)       (5) = (3) + (4)"
666 PRINT
667 PRINT "   YEAR   AMOUNT       AMOUNT        ACCRUED     LOAN BALANCE"
668 PRINT "          RECEIVED     RECEIVED      INTEREST    (ACCUM. DEBT)"
669 PRINT
670 PRINT "                    (CUMULATIVE) (CUMULATIVE) "
672 PRINT "____________________________________________________________"
674 PRINT
680 FOR J=1 TO N1
690 PRINT USING "###  ######.##     #######.##     #######.##    #########.##";
J,12*M,12*M*J,B(J),A(J)
698 NEXT J
700 PRINT               " ______"
701 PRINT
702 V1=V*((1+(R/100))^(N1))
704 PRINT
705 PRINT "AFTER "N1" YEARS, THE APPRECIATED VALUE OF YOUR HOME WILL BE $"V1
706 PRINT
707 PRINT "AFTER "N1" YEARS, THE NET EQUITY IN THE HOUSE WILL BE $"(V1-L)
710 PRINT
720 PRINT " WOULD YOU LIKE TO START AGAIN? (Y OR N)"
730 INPUT E$
740 IF E$="N" THEN 770
750 ERASE A,B,I,V
760 GOTO 100
770 PRINT
790 END
```

APPENDIX

14 PRICE-LEVEL ADJUSTED MORTGAGE— Sample Run

```
THIS PROGRAM WILL CONSTRUCT THE AMORTIZATION SCHEDULE FOR THE PRICE
LEVEL-ADJUSTED MORTGAGE (PLAM).

ENTER THE LOAN AMOUNT
? 100000

ENTER THE ANNUAL REAL INTEREST RATE IN PERCENT
? 3

ENTER THE TERM OF THE LOAN IN YEARS
? 30

YOUR MONTHLY PAYMENT FOR THE FIRST YEAR WILL BE $ 421.6017

WOULD YOU LIKE TO CALCULATE YOUR FUTURE MONTHLY PAYMENTS? (Y OR N)
? Y

FOR HOW MANY YEARS
? 5

ENTER THE EXPECTED ANNUAL INFLATION RATE FOR YEAR 1 IN PERCENT
? 4
ENTER THE EXPECTED ANNUAL INFLATION RATE FOR YEAR 2 IN PERCENT
? 5
ENTER THE EXPECTED ANNUAL INFLATION RATE FOR YEAR 3 IN PERCENT
? 6
ENTER THE EXPECTED ANNUAL INFLATION RATE FOR YEAR 4 IN PERCENT
? 7
```

ENTER THE EXPECTED ANNUAL INFLATION RATE FOR YEAR 5 IN PERCENT
? 8

. . . WORKING . . .

WOULD YOU LIKE TO SEE THE RESULTS? (Y OR N)
? Y

FOR HOW MANY MONTHS
? 25

AMORTIZATION SCHEDULE

MONTH	(1) MONTHLY PAYMENT	(2) INTEREST PAID	(3) PRINCIPAL PAID	(4) MORTGAGE BALANCE
1	421.60	250.00	171.60	99828.40
2	421.60	249.57	172.03	99656.37
3	421.60	249.14	172.46	99483.91
4	421.60	248.71	172.89	99311.02
5	421.60	248.28	173.32	99137.69
6	421.60	247.84	173.76	98963.93
7	421.60	247.41	174.19	98789.74
8	421.60	246.97	174.63	98615.11
9	421.60	246.54	175.06	98440.05
10	421.60	246.10	175.50	98264.55
11	421.60	245.66	175.94	98088.61
12	421.60	245.22	176.38	101828.70
13	438.47	254.57	183.89	101644.80
14	438.47	254.11	184.35	101460.50
15	438.47	253.65	184.81	101275.60
16	438.47	253.19	185.28	101090.40
17	438.47	252.73	185.74	100904.60
18	438.47	252.26	186.20	100718.40
19	438.47	251.80	186.67	100531.70
20	438.47	251.33	187.14	100344.60
21	438.47	250.86	187.60	100157.00
22	438.47	250.39	188.07	99968.93
23	438.47	249.92	188.54	99780.38
24	438.47	249.45	189.01	104570.90
25	460.39	261.43	198.96	104372.00

. . . MORE? Y OR N
? Y

AMORTIZATION SCHEDULE

YEAR	(1) MONTHLY PAYMENT (NOMINAL)	(2) MONTHLY PAYMENT (REAL)	(3) INTEREST PAID	(4) PRINCIPAL PAID	(5) MORTGAGE BALANCE (NOMINAL)
1	421.60	421.60	2971.45	2087.77	101828.70
2	438.47	417.59	3024.26	2237.32	104570.90
3	460.39	409.74	3104.02	2420.64	108279.30
4	488.01	398.36	3212.22	2643.93	113029.80
5	522.17	383.81	3351.03	2915.05	118924.00

WOULD YOU LIKE TO START AGAIN? (Y OR N)
? N

APPENDIX

15 A Price-Level Adjusted Mortgage Program

```
76 PRINT
78 PRINT " A PRICE LEVEL ADJUSTED MORTGAGE PROGRAM"
80 PRINT
82 PRINT "THIS PROGRAM WILL CONSTRUCT THE AMORTIZATION SCHEDULE FOR THE"
84 PRINT "PRICE LEVEL-ADJUSTED MORTGAGE (PLAM)."
100 PRINT
110 DIM A(360),B(360),C(360),D(360),E(360),F(360),M(360),N(360),R(360)
120 PRINT
130 PRINT "ENTER THE LOAN AMOUNT"
140 INPUT L
150 PRINT
160 PRINT "ENTER THE ANNUAL REAL INTEREST RATE IN PERCENT"
170 INPUT I1
190 I=I1/1200
200 PRINT
210 PRINT "ENTER THE TERM OF THE LOAN IN YEARS"
220 INPUT N1
230 N=12*N1
240 M=(L*I)/(1-(1+I)^(-N))
250 PRINT
260 PRINT "YOUR MONTHLY PAYMENT FOR THE FIRST YEAR WILL BE $"M
270 PRINT
280 PRINT "WOULD YOU LIKE TO CALCULATE YOUR FUTURE MONTHLY PAYMENTS? (Y OR N)"
290 INPUT B$
300 IF B$="N" THEN 895
```

```
310 PRINT
320 PRINT "FOR HOW MANY YEARS"
330 INPUT N2
340 PRINT
360 FOR J=1 TO N2
370 PRINT "ENTER THE EXPECTED ANNUAL INFLATION RATE FOR YEAR "J" IN PERCENT"
380 INPUT R(J)
385 R(J)=R(J)/100
390 NEXT J
400 PRINT
410 PRINT
420 PRINT ". . . WORKING . . ."
430 PRINT
440 PRINT
450 A(0)=L
460 Q=0
470 M(1)=M
480 FOR T=1 TO N2
490 FOR J=1 TO 12
500 Q=Q+1
510 B(Q)=A(Q-1)*I
520 C(Q)=M(T)-B(Q)
530 A(Q)=A(Q-1)-C(Q)
540 D(Q)=M(T)
545 NEXT J
547 N(T)=M(T)/((1+R(T))^(T-1))
550 A(Q)=A(Q)*(1+R(T))
555 M(T+1)=(A(Q)*I)/(1-(1+I)^((12*T)-N))
560 NEXT T
570 S=0
580 Q=0
590 S1=0
600 FOR T=1 TO N2
610 FOR J=1 TO 12
620 Q=Q+1
630 S=S+B(Q)
640 S1=S1+C(Q)
650 NEXT J
660 E(T)=S
670 F(T)=S1
680 S=0
690 S1=0
```

```
700 NEXT T
710 PRINT
720 PRINT "WOULD YOU LIKE TO SEE THE RESULTS? (Y OR N)"
730 INPUT B$
740 IF B$="N" THEN 900
750 PRINT
760 PRINT "FOR HOW MANY MONTHS"
761 INPUT N4
762 PRINT
763 PRINT
764 PRINT "                    AMORTIZATION SCHEDULE"
765 PRINT
766 PRINT "              (1)          (2)          (3)          (4) "
767 PRINT
768 PRINT "    MONTH   MONTHLY     INTEREST    PRINCIPAL    MORTGAGE"
769 PRINT "            PAYMENT       PAID        PAID       BALANCE "
770 PRINT "______________________________________________________________"
780 PRINT
790 FOR J=1 TO N4
800 PRINT USING " ###      #####.##      #####.##      #####.##     #########.##";
J,D(J),B(J),C(J),A(J)
810 NEXT J
820 PRINT
830 PRINT ". . . MORE? (Y OR N)"
840 INPUT C$
850 IF C$="N" THEN 905
851 PRINT
852 PRINT
853 PRINT "                    AMORTIZATION SCHEDULE"
855 PRINT "          (1)        (2)        (3)        (4)        (5) "
856 PRINT
857 PRINT "   YEAR MONTHLY   MONTHLY  INTEREST PRINCIPAL MORTGAGE "
858 PRINT "        PAYMENT   PAYMENT    PAID      PAID     BALANCE "
859 PRINT "       (NOMINAL)  (REAL)                       (NOMINAL)"
860 PRINT "______________________________________________________________"
862 PRINT
870 FOR J=1 TO N2
880 PRINT USING "##  ####.##     #####.##    #####.##    #####.##    #########.##";
J,M(J),N(J),E(J),F(J),A(12*J)
890 NEXT J
895 PRINT
```

```
900 PRINT
905 PRINT
910 PRINT "WOULD YOU LIKE TO START AGAIN? (Y OR N)"
920 INPUT D$
930 IF D$="N" THEN 960
940 ERASE A,B,C,D,E,F,M,N,R
950 GOTO 100
960 PRINT
980 END
```

APPENDIX

16 15-Year Versus 30-Year Fixed Rate Mortgage Program—Sample Run

```
THIS PROGRAM WILL HELP YOU CHOOSE BETWEEN THE 15-YEAR FIXED-RATE MORTGAGE
AND THE 30-YEAR FIXED-RATE MORTGAGE. THE EVALUATION IS BASED ON MONTHLY
PAYMENT SAVINGS, TAX SAVINGS, AND PAY-OFF BALANCES OVER A 15-YEAR
PERIOD.

ENTER THE LOAN AMOUNT
? 100000

ENTER THE ANNUAL INTEREST RATE ON THE 30-YEAR MORTGAGE IN %
? 8.75

ENTER THE NUMBER OF POINTS OF THE 30-YEAR MORTGAGE
? 2.75

ENTER THE NUMBER OF POINTS OF THE 15-YEAR MORTGAGE
? 3.75

ENTER THE ANNUAL INTEREST RATE ON THE 15-YEAR MORTGAGE IN %
? 8.25

ENTER YOUR MARGINAL TAX RATE IN PERCENT
? 28

ENTER THE BEST ANNUAL INTEREST RATE YOU CAN EARN ON YOUR
SAVINGS (IN PERCENT AND BEFORE TAXES).
? 8.25
```

. . . WORKING . . .

WOULD YOU LIKE TO SEE THE RESULTS? (Y OR N)
? Y

FOR HOW MANY MONTHS?
? 3

MONTH	(1) MORTGAGE PAYMENT 15-YEAR	(2) MORTGAGE PAYMENT 30-YEAR	(3) = (1) − (2) PAYMENT DIFFERENCE	(4) INTEREST PAID 30-YEAR	(5) INTEREST PAID 15-YEAR
1	970.14	786.70	183.44	729.17	687.50
2	970.14	786.70	183.44	728.75	685.56
3	970.14	786.70	183.44	728.32	683.60

WOULD YOU LIKE TO SEE MORE RESULTS? (Y OR N)
? Y

MONTH	(6) = (4) − (5) DIFFERENCE IN INTEREST	(7) = (6) * .28 TAX SAVINGS	(8) = (3) + (7) TATS	(9) PV OF (8)	(10) PV OF TATS (CUMULATIVE)
1	41.67	11.67	195.11	194.14	194.14
2	43.19	12.09	195.53	193.61	387.76
3	44.72	12.52	195.96	193.08	580.84

(8) = TATS = TOTAL AFTER-TAX SAVINGS
(9) = PV OF (8) = PRESENT VALUE OF THE TOTAL AFTER-TAX SAVINGS
(10) = PV OF TATS = PRESENT VALUE OF THE TOTAL AFTER-TAX SAVINGS

WOULD YOU LIKE TO SEE MORE RESULTS? (Y OR N)
? Y

MONTH	(11) MORTGAGE BALANCE 30-YEAR	(12) MORTGAGE BALANCE 15-YEAR	(13) = (11) − (12) DIFFERENCE	(14) PRESENT VALUE OF (13)
1	99942.47	99717.36	225.11	224.00
2	99884.52	99432.78	451.74	447.30
3	99826.14	99146.24	679.91	669.91

WOULD YOU LIKE TO SEE MORE RESULTS? (Y OR N)
? Y

YEAR	(15) PRESENT VALUE OF THE TOTAL AFTER-TAX SAVINGS OF THE 30-YEAR MORTGAGE (CUMULATIVE)	(16) PRESENT VALUE OF THE THE DIFFERENCE IN MORTGAGE BALANCES
1	2295.24	2642.79
2	4518.83	5191.50
3	6676.20	7652.74
4	8772.52	10032.85
5	10812.68	12337.79
6	12801.30	14573.19
7	14742.78	16744.45
8	16641.31	18856.62
9	18500.85	20914.52
10	20325.17	22922.71
11	22117.86	24885.52
12	23882.33	26807.08
13	25621.83	28691.28
14	27339.47	30541.85
15	29038.19	32362.34

YOUR CROSSOVER MONTH IS MONTH 26
IF YOU PLAN TO PREPAY THE LOAN BEFORE THE CROSSOVER MONTH,
THE 30-YEAR MORTGAGE WOULD BE BETTER FOR YOU. OTHERWISE,
THE 15-YEAR MORTGAGE WOULD BE BETTER FOR YOU.

APPENDIX

17 15-Year Versus 30-Year Fixed Rate Mortgage Program

```
66 PRINT
67 PRINT "FIFTEEN-YEAR VERSUS THIRTY-YEAR FIXED-RATE MORTGAGES"
69 PRINT
70 PRINT "THIS PROGRAM WILL HELP YOU CHOOSE BETWEEN THE 15-YEAR FIXED-RATE"
72 PRINT "MORTGAGE AND THE 30-YEAR FIXED-RATE MORTGAGE. THE EVALUATION IS"
74 PRINT "BASED ON MONTHLY PAYMENT SAVINGS, TAX SAVINGS, AND PAY-OFF BALANCES"
75 PRINT "OVER A 15-YEAR PERIOD."
77 PRINT
100 PRINT
109 PRINT
110 PRINT "ENTER THE LOAN AMOUNT"
120 INPUT A
130 PRINT
160 PRINT
170 PRINT "ENTER THE ANNUAL INTEREST RATE ON THE 30-YEAR MORTGAGE IN %"
180 INPUT I1
190 I1=I1/100
192 PRINT
194 PRINT "ENTER THE NUMBER OF POINTS OF THE 30-YEAR MORTGAGE"
196 INPUT P1
198 P1=P1/100
200 P=P1*A
202 PRINT
204 PRINT "ENTER THE NUMBER OF POINTS OF THE 15-YEAR MORTGAGE"
206 INPUT P2
```

```
208 P2=P2/100
210 P3=P2*A
212 PRINT
214 PRINT "ENTER THE ANNUAL INTEREST RATE ON THE 15-YEAR MORTGAGE IN %"
220 INPUT I2
221 I2=I2/100
222 PRINT
223 PRINT "ENTER YOUR MARGINAL TAX RATE IN PERCENT"
224 INPUT T1
226 T1=T1/100
228 PRINT
230 PRINT "ENTER THE BEST ANNUAL INTEREST RATE YOU CAN EARN ON YOUR"
232 PRINT "SAVINGS (IN PERCENT AND BEFORE TAXES)."
234 INPUT R
236 R=R*(1-T1)
238 R=R/100
239 R=R/12
240 PRINT
242 PRINT
244 PRINT " . . . WORKING . . ."
246 PRINT
248 PRINT
250 M1=(A*(I1/12))/(1-((1+(I1/12))^(-360)))
260 M2=(A*(I2/12))/(1-((1+(I2/12))^(-180)))
262 P4=P*(1-T1)
264 P5=P3*(1-T1)
266 P6=P5-P4
270 PRINT
280 DIM A(481),B(481),C(481),D(481),E(481),F(481),G(481),H(481),
I(481),K(481),L(481),M(481),N(481),O(481),P(481),Q(481),R(481),S(481)
300 A(0)=A
305 D(0)=A
310 FOR J=1 TO 180
320 B(J)=A(J-1)*(I1/12)
330 C(J)=M1-B(J)
340 A(J)=A(J-1)-C(J)
360 E(J)=D(J-1)*(I2/12)
370 F(J)=M2-E(J)
380 D(J)=D(J-1)-F(J)
390 NEXT J
400 FOR J=1 TO 180
410 G(J)=M1
```

```
420 H(J)=M2
430 I(J)=H(J)-G(J)
440 K(J)=B(J)-E(J)
450 L(J)=K(J)*T1
460 M(J)=I(J)+L(J)
465 NEXT J
470 PRINT
530 FOR J=1 TO 180
540 N(J)=M(J)*(1/((1+R)^J))
550 O(J)=A(J)-D(J)
560 P(J)=O(J)*(1/((1+R)^J))
570 NEXT J
580 S1=0
590 FOR J=1 TO 180
600 S1= S1+N(J)
610 Q(J)=S1
620 NEXT J
626 Q=0
627 S2=0
628 FOR T=1 TO 15
629 FOR J=1 TO 12
630 Q=Q+1
631 S2=S2+N(Q)
632 NEXT J
633 R(T)=S2
634 NEXT T
635 FOR J=1 TO 15
636 S(J)=P(12*J)
637 NEXT J
638 PRINT
640 PRINT "WOULD YOU LIKE TO SEE THE RESULTS? (Y OR N)"
650 INPUT A$
660 IF A$="N" THEN 910
670 PRINT
680 PRINT "FOR HOW MANY MONTHS?"
690 INPUT N2
692 PRINT "          (1)        (2)     (3) = (1) - (2)     (4)        (5)
693 PRINT
694 PRINT "MONTH MORTGAGE MORTGAGE      PAYMENT       INTEREST  INTEREST"
695 PRINT "      PAYMENT  PAYMENT      DIFFERENCE       PAID      PAID"
696 PRINT "      15-YEAR  30-YEAR                     30-YEAR   15-YEAR"
702 PRINT "______________________________________________________________"
```

```
704 PRINT
710 FOR J=1 TO N2
720 PRINT USING "###  ####.##  ####.##  ####.##  ####.##  ###.##";
J,H(J),G(J),I(J),B(J),E(J)
725 NEXT J
726 PRINT
727 PRINT "WOULD YOU LIKE TO SEE MORE RESULTS? (Y OR N)"
728 INPUT E$
729 IF E$="N" THEN 910
731 PRINT
732 PRINT
733 PRINT "           (6) = (4) - (5)   (7) = (6) * "T1"  (8) = (3) + (7)   (9)          (10)"
734 PRINT
735 PRINT "MONTH   DIFFERENCE  TAX SAVINGS TATS  PV OF (8)   PV OF TATS"
736 PRINT "        IN INTEREST                              (CUMULATIVE)"
740 PRINT " ______________________________________________________________"
742 PRINT
750 FOR J=1 TO N2
760 PRINT USING "###      ####.##        ####.##     ####.##    ####.##       #####.##";
J,K(J),L(J),M(J),N(J),Q(J)
762 NEXT J
763 PRINT " ______________________________________________________________"
765 PRINT
766 PRINT "(8) = TATS = TOTAL AFTER-TAX SAVINGS"
767 PRINT "(9) = PV OF (8) = PRESENT VALUE OF THE TOTAL AFTER-TAX SAVINGS"
768 PRINT "(10) = PV OF TATS = PRESENT VALUE OF THE TOTAL AFTER-TAX SAVINGS"
769 PRINT
772 PRINT "WOULD YOU LIKE TO SEE MORE RESULTS? (Y OR N)"
773 INPUT F$
774 IF F$="N" THEN 905
776 PRINT
777 PRINT
778 PRINT "         (11)       (12)     (13) = (11) - (12)     (14) "
782 PRINT
783 PRINT "       MORTGAGE   MORTGAGE     DIFFERENCE       PRESENT"
784 PRINT "MONTH   BALANCE    BALANCE                     VALUE OF (13)"
785 PRINT "        30-YEAR    15-YEAR                     "
786 PRINT "____________________________________________________________"
790 PRINT
800 FOR J=1 TO N2
810 PRINT USING "###  #########.##   #########.##      #########.##      #########.##";
J,A(J),D(J),O(J),P(J)
```

```
812 NEXT J
815 PRINT
816 PRINT "WOULD YOU LIKE TO SEE MORE RESULTS? (Y OR N)"
817 INPUT G$
818 IF G$="N" THEN 906
821 PRINT
822 PRINT
823 PRINT "                    (15)                        (16) "
824 PRINT
825 PRINT "   YEAR    PRESENT VALUE OF THE      PRESENT VALUE OF THE "
826 PRINT "           TOTAL AFTER-TAX SAVINGS     THE DIFFERENCE IN"
827 PRINT "           OF THE 30-YEAR MORTGAGE     MORTGAGE BALANCES"
828 PRINT "                (CUMULATIVE)                              "
829 PRINT "_____________________________________________________________"
830 PRINT
840 FOR J=1 TO 15
850 PRINT USING "###         #########.##              #########.##";
J,R(J),S(J)
860 NEXT J
862 PRINT
864 FOR J=1 TO 180
866 IF (Q(J)+P6) > P(J) THEN 872
868 PRINT (Q(J)+P6), P(J)
870 GOTO 874
872 NEXT J
873 GOTO 902
874 PRINT
876 PRINT "YOUR CROSSOVER MONTH IS MONTH "J
878 PRINT "IF YOU PLAN TO PREPAY THE LOAN BEFORE THE CROSSOVER MONTH,"
880 PRINT "THE 30-YEAR MORTGAGE WOULD BE BETTER FOR YOU. OTHERWISE,"
882 PRINT "THE 15-YEAR MORTGAGE WOULD BE BETTER FOR YOU."
884 GOTO 950
902 PRINT
903 IF P(180) > (Q(180)+P6) THEN 912
904 PRINT
905 PRINT "GIVEN THE INFORMATION THAT WAS SUPPLIED, THE 30-YEAR MORTGAGE WOULD"
906 PRINT "BE MORE SUITABLE FOR YOU FINANCIALLY. THE PRESENT VALUE OF THE "
907 PRINT "CUMULATIVE, TOTAL AFTER-TAX SAVINGS ASSOCIATED WITH THE 30-YEAR"
908 PRINT "MORTGAGE OVER THE FIRST 15-YEAR PERIOD ($"(Q(180)+P6)") EXCEEDS"
909 PRINT "THE PRESENT VALUE OF THE PAY-OFF BALANCE OF THE 30-YEAR MORTGAGE"
910 PRINT "($"P(180)") AT THE END OF 15 YEARS."
911 GOTO 919
```

```
912 PRINT
913 PRINT "GIVEN THE INFORMATION THAT WAS SUPPLIED, THE 15-YEAR MORTGAGE WOULD"
914 PRINT "BE MORE SUITABLE FOR YOU FINANCIALLY. THE PRESENT VALUE OF THE"
915 PRINT "CUMULATIVE, TOTAL AFTER-TAX SAVINGS ASSOCIATED WITH THE 30-YEAR"
916 PRINT "MORTGAGE OVER THE FIRST 15-YEAR PERIOD ($"(Q(180)+P6)") IS SMALLER"
917 PRINT "THAN THE PRESENT VALUE OF THE PAY-OFF BALANCE OF THE 30-YEAR "
918 PRINT "MORTGAGE ($"P(180)") AT THE END OF 15 YEARS."
919 PRINT
920 PRINT "WOULD YOU LIKE TO START AGAIN? (Y OR N)"
930 INPUT C$
940 IF C$="N" THEN 950
942 ERASE A,B,C,D,E,F,G,H,I,K,L,M,N,O,P,Q,R,S
945 GOTO 100
950 PRINT
970 END
```

APPENDIX

18 A MORTGAGE REFINANCING PROGRAM—Sample Run

```
THIS PROGRAM WILL HELP YOU DECIDE WHETHER OR NOT YOU SHOULD
REFINANCE YOUR MORTGAGE AT THIS TIME. YOU MAY WANT TO REFINANCE
TO TAKE ADVANTAGE OF A LOWER INTEREST RATE OR TO USE THE EQUITY
IN YOUR HOME FOR OTHER INVESTMENTS.

ENTER THE ORIGINAL AMOUNT OF THE OLD (EXISTING) LOAN
? 100000

ENTER THE ORIGINAL TERM OF THE OLD LOAN IN YEARS
? 30

ENTER THE ANNUAL INTEREST RATE OF THE OLD LOAN IN PERCENT
? 12

ENTER THE REMAINING TERM OF THE OLD LOAN IN MONTHS
? 336

ENTER THE PREPAYMENT PENALTY ON THE OLD LOAN IN DOLLARS
? 0

WILL THIS PENALTY BE AN OUT-OF-POCKET EXPENSE? (Y OR N)
? Y

THE MONTHLY PAYMENT OF THE OLD LOAN IS $ 1028.613

THE CURRENT BALANCE OF THE OLD LOAN IS $ 99228.21

ENTER YOUR MARGINAL TAX RATE IN PERCENT
? 28
```

```
ENTER THE AMOUNT OF THE NEW LOAN (AMOUNT YOU WISH TO BORROW NOW)
DON'T INCLUDE POINTS AND OTHER CLOSING COSTS EVEN IF THEY
WILL BE ADDED TO THE LOAN. THEY WILL BE INCLUDED AUTOMATICALLY.
? 99228.21

ENTER THE ANNUAL INTEREST RATE ON THE NEW LOAN IN PERCENT
? 10

ENTER THE TERM OF THE NEW LOAN IN YEARS
? 30

ENTER THE NUMBER OF POINTS OF THE NEW LOAN
? 2

YOUR POINTS WILL AMOUNT TO $ 1984.564. HOW MUCH OF THIS COST WILL
BE AN OUT-OF-POCKET EXPENSE?
? 1984.564

ENTER OTHER CLOSING COSTS
? 950

HOW MUCH OF THIS COST WILL BE AN OUT-OF-POCKET EXPENSE?
? 950

ENTER THE BEST ANNUAL INTEREST RATE YOU CAN EARN ON YOUR SAVINGS
IN PERCENT AND BEFORE TAXES
? 9.25

 . . . WORKING . . .

WOULD YOU LIKE TO SEE THE RESULTS? (Y OR N)
? Y

THE MONTHLY PAYMENT OF THE NEW LOAN IS $ 870.7992

THE OUT-OF-POCKET CLOSING COSTS AND CLOSING COSTS ADDED TO THE
LOAN ARE $ 2934.564 AND $ 2.441406E-4 RESPECTIVELY.

THE NET PROCEEDS FROM THE NEW LOAN IS $-2934.563

 . . . MORE? (Y OR N)
? Y

FOR HOW MANY PERIODS?
? 2
```

MONTH	(1) MONTHLY PAYMENT (OLD LOAN)	(2) MONTHLY PAYMENT (NEW LOAN)	(3) = (1) - (2) PAYMENT DIFFERENCE	(4) INTEREST (OLD LOAN)	(5) INTEREST (NEW LOAN)
1	1028.61	870.80	157.81	992.28	826.90
2	1028.61	870.80	157.81	991.92	826.54

. . . MORE? Y OR N
? Y

MONTH	(6)=(4)-(5)-K INTEREST DIFFERENCE	(7) = (6) * T TAX SAVINGS OF OLD LOAN	(8) = (3) - (7) PAYMENT DIFFERENCE (AFTER-TAX)	(9) PRESENT VALUE OF (8) @ .555%
1	159.87	44.76	113.05	112.43
2	159.87	44.76	113.05	111.81

K = AMORTIZED POINTS = $ 5.512678
T = MARGINAL TAX RATE = 28%

. . . MORE? (Y OR N)
? Y

MONTH	(10) BALANCE OLD LOAN	(11) BALANCE NEW LOAN MINUS TS	(12) = (10) - (11) DIFFERENCE BETWEEN BALANCES	(13) PRESENT VALUE OF (12) @ .555%
1	99191.88	98630.18	561.70	558.60
2	99155.18	98587.46	567.73	561.48

TS = TAX SAVINGS RESULTING FROM THE WRITEOFF OF THE UNAMORTIZED POINTS.

. . . MORE? (Y OR N)
? Y

YEAR	(14) PRESENT VALUE OF AFTER-TAX PAYMENT DIFFERENCE	(15) PRESENT VALUE OF AFTER-TAX PAYMENT DIFFERENCE (CUMULATIVE)	(16) = (13) + (15) PRESENT VALUE OF AFTER-TAX PAY. DIFF. (CUM.) & PRESENT VALUE OF DIFFERENCE IN BALANCES
1	1308.90	1308.90	1896.54
2	1224.96	2533.86	3146.47

```
3      1146.73      3680.59      4310.85
4      1073.86      4754.45      5394.72
5      1006.04      5760.49      6402.77
6       942.98      6703.47      7339.36

YOUR CROSSOVER MONTH IS MONTH 22
IN GENERAL, IF YOU PLAN TO PREPAY THE LOAN BEFORE THE CROSSOVER
MONTH, REFINANCING MAY NOT BE TO YOUR ADVANTAGE.

DO YOU THINK THE LOAN WILL BE PREPAID? (Y OR N)
? N

WOULD YOU LIKE TO START AGAIN? (Y OR N)
? N
```

APPENDIX

19 A MORTGAGE REFINANCING PROGRAM

```
40 PRINT
42 PRINT "A MORTGAGE REFINANCING PROGRAM"
44 PRINT
46 PRINT "THIS PROGRAM WILL HELP YOU DECIDE WHETHER OR NOT YOU SHOULD "
48 PRINT "REFINANCE YOUR MORTGAGE AT THIS TIME. YOU MAY WANT TO REFINANCE"
50 PRINT "TO TAKE ADVANTAGE OF A LOWER INTEREST RATE OR TO USE THE EQUITY"
52 PRINT "IN YOUR HOME FOR OTHER INVESTMENTS."
54 PRINT
56 PRINT "ENTER THE ORIGINAL AMOUNT OF THE OLD (EXISTING) LOAN"
58 INPUT L1
60 PRINT
62 PRINT "ENTER THE ORIGINAL TERM OF THE OLD LOAN IN YEARS"
64 INPUT N2
66 PRINT
68 PRINT "ENTER THE ANNUAL INTEREST RATE OF THE OLD LOAN IN PERCENT"
70 INPUT I2
72 I2=I2/100
74 PRINT
76 PRINT "ENTER THE REMAINING TERM OF THE OLD LOAN IN MONTHS"
78 INPUT N3
79 N5=N3/12
80 N5=INT(N5)
81 N4=12*N2
82 PRINT
83 PRINT "ENTER THE PREPAYMENT PENALTY ON THE OLD LOAN IN DOLLARS"
84 INPUT PP1
85 PP=PP1*(1-T)
86 PRINT
```

```
87 PRINT "WILL THIS PENALTY BE AN OUT-OF-POCKET EXPENSE? (Y OR N)"
88 INPUT B$
89 IF B$="N" THEN 93
90 PP=-1*PP1*T
91 PP2=PP1
92 GOTO 94
93 PP2=0
94 M1=L1*(I2/12)/(1-((1+(I2/12))^(-N4)))
96 B=(M1/(I2/12))*(1-((1+(I2/12))^(-N3)))
98 PRINT
100 PRINT "THE MONTHLY PAYMENT OF THE OLD LOAN IS $"M1
102 PRINT
104 PRINT "THE CURRENT BALANCE OF THE OLD LOAN IS $"B
106 PRINT
110 DIM A(481),B(481),C(481),D(481),E(481),F(481),G(481),H(481),
I(481),K(481),L(481),M(481),N(481),P(481),Q(481),R(481),S(481),T(481)
112 PRINT "ENTER YOUR MARGINAL TAX RATE IN PERCENT"
114 INPUT T1
116 T=T1/100
118 PRINT
120 PRINT "ENTER THE AMOUNT OF THE NEW LOAN (AMOUNT YOU WISH TO BORROW NOW)"
122 PRINT "DON'T INCLUDE POINTS AND OTHER CLOSING COSTS EVEN IF THEY"
124 PRINT "WILL BE ADDED TO THE LOAN. THEY WILL BE INCLUDED AUTOMATICALLY."
130 INPUT L
140 PRINT
150 PRINT "ENTER THE ANNUAL INTEREST RATE ON THE NEW LOAN IN PERCENT"
160 INPUT I1
170 I=I1/100
172 PRINT
174 PRINT "ENTER THE TERM OF THE NEW LOAN IN YEARS"
176 INPUT N1
178 N=12*N1
180 PRINT
182 PRINT "ENTER THE NUMBER OF POINTS OF THE NEW LOAN"
184 INPUT P1
186 P1=P1/100
188 P15=P1*L
190 PRINT
192 PRINT "YOUR POINTS WILL AMOUNT TO $"P15". HOW MUCH OF THIS COST WILL"
194 PRINT "BE AN OUT-OF-POCKET EXPENSE?"
196 INPUT P10
198 PRINT
```

```
200 PRINT "ENTER OTHER CLOSING COSTS"
202 INPUT C1
203 PRINT
204 PRINT "HOW MUCH OF THIS COST WILL BE AN OUT-OF-POCKET EXPENSE?"
206 INPUT C4
208 IF (L-B) > 2 THEN 212
210 GOTO 244
212 PRINT
214 PRINT "YOUR NEW LOAN AMOUNT EXCEEDS THE CURRENT BALANCE. IS THE EXTRA"
216 PRINT "MONEY FOR IMPROVING YOUR PRINCIPAL RESIDENCE? (Y OR N)"
218 INPUT A$
220 IF A$="N" THEN 244
224 B1=L-B
226 P13=P1*B
228 P14=P1*B1
230 PRINT
232 P14=(P14/P15)*P10
234 P13=(P13/P15)*P10
236 P12=P13/N
238 P=B1-P10+(P14*T)-C4
240 L=L+(P15-P10)+(C1-C4)+PP2
241 C5=(P15-P10)+(C1-C4)+PP2
242 GOTO 250
244 P12=P10/N
246 P=P10+C4+PP
248 L=L+(P15-P10)+(C1-C4)+PP2
249 C5=(P15-P10)+(C1-C4)+PP2
250 PRINT
350 PRINT
540 PRINT
550 PRINT "ENTER THE BEST ANNUAL INTEREST RATE YOU CAN EARN ON YOUR SAVINGS"
560 PRINT "IN PERCENT AND BEFORE TAXES"
570 INPUT R1
572 PRINT
573 PRINT
574 PRINT ". . . WORKING . . . "
575 PRINT
576 PRINT
580 R2=R1*(1-T)
590 R=R2/100
592 R5=R2/12
595 M=L*(I/12)/(1-((1+(I/12))^(-N)))
```

```
620 NP=L-P-B-PP
625 S=0
630 A(0)=L
640 D(0)=B
650 FOR J=1 TO N3
660 M2=M1-M
670 B(J)=A(J-1)*(I/12)
680 C(J)=M-B(J)
690 A(J)=A(J-1)-C(J)
692 T(J)=A(J)-((P10-((J)*(P10/N)))*T)
700 E(J)=D(J-1)*(I2/12)
710 F(J)=M1-E(J)
720 D(J)=D(J-1)-F(J)
730 G(J)=E(J)-B(J)-P12
740 H(J)=T*G(J)
750 I(J)=D(J)-T(J)
760 K(J)=M2-H(J)
770 L(J)=K(J)/((1+(R/12))^(J))
780 M(J)=I(J)/((1+(R/12))^(J))
784 S=S+L(J)
786 S(J)=S
790 NEXT J
800 Q=0
810 S=0
820 S1=0
830 FOR I=1 TO N5
840 FOR J=1 TO 12
850 Q=Q+1
860 S=S+L(Q)
870 NEXT J
880 N(I)=S
890 S=0
900 NEXT I
910 FOR J=1 TO N5
920 S1=S1+N(J)
930 P(J)=S1
940 NEXT J
950 FOR J=1 TO N5
960 Q(J)=P(J)+M(12*J)
970 NEXT J
980 PRINT
990 PRINT "WOULD YOU LIKE TO SEE THE RESULTS? (Y OR N)"
```

```
1000 INPUT B$
1010 IF B$="N" THEN 1680
1020 PRINT
1030 PRINT "THE MONTHLY PAYMENT OF THE NEW LOAN IS $"M
1040 PRINT
1050 PRINT "THE OUT-OF-POCKET CLOSING COSTS AND CLOSING COSTS ADDED TO THE"
1052 PRINT "LOAN ARE $"P" AND $"C5" RESPECTIVELY."
1100 PRINT
1110 PRINT "THE NET PROCEEDS FROM THE NEW LOAN IS $"NP
1120 PRINT
1130 PRINT ". . . MORE? (Y OR N)"
1140 INPUT C$
1150 IF C$="N" THEN 1680
1155 PRINT
1160 PRINT "FOR HOW MANY PERIODS"
1170 INPUT N6
1173 PRINT
1174 PRINT "          (1)        (2)     (3)=(1)-(2)     (4)        (5)"
1175 PRINT
1176 PRINT "MONTH   MONTHLY    MONTHLY     PAYMENT     INTEREST   INTEREST "
1177 PRINT "        PAYMENT    PAYMENT   DIFFERENCE  (OLD LOAN) (NEW LOAN)"
1178 PRINT "       (OLD LOAN) (NEW LOAN)                                    "
1179 PRINT " ______________________________________________________________"
1180 PRINT
1181 FOR J=1 TO N6
 1190 PRINT USING "### ####.##   ####.##     ####.##     ####.##    ####.##";
J,M1,M,M2,E(J),B(J)
1200 NEXT J
1210 PRINT
1220 PRINT ". . . MORE? (Y OR N)"
1230 INPUT D$
1240 IF D$="N" THEN 1680
1243 PRINT
1244 PRINT "(6) = (4) - (5) - K   (7) = (6) * T   (8) = (3) - (7)   (9)   "
1245 PRINT
1247 PRINT "MONTH    INTEREST   TAX SAVINGS    PAYMENT     PRESENT"
1248 PRINT "        DIFFERENCE  OF OLD LOAN   DIFFERENCE   VALUE OF "
1249 PRINT "                                  (AFTER-TAX)  (8) @ "R5"%"
1250 PRINT " _______________________________________________________"
1251 PRINT
1260 FOR J=1 TO N6
1270 PRINT USING "###   ####.##      ####.##       ####.##      ####.##";
J,G(J),H(J),K(J),L(J)
```

```
1280 NEXT J
1281 PRINT " ____________________________________________________________"
1282 PRINT "K = AMORTIZED POINTS = $"P12
1283 PRINT "T = MARGINAL TAX RATE = "T1"%"
1290 PRINT
1300 PRINT ". . . MORE? (Y OR N)"
1310 INPUT E$
1320 IF E$="N" THEN 1680
1323 PRINT
1324 PRINT "             (10)         (11)      (12)=(10)-(11)       (13) "
1325 PRINT
1327 PRINT "MONTH     BALANCE     BALANCE      DIFFERENCE    PRESENT VALUE"
1328 PRINT "          OLD LOAN    NEW LOAN       BETWEEN      OF (12) @ "R5"
1329 PRINT "                      MINUS TS      BALANCES          %"
1330 PRINT " ______________________________________________________________"
1332 PRINT
1340 FOR J=1 TO N6
1350 PRINT USING "###   ######.##     ######.##         ######.##          ######.##";
J,D(J),T(J),I(J),M(J)
1360 NEXT J
1370 PRINT
1372 PRINT " ____________________________________________________________"
1373 PRINT
1374 PRINT "TS = TAX SAVINGS RESULTING FROM THE WRITEOFF OF THE UNAMORTIZED"
1376 PRINT " POINTS."
1377 PRINT
1380 PRINT " . . . MORE? (Y OR N)"
1390 INPUT F$
1400 IF F$="N" THEN 1680
1403 PRINT
1404 PRINT "               (14)               (15)           (16)=(13)+(15) "
1405 PRINT
1407 PRINT "YEAR    PRESENT VALUE OF PRESENT VALUE OF  PRESENT VALUE OF "
1408 PRINT "          AFTER-TAX PAY-   AFTER-TAX PAY-  AFTER-TAX PAY. DIFF.
1409 PRINT "         MENT DIFFERENCE  MENT DIFFERENCE   (CUM.) & PRESENT "
1410 PRINT "                            (CUMULATIVE)   VALUE OF DIFFERENCE"
1411 PRINT "                                                IN BALANCES"
1412 PRINT " ______________________________________________________________"
1413 PRINT
1420 FOR J=1 TO N5
1430 PRINT USING "##      ######.##               ######.##            #######.##";
J,N(J),P(J),Q(J)
```

```
1440 NEXT J
1442 PRINT " ____________________________________________________________"
1444 PRINT
1445 IF P < 300 THEN 1462
1446 FOR J=1 TO N3
1448 IF P > (S(J)+M(J)) THEN 1454
1450 PRINT P,(S(J)+M(J))
1452 GOTO 1456
1453 PRINT
1454 NEXT J
1455 GOTO 1462
1456 PRINT
1458 PRINT "YOUR CROSS-OVER MONTH IS MONTH "J
1460 PRINT "IN GENERAL, IF YOU PLAN TO PREPAY THE LOAN BEFORE THE CROSSOVER"
1461 PRINT "MONTH, REFINANCING MAY NOT BE TO YOUR ADVANTAGE."
1462 PRINT
1464 PRINT "DO YOU THINK THE LOAN WILL BE PREPAID? (Y OR N)"
1470 INPUT G$
1480 IF G$="N" THEN 1680
1490 PRINT
1500 PRINT "IN HOW MANY YEARS?"
1502 INPUT N7
1504 N8=12*N7
1508 PRINT
1510 PRINT "YOUR BALANCE AFTER "N7" YEARS IS $"A(N8)
1512 PRINT
1540 PRINT "WHAT IS THE PREPAYMENT PENALTY ON THE NEW LOAN IN DOLLARS?"
1550 INPUT P3
1560 P4=P3*(1-T)
1570 P5= P4/((1+(R/12))^(N8))
1580 PRINT
1600 P6=Q(N7)+NP-P5
1610 IF P6<0 THEN 1650
1620 PRINT
1630 PRINT "SINCE THE AFTER-TAX NET BENEFIT OF REFINANCING ($"P6") IS"
1640 PRINT "POSITIVE, YOU SHOULD REFINANCE"
1645 GOTO 1680
1650 PRINT
1660 PRINT "SINCE THE AFTER-TAX NET BENEFIT OF REFINANCING ($"P6") IS"
1670 PRINT "NEGATIVE, YOU SHOULD NOT REFINANCE AT THIS TIME"
1680 PRINT
```

```
1682 PRINT
1684 PRINT
1686 PRINT
1688 PRINT
1690 PRINT
1700 PRINT "WOULD YOU LIKE TO START AGAIN? (Y OR N)"
1710 INPUT H$
1715 IF H$="N" THEN 1740
1720 ERASE A,B,C,D,E,F,G,H,I,K,L,M,N,P,Q,R,S,T
1730 GOTO 54
1740 PRINT
1760 END
```

APPENDIX

20 Biweekly Versus Monthly Payment Mortgage Program

```
57 PRINT
58 PRINT "BIWEEKLY VERSUS MONTHLY PAYMENT MORTGAGE PROGRAM"
60 PRINT
62 PRINT "THIS PROGRAM WILL COMPARE THE MONTHLY MORTGAGE PAYMENT PLAN AND THE "
64 PRINT "BIWEEKLY MORTGAGE PAYMENT PLAN"
66 PRINT
90 DIM A(600),B(600),C(600),D(600),E(600),F(600),G(600),H(600),
I(600),K(600),L(600),M(600),N(600),P(600),Q(600)
100 PRINT
110 PRINT "ENTER THE LOAN AMOUNT"
120 INPUT A
130 PRINT
140 PRINT "ENTER THE ANNUAL INTEREST RATE OF THE BIWEEKLY PAYMENT MORTGAGE"
142 PRINT "IN PERCENT"
150 INPUT I
155 I=I/100
156 PRINT "ENTER THE ANNUAL INTEREST RATE OF THE MONTHLY PAYMENT MORTGAGE"
157 PRINT "IN PERCENT"
158 INPUT K
159 K=K/100
160 PRINT
170 PRINT "ENTER THE TERM OF THE LOAN IN YEARS"
180 INPUT N
190 PRINT
200 M=A*(I/12)/(1-((1+(I/12))^(-12*N)))
```

```
210 M1=M/2
211 M=0
212 M=A*(K/12)/(1-((1+(K/12))^(-12*N)))
220 A1=LOG(1-(A*(I/26)/M1))
230 A2=LOG(1+(I/26))
240 N1=(LOG(1)-A1)/A2
245 N3=N1/26
246 N4=INT(N3)
247 N2=26*N4
248 N6=12*N4
256 PRINT
257 PRINT "ENTER YOUR MARGINAL TAX RATE IN PERCENT"
258 INPUT T
259 T=T/100
260 PRINT
263 PRINT
264 PRINT "ENTER THE BEST INTEREST RATE YOU CAN EARN ON YOUR SAVINGS (IN"
265 PRINT "PERCENT AND BEFORE TAXES)"
266 INPUT R1
267 R2=R1*(1-T)
268 R=R2/100
270 PRINT
271 PRINT "YOUR MONTHLY PAYMENT IS $"M
272 PRINT
273 PRINT "IF YOU PAY $"M1" BIWEEKLY, YOUR MORTGAGE WILL BE PAID OFF FULLY"
274 PRINT "IN "N3" YEARS."
275 PRINT
276 PRINT
277 PRINT ". . . WORKING . . ."
278 PRINT
279 PRINT
280 A(0)=A
290 D(0)=A
300 FOR J=1 TO N6
310 B(J)=A(J-1)*(K/12)
320 C(J)=M-B(J)
330 A(J)=A(J-1)-C(J)
340 NEXT J
350 FOR J=1 TO N2
360 E(J)=D(J-1)*(I/26)
370 F(J)=M1-E(J)
380 D(J)=D(J-1)-F(J)
```

```
390 NEXT J
400 S=0
410 S1=0
420 S2=0
430 S3=0
440 S4=0
445 Q=0
450 FOR I=1 TO N4
460 FOR J=1 TO 12
465 Q=Q+1
470 S=S+B(Q)
480 NEXT J
490 G(I)=S/26
500 S=0
510 NEXT I
520 Q=0
530 FOR I=1 TO N4
540 FOR J=1 TO 26
550 Q=Q+1
560 H(Q)=(G(I)*T)/((1+(R/26))^(Q))
561 NEXT J
562 NEXT I
563 Q=0
564 FOR I=1 TO N4
565 FOR J=1 TO 26
566 Q=Q+1
567 S1=S1+H(Q)
568 NEXT J
569 I(I)=S1
570 S1=0
571 NEXT I
572 FOR J=1 TO N4
573 S2=S2+I(J)
574 K(J)=S2
575 NEXT J
576 FOR J=1 TO N6
577 L(J)=M/((1+(R/12))^(J))
578 M(J)=(A(J)/((1+(R/12))^(J)))
579 NEXT J
590 PRINT
595 GOTO 900
600 PRINT ". . RESULTS? (Y OR N)"
```

```
610 INPUT B$
620 IF B$="N" THEN 2661
630 PRINT
631 PRINT "FOR HOW MANY PERIODS?"
632 INPUT M2
633 PRINT
634 PRINT "          (1)        (2)        (3)      (4)         (5)"
635 PRINT
636 PRINT "MONTH  INTEREST  PRINCIPAL  BALANCE  PV OF M  PV OF BALANCE"
637 PRINT "         (MPM)    PAID (MPM)   (MPM)              (3) @ "R2"%"
638 PRINT "_______________________________________________________________"
639 PRINT
640 FOR J=1 TO M2
650 PRINT USING "###  ####.##     ####.##    #######.##   ####.##     #######.##";
J,B(J),C(J),A(J),L(J),M(J)
660 NEXT J
662 PRINT
663 PRINT "MPM = MONTHLY PAYMENT MORTGAGE"
664 PRINT "PV OF M = PRESENT VALUE OF THE MONTHLY PAYMENTS"
665 PRINT "PV OF BALANCE = PRESENT VALUE OF THE MORTGAGE BALANCE (3)"
666 PRINT "ALL PRESENT VALUES IN THIS OUTPUT ARE AT "R2"%"
670 PRINT
680 PRINT "MORE?"
690 INPUT C$
700 IF C$="N" THEN 2662
702 PRINT
703 PRINT "           (6)        (7)        (8)            (9) "
704 PRINT
705 PRINT "BIWEEKLY INTEREST  PRINCIPAL  BALANCE PRESENT VALUE OF TAX"
706 PRINT " PERIOD    (BPM)    PAID(BPM)   (BPM)     SAVINGS (BPM) "
707 PRINT "_______________________________________________________________"
708 PRINT
720 FOR J=1 TO M2
730 PRINT USING "###  ####.##      ####.##    #######.##        #####.##";
J,E(J),F(J),D(J),H(J)
734 NEXT J
736 PRINT
737 PRINT "BPM = BIWEEKLY PAYMENT MORTGAGE"
742 PRINT
743 PRINT ". . . MORE? (Y OR N)"
744 INPUT K$
745 IF K$="N" THEN 2670
```

```
746 PRINT
747 PRINT "FOR HOW MANY YEARS?"
748 INPUT Y1
749 PRINT
750 PRINT "              (10)          (11)                 (12) "
752 PRINT
755 PRINT "YEAR     BIWEEKLY  PRESENT VALUE OF  PRESENT VALUE OF TAX"
757 PRINT "         INTEREST    TAX SAVINGS     SAVINGS (CUMULATIVE)"
759 PRINT "          (MPM)     @ "R2"% (MPM)      @ "R2"% (MPM) "
760 PRINT "___________________________________________________________"
762 PRINT
764 FOR J=1 TO Y1
766 PRINT USING "##     ####.##        ####.##            ######.##";
J,G(J),I(J),K(J)
768 NEXT J
770 PRINT
772 PRINT "MPM = MONTHLY PAYMENT MORTGAGE"
780 PRINT
782 PRINT
784 PRINT ". . . WORKING . . ."
786 PRINT
788 PRINT
900 ERASE A,B,C
910 DIM A(600),B(600),C(600)
915 Q=0
920 FOR I=1 TO N4
930 FOR J=1 TO 12
935 Q=Q+1
940 S3=S3+L(Q)
950 NEXT J
960 A(I)=S3
970 S3=0
980 NEXT I
990 FOR J=1 TO N4
1000 S4=S4+A(J)
1010 N(J)=S4
1020 NEXT J
1030 FOR J=1 TO N4
1040 B(J)=M(J*12)
1050 NEXT J
1060 FOR J=1 TO N4
1070 C(J)=N(J)-K(J)+B(J)
```

```
1080 NEXT J
1085 GOTO 1250
1170 PRINT
1180 PRINT ". . . MORE? (Y OR N)"
1190 INPUT Q$
1200 IF Q$="N" THEN 2669
1202 PRINT
1203 PRINT "          (13)        (14)          (15)   (16)=(14)-(12)+(15)"
1204 PRINT
1205 PRINT "YEAR    PV OF M     PV OF M     PV OF BALANCE  PV OF AFTER-TAX"
1206 PRINT "         (MPM)   (CUMULATIVE)      (MPM)        COST OF MPM"
1207 PRINT " ______________________________________________________________"
1208 PRINT
1210 FOR J=1 TO Y1
1212 PRINT USING "## #####.##     #######.##        ########.##        ##########.##";
J,A(J),N(J),B(J),C(J)
1214 NEXT J
1215 PRINT
1216 PRINT "MPM = MONTHLY PAYMENT MORTGAGE"
1217 PRINT "PV OF M = PRESENT VALUE OF THE MONTHLY PAYMENTS"
1218 PRINT "PV = PRESENT VALUE @ "R2"%"
1219 PRINT
1220 PRINT
1222 PRINT ". . . WORKING . . . ."
1224 PRINT
1226 PRINT
1250 ERASE G,H,I,M,A,L
1260 DIM G(600),H(600),I(600),M(600),A(600),L(600)
1270 S=0
1280 S1=0
1290 S2=0
1300 S3=0
1310 S4=0
1315 Q=0
1320 FOR I=1 TO N4
1330 FOR J=1 TO 26
1335 Q=Q+1
1340 S=S+E(Q)
1350 NEXT J
1360 G(I)=S/26
1370 S=0
1380 NEXT I
```

```
1390 Q=0
1400 FOR I=1 TO N4
1410 FOR J=1 TO 26
1420 Q=Q+1
1430 H(Q)=(G(I)*T)/((1+(R/26))^(Q))
1440 NEXT J
1450 NEXT I
1455 Q=0
1460 FOR I=1 TO N4
1470 FOR J=1 TO 26
1475 Q=Q+1
1480 S1=S1+H(Q)
1490 NEXT J
1500 I(I)=S1
1505 S1=0
1510 NEXT I
1520 FOR J=1 TO N4
1530 S2=S2+I(J)
1540 A(J)=S2
1550 NEXT J
1560 FOR J=1 TO N2
1570 L(J)=M1/((1+(R/26))^(J))
1580 M(J)=D(J)/((1+(R/26))^(J))
1590 NEXT J
1600 ERASE E,F,D
1610 DIM E(600),F(600),D(600)
1615 Q=0
1620 FOR I=1 TO N4
1630 FOR J=1 TO 26
1635 Q=Q+1
1640 S3=S3+L(Q)
1650 NEXT J
1660 E(I)=S3
1670 S3=0
1680 NEXT I
1690 FOR J=1 TO N4
1700 S4=S4+E(J)
1710 F(J)=S4
1720 P(J)=M(J*26)
1730 Q(J)=F(J)-A(J)+P(J)
1740 NEXT J
1745 GOTO 1920
```

```
1750 PRINT
1760 PRINT "MORE?"
1770 INPUT E$
1780 IF E$="N" THEN 2665
1782 PRINT
1783 PRINT "                    (17)                 (18)               (19) "
1784 PRINT
1785 PRINT "BIWEEKLY  PRESENT VALUE OF  PRESENT VALUE OF  PRESENT VALUE OF"
1786 PRINT " PERIOD     TAX SAVINGS @     BIWEEKLY PAY-    BALANCE (BPM)"
1787 PRINT "              "R2"% (BPM)   MENTS @ "R2"% (BPM)     @ "R2"%"
1788 PRINT " ______________________________________________________________"
1790 PRINT
1800 FOR J=1 TO M2
1810 PRINT USING "###       ####.##              ####.##            #######.##";
J,H(J),L(J),M(J)
1820 NEXT J
1822 PRINT
1824 PRINT "BPM = BIWEEKLY PAYMENT MORTGAGE"
1830 PRINT
1840 PRINT "MORE?"
1845 INPUT F$
1850 IF F$="N" THEN 2666
1852 PRINT
1853 PRINT "           (20)           (21)                (22)"
1854 PRINT
1855 PRINT "YEAR     BIWEEKLY  PRESENT VALUE OF  PRESENT VALUE OF TAX"
1856 PRINT "         INTEREST  TAX SAVINGS (BPM) SAVINGS (CUMULATIVE)"
1857 PRINT "           (BPM)                                (BPM) "
1858 PRINT " _____________________________________________________"
1859 PRINT
1880 FOR J=1 TO M2
1890 PRINT USING "##      ###.##            ####.##                #####.##";
J,G(J),I(J),A(J)
1892 NEXT J
1894 PRINT
1895 PRINT ". . . MORE? (Y OR N)"
1896 INPUT L$
1897 IF L$="N" THEN 2672
1898 PRINT
1899 PRINT "        (23)         (24)             (25)               (26)"
1900 PRINT
1902 PRINT "YEAR  PV OF BP    PV OF BP    PV OF BALANCE  PRESENT VALUE OF"
```

```
1903 PRINT "              (CUMULATIVE)    (BPM)    AFTER-TAX COST OF"
1904 PRINT "                                                   BPM"
1905 PRINT " ________________________________________________________"
1906 PRINT
1907 FOR J=1 TO Y1
1908 PRINT USING "## #####.##    ######.##      #######.##      #########.##";
J,E(J),F(J),P(J),Q(J)
1910 NEXT J
1911 PRINT
1912 PRINT "BPM = BIWEEKLY PAYMENT MORTGAGE"
1913 PRINT "PV OF BP = PRESENT VALUES OF BIWEEKLY PAYMENTS @ "R2"%"
1914 PRINT "PV = PRESENT VALUE @ "R2"%"
1915 PRINT
1920 PRINT "WOULD YOU LIKE TO SEE THE SUMMARY RESULTS? (Y OR N)"
1930 INPUT I$
1940 IF I$="N" THEN 2667
1950 PRINT
1960 PRINT "FOR HOW MANY YEARS?"
1970 INPUT V
1985 PRINT
1990 PRINT    "     (1)     (2)          (3)      (4) = (1) - (2) + (3)"
2000 PRINT
2010 PRINT "YEAR    PV OF MP     PV OF TS     PV OF PB     PV OF NMP"
2020 PRINT "      (CUMULATIVE) (CUMULATIVE)                  AND PB"
2022 PRINT " ________________________________________________________"
2030 PRINT
2035 FOR J=1 TO V
2040 PRINT USING "## #########.##     #########.##     #########.##     ##########.##";
J,N(J),K(J),B(J),C(J)
2050 NEXT J
2060 PRINT
2070 PRINT "(1) = PV OF MP = PRESENT VALUE OF THE MONTHLY PAYMENTS AT "R*100"%"
2080 PRINT "(2) = PV OF TS = PRESENT VALUE OF THE TAX SAVINGS AT "R*100"%"
2090 PRINT "(3) = PV OF PB = PRESENT VALUE OF THE PAY-OFF BALANCE AT "R*100"%"
2100 PRINT "(4) = PV OF NMP AND PB = PRESENT VALUE OF THE NET (AFTER-TAX)"
2110 PRINT "MONTHLY PAYMENTS AND THE PAY-OFF BALANCE"
2120 PRINT
2130 PRINT ". . . MORE? (Y OR N)"
2140 INPUT L$
2150 IF L$="N" THEN 2668
2160 PRINT
2180 PRINT        "(1)         (2)          (3)          (4)=(1)-(2)+(3)"
```

```
2190 PRINT
2200 PRINT "YEAR     PV OF BP      PV OF TS      PV OF PB      PV OF NBP"
2210 PRINT "       (CUMULATIVE) (CUMULATIVE)                     AND PB"
2212 PRINT " _____________________________________________________________"
2220 PRINT
2225 FOR J=1 TO V
2230 PRINT USING "## #########.##     #########.##     #########.##     ##########.##";
J,F(J),A(J),P(J),Q(J)
2240 NEXT J
2250 PRINT
2260 PRINT "(1) = PV OF BP = PRESENT VALUE OF THE BIWEEKLY PAYMENTS @ "R*100"%"
2270 PRINT "(2) = PV OF TS = PRESENT VALUE OF THE TAX SAVINGS @ "R*100"%"
2280 PRINT "(3) = PV OF PB = PRESENT VALUE OF THE PAY-OFF BALANCE @ "R*100"%"
2290 PRINT "(4) = PV OF NBP AND PB = PRESENT VALUE OF THE NET (AFTER-TAX)"
2300 PRINT "BIWEEKLY PAYMENTS AND THE PAY-OFF BALANCE"
2310 PRINT
2320 IF C(N4) < Q(N4) THEN 2410
2330 PRINT
2340 PRINT "SINCE THE SUM OF THE PRESENT VALUES OF THE AFTER-TAX MONTHLY "
2350 PRINT "PAYMENTS AND THE PAY-OFF BALANCE IN YEAR "N4" ($ "C(N4)") EXCEEDS"
2360 PRINT "THE SUM OF THE PRESENT VALUES OF THE AFTER-TAX BIWEEKLY PAYMENTS"
2370 PRINT "AND THE PAY-OFF BALANCE IN YEAR "N4" ($"Q(N4)"), THE BIWEEKLY"
2380 PRINT "PAYMENT PLAN IS BETTER FOR YOU FINANCIALLY. THIS ANALYSIS ASSUMES"
2390 PRINT "THAT THE LOAN WILL NOT BE PAID OFF BEFORE YEAR "N4
2400 GOTO 2470
2405 PRINT
2410 PRINT "SINCE THE SUM OF THE PRESENT VALUES OF THE AFTER-TAX MONTHLY"
2420 PRINT "PAYMENTS AND THE PAY-OFF BALANCE IN YEAR "N4" ($"C(N4)") IS SMALLER"
2430 PRINT "THAN THE SUM OF THE PRESENT VALUES OF THE AFTER-TAX BIWEEKLY"
2440 PRINT "PAYMENTS AND THE PAY-OFF BALANCE IN YEAR "N4" ($"Q(N4)"), THE "
2450 PRINT "MONTHLY PAYMENT PLAN IS BETTER FOR YOU FINANCIALLY. THIS ANALYSIS"
2460 PRINT "ASSUMES THAT THE LOAN WILL NOT BE PAID OFF BEFORE YEAR "N4"."
2470 GOTO 2655
2480 PRINT "DO YOU THINK THE LOAN WILL BE PREPAID? (Y OR N)"
2490 INPUT M$
2500 IF M$="N" THEN 2625
2510 PRINT
2520 PRINT "IN HOW MANY YEARS?"
2530 INPUT Z
2540 IF C(Z) > Q(Z) THEN 2590
2550 PRINT
2560 PRINT "IF THE LOAN IS PREPAID IN YEAR "Z", THE MONTHLY PAYMENT PLAN WOULD"
```

```
2570 PRINT "BE BETTER FOR YOU."
2580 GOTO 2620
2590 PRINT
2600 PRINT "IF THE LOAN IS PREPAID IN YEAR "Z", THE BIWEEKLY PAYMENT PLAN "
2610 PRINT "WOULD BE BETTER FOR YOU."
2620 PRINT
2630 PRINT "WOULD YOU LIKE TO START AGAIN? (Y OR N)"
2640 INPUT N$
2650 IF N$="N" THEN 2670
2655 ERASE A,B,C,D,E,F,G,H,I,K,L,M,N,P,Q
2657 GOTO 66
2660 PRINT
2661 PRINT
2662 PRINT
2663 PRINT
2664 PRINT
2665 PRINT
2666 PRINT
2667 PRINT
2668 PRINT
2669 PRINT
2670 PRINT
2672 PRINT
2750 PRINT "IT WAS A PLEASURE WORKING WITH YOU "A$". COME AGAIN."
2760 END
```

APPENDIX

21 Lower Interest Rate Versus More Points Program—Sample Run

```
THIS PROGRAM WILL HELP YOU DETERMINE WHETHER OR
NOT IT IS A GOOD IDEA TO PAY MORE POINTS FOR A LOWER INTEREST
RATE ON A LOAN.

ENTER THE LOAN AMOUNT
? 100000

ENTER YOUR MARGINAL TAX RATE IN PERCENT
? 28

ENTER THE BEST INTEREST RATE YOU CAN EARN ON YOUR SAVINGS (BEFORE
TAXES AND IN PERCENT)
? 9.25

ENTER THE TERM OF THE LOAN IN YEARS
? 30

FIRST MORTGAGE = MORTGAGE WITH THE HIGHER INTEREST RATE

ALTERNATIVE MORTGAGE = MORTGAGE WITH THE LOWER INTEREST RATE

ENTER THE INTEREST RATE OF THE FIRST MORTGAGE IN PERCENT
? 10.25

ENTER THE INTEREST RATE OF THE ALTERNATIVE MORTGAGE IN PERCENT
? 10

ENTER THE NUMBER OF POINTS OF THE FIRST MORTGAGE
? 1
```

```
ENTER THE NUMBER OF POINTS OF THE ALTERNATIVE MORTGAGE
? 2

.1025            .1            .0666
THE AFTER-TAX COSTS OF THE POINTS ASSOCIATED WITH THE FIRST
MORTGAGE AND THE SECOND MORTGAGE ARE $ 720 AND $ 1440 RESPECTIVELY.

THE MONTHLY PAYMENT OF THE FIRST MORTGAGE IS $ 896.1009

THE MONTHLY PAYMENT OF THE ALTERNATIVE MORTGAGE IS $ 877.5722

THE DIFFERENCE IN THE MONTHLY PAYMENTS IS $ 18.52869

 . . . WORKING . . .

WOULD YOU LIKE TO SEE THE RESULTS? (Y OR N)
? Y

FOR HOW MANY MONTHS?
? 2
```

MONTH	(1) PAYMENT DIFFERENCE	(2) INTEREST FIRST MORTGAGE	(3) INTEREST ALTERNATIVE MORTGAGE	(4) = (2) – (3) DIFFERENCE IN INTEREST
1	18.53	854.17	833.33	20.83
2	18.53	853.81	832.96	20.84

```
 . . . MORE? Y OR N
? Y
```

MONTH	(5) = (4) * .28 TAX SAVINGS	(6) = (1) – (5) AFTER-TAX PAYMENT DIFFERENCE	(7) PRESENT VALUE OF (6) @ 6.660001%
1	5.83	12.70	12.63
2	5.84	12.69	12.55

```
 . . . MORE? (Y OR N)
? Y
```

MONTH	(8) BALANCE FIRST MORTGAGE	(9) BALANCE ALTERNATIVE MORTGAGE	(10) = (8) – (9) DIFFERENCE BETWEEN BALANCES	(11) PRESENT VALUE OF (10) @ 6.660001%
1	99958.06	99955.76	2.30	2.29
2	99915.77	99911.15	4.62	4.57

. . . MORE? (Y OR N)
? Y

FOR HOW MANY YEARS?
? 2

YEAR	(12) PV OF ATDP	(13) PV OF ATDP (CUMULATIVE)	(14) PV OF DMB	(15) = (13) + (14) PV OF ATDP + PV OF DMB
1	146.80	146.80	26.53	173.33
2	136.98	283.79	50.99	334.78

(12) = PV OF ATDP=PRESENT VALUE OF AFTER-TAX DIFFERENCE IN PAYMENTS
(13) = PV OF ATDP=PRESENT VALUE OF THE AFTER-TAX DIFFERENCE IN THE PAYMENTS (CUMULATIVE) @ 6.660001 %
(14) = PV OF DMB=PRESENT VALUE OF THE DIFFERENCE IN THE MORTGAGE BALANCES @ 6.66001 %
(15) = TOTAL AFTER-TAX BENEFITS FROM THE MORTGAGE WITH THE LOWER INTEREST RATE BUT MORE POINTS

DO YOU THINK THE LOAN WILL BE PREPAID? (Y OR N)
? N

IF THE LOAN IS PAID OFF IN YEAR 30, THE AFTER-TAX COST ($ 0) OF THE EXCESS POINTS ASSOCIATED WITH THE ALTERNATIVE MORTGAGE (THE MORTGAGE WITH THE LOWER INTEREST RATE) WILL BE SMALLER THAN THE TOTAL AFTER-TAX SAVINGS GENERATED BY THAT MORTGAGE ($ 1999.761). GIVEN THE INFORMATION SUPPLIED, THE MORTGAGE WITH THE LOWER INTEREST RATE BUT A LARGER NUMBER OF POINTS WOULD BE BETTER FOR YOU.

IF THE POINTS ARE NOT DEDUCTIBLE IN THE CURRENT PERIOD, THE COST OF THE EXCESS POINTS ($ 1000) ASSOCIATED WITH THE ALTERNATIVE MORTGAGE WILL BE SMALLER THAN THE TOTAL AFTER-TAX SAVINGS ($ 1999.761) GENERATED BY THAT MORTGAGE. GIVEN THE INFORMATION SUPPLIED, THE ALTERNATIVE MORTGAGE WOULD BE BETTER FOR YOU.

WOULD YOU LIKE TO START AGAIN? (Y OR N)
? N

APPENDIX

22 Lower Interest Rate Versus More Points Program

```
69 PRINT
72 PRINT "LOWER INTEREST RATE VERSUS MORE POINTS PROGRAM"
74 PRINT
76 PRINT "THIS PROGRAM WILL HELP YOU DETERMINE WHETHER OR "
78 PRINT "NOT IT IS A GOOD IDEA TO PAY MORE POINTS FOR A LOWER INTEREST "
80 PRINT "RATE ON A LOAN."
82 PRINT
90 DIM A(481),B(481),C(481),D(481),E(481),F(481),G(481),H(481),
I(481),K(481),L(481),M(481),N(481),P(481),Q(481),R(481)
100 PRINT
110 PRINT "ENTER THE LOAN AMOUNT"
120 INPUT A
130 PRINT
140 PRINT "ENTER YOUR MARGINAL TAX RATE IN PERCENT"
150 INPUT T1
160 T=T1/100
170 PRINT
180 PRINT "ENTER THE BEST INTEREST RATE YOU CAN EARN ON YOUR SAVINGS (BEFORE"
190 PRINT "TAXES AND IN PERCENT)"
200 INPUT R1
210 R2=R1*(1-T)
220 R=R2/100
230 PRINT
240 PRINT "ENTER THE TERM OF THE LOAN IN YEARS"
250 INPUT N
```

```
252 PRINT
253 PRINT "FIRST MORTGAGE = MORTGAGE WITH THE HIGHER INTEREST RATE"
254 PRINT
255 PRINT "ALTERNATIVE MORTGAGE = MORTGAGE WITH THE LOWER INTEREST RATE "
257 PRINT
258 PRINT "ENTER THE INTEREST RATE OF THE FIRST MORTGAGE IN PERCENT"
259 INPUT I1
260 I=I1/100
262 PRINT
263 PRINT "ENTER THE INTEREST RATE OF THE ALTERNATIVE MORTGAGE IN PERCENT"
264 INPUT I2
265 I3=I2/100
270 PRINT
280 PRINT "ENTER THE NUMBER OF POINTS OF THE FIRST MORTGAGE"
290 INPUT P1
300 P5=(P1/100)*A
310 PRINT
320 PRINT "ENTER THE NUMBER OF POINTS OF THE ALTERNATIVE MORTGAGE"
330 INPUT P2
340 P6=(P2/100)*A
390 P=P5*(1-T)
400 P3=P6*(1-T)
410 P7=P6-P5
420 PRINT
430 PRINT "THE AFTER-TAX COSTS OF THE POINTS ASSOCIATED WITH THE FIRST "
440 PRINT "MORTGAGE AND THE SECOND MORTGAGE ARE $"P" AND $"P3" RESPECTIVELY."
450 M=A*(I/12)/(1-((1+(I/12))^(-12*N)))
460 M1=A*(I3/12)/(1-((1+(I3/12))^(-12*N)))
470 PRINT
480 PRINT "THE MONTHLY PAYMENT OF THE FIRST MORTGAGE IS $"M
490 PRINT
495 PRINT
500 PRINT "THE MONTHLY PAYMENT OF THE ALTERNATIVE MORTGAGE IS $"M1
510 M2=M-M1
520 PRINT
530 PRINT "THE DIFFERENCE IN THE MONTHLY PAYMENTS IS $"M2
540 PRINT
550 PRINT
560 PRINT " . . . WORKING . . . "
570 PRINT
580 PRINT
```

```
590 A(0)=A
600 D(0)=A
610 FOR J=1 TO 12*N
620 B(J)=A(J-1)*(I/12)
630 C(J)=M-B(J)
640 A(J)=A(J-1)-C(J)
650 E(J)=D(J-1)*(I3/12)
660 F(J)=M1-E(J)
670 D(J)=D(J-1)-F(J)
680 G(J)=B(J)-E(J)
690 H(J)=G(J)*T
700 I(J)=M2-H(J)
710 K(J)=I(J)/((1+(R/12))^(J))
720 L(J)=A(J)-D(J)
730 M(J)=L(J)/((1+(R/12))^(J))
740 NEXT J
750 Q=0
760 S=0
770 FOR I=1 TO N
780 FOR J=1 TO 12
790 Q=Q+1
800 S=S+K(Q)
810 NEXT J
820 N(I)=S
830 S=0
840 NEXT I
850 S1=0
860 FOR J=1 TO N
870 S1=S1+N(J)
880 P(J)=S1
890 Q(J)=M(12*J)
900 R(J)=P(J)+Q(J)
910 NEXT J
920 PRINT
930 PRINT "WOULD YOU LIKE TO SEE THE RESULTS? (Y OR N)"
940 INPUT B$
950 IF B$="N" THEN 2020
960 PRINT
970 PRINT "FOR HOW MANY MONTHS?"
972 INPUT N1
974 PRINT
```

```
975 PRINT "            (1)          (2)            (3)       (4) = (2) - (3) "
976 PRINT
977 PRINT "MONTH    PAYMENT    INTEREST     INTEREST    DIFFERENCE IN"
978 PRINT "        DIFFERENCE   FIRST    ALTERNATIVE     INTEREST"
979 PRINT "                    MORTGAGE    MORTGAGE                  "
980 PRINT "_______________________________________________________________"
990 PRINT
1000 FOR J=1 TO N1
1010 PRINT USING "### ####.##        ####.##          ####.##           ####.##";
J,M2,B(J),E(J),G(J)
1020 NEXT J
1030 PRINT
1040 PRINT " . . . MORE? (Y OR N)"
1050 INPUT C$
1060 IF C$="N" THEN 2021
1062 PRINT
1063 PRINT "           (5) = (4) * "T"    (6) = (1) - (5)          (7)"
1064 PRINT
1065 PRINT "MONTH           TAX        AFTER-TAX PAYMENT  PRESENT VALUE "
1066 PRINT "              SAVINGS          DIFFERENCE     OF (6) @ "R2"%"
1067 PRINT " ____________________________________________________________"
1080 FOR J=1 TO N1
1090 PRINT USING "###         ####.##               ####.##             ####.##";
J,H(J),I(J),K(J)
1100 NEXT J
1110 PRINT
1120 PRINT ". . . MORE? (Y OR N)"
1130 INPUT D$
1140 IF D$="N" THEN 2022
1142 PRINT
1143 PRINT "           (8)          (9)       (10) = (8) - (9)       (11) "
1144 PRINT
1145 PRINT "MONTH  BALANCE     BALANCE       DIFFERENCE     PRESENT VALUE"
1146 PRINT "         FIRST   ALTERNATIVE      BETWEEN     OF (10) @ "R2"%"
1147 PRINT "       MORTGAGE   MORTGAGE       BALANCES                     "
1148 PRINT " _____________________________________________________________"
1149 PRINT
1150 PRINT
1160 FOR J=1 TO N1
1170 PRINT USING "### #######.##      #######.##         #######.##        #######.##";
J,A(J),D(J),L(J),M(J)
1180 NEXT J
1190 PRINT
```

```
1200 PRINT ". . . MORE? (Y OR N)"
1210 INPUT E$
1220 IF E$="N" THEN 2024
1230 PRINT
1240 PRINT "FOR HOW MANY YEARS?"
1250 INPUT N2
1260 PRINT
1270 PRINT "            (12)          (13)          (14)      (15)=(13)+(14)"
1280 PRINT
1290 PRINT "YEAR     PV OF ATDP    PV OF ATDP    PV OF DMB      PV OF ATDP"
1300 PRINT "                      (CUMULATIVE)                  + PV OF DMB"
1310 PRINT " ______________________________________________________________"
1320 PRINT
1330 FOR J=1 TO N2
1340 PRINT USING "##    ########.##      #########.##      #########.##      ########.##";
J,N(J),P(J),Q(J),R(J)
1345 NEXT J
1350 PRINT " ______________________________________________________________"
1360 PRINT
1365 PRINT "(12)=PV OF ATDP=PRESENT VALUE OF AFTER-TAX DIFFERENCE IN PAYMENTS"
1370 PRINT "(13)=PV OF ATDP=PRESENT VALUE OF THE AFTER-TAX DIFFERENCE IN THE "
1380 PRINT "PAYMENTS (CUMULATIVE) @ "R2"%"
1390 PRINT "(14)=PV OF DMB=PRESENT VALUE OF THE DIFFERENCE IN THE MORTGAGE"
1400 PRINT "BALANCES @ "R2"%"
1410 PRINT "(15)=TOTAL AFTER-TAX BENEFITS FROM THE MORTGAGE WITH THE LOWER"
1415 PRINT " INTEREST RATE BUT MORE POINTS"
1420 PRINT
1430 PRINT "DO YOU THINK THE LOAN WILL BE PREPAID? (Y OR N)"
1440 INPUT F$
1450 IF F$="N" THEN 1680
1460 PRINT
1470 PRINT "AFTER HOW MANY YEARS?"
1480 INPUT N3
1490 P4=P3-P
1500 IF P4 < R(N3) THEN 1590
1510 PRINT
1520 PRINT "IF THE LOAN IS PAID OFF IN YEAR "N3", THE AFTER-TAX COST ($"P4")"
1530 PRINT "OF THE EXCESS POINTS ASSOCIATED WITH THE ALTERNATIVE MORTGAGE"
1540 PRINT "THE MORTGAGE WITH THE LOWER INTEREST RATE) WILL EXCEED THE"
1550 PRINT "TOTAL AFTER-TAX SAVINGS GENERATED BY THAT MORTGAGE ($"R(N3)")."
1560 PRINT "GIVEN THE INFORMATION SUPPLIED, THE MORTGAGE WITH THE HIGHER"
1570 PRINT "INTEREST RATE BUT FEWER POINTS IS BETTER FOR YOU."
```

```
1580 GOTO 1700
1590 PRINT
1600 PRINT "IF THE LOAN IS PAID OFF IN YEAR "N3", THE AFTER-TAX COST ($"P4")"
1610 PRINT "OF THE EXCESS POINTS ASSOCIATED WITH THE ALTERNATIVE MORTGAGE"
1620 PRINT "(THE MORTGAGE WITH THE LOWER INTEREST RATE) WILL BE SMALLER"
1630 PRINT "THAN THE TOTAL AFTER-TAX SAVINGS GENERATED BY THAT MORTGAGE "
1640 PRINT "($"R(N3)"). GIVEN THE INFORMATION SUPPLIED, THE MORTGAGE WITH THE"
1650 PRINT " LOWER INTEREST RATE BUT A LARGER NUMBER OF POINTS WOULD BE BETTER"
1660 PRINT "FOR YOU."
1670 GOTO 1710
1680 N3=N
1690 GOTO 1500
1700 PRINT
1710 PRINT
1720 IF P7 < R(N3) THEN 1810
1730 PRINT
1740 PRINT "IF THE POINTS ARE NOT DEDUCTIBLE IN THE CURRENT PERIOD, THE COST"
1750 PRINT " OF THE EXCESS POINTS ($"P7") ASSOCIATED WITH THE ALTERNATIVE"
1760 PRINT "MORTGAGE WILL EXCEED THE TOTAL AFTER-TAX SAVINGS GENERATED BY THAT"
1770 PRINT "MORTGAGE ($"R(N3)"). GIVEN THE INFORMATION SUPPLIED, THE"
1780 PRINT "FIRST MORTGAGE WOULD BE BETTER FOR YOU."
1790 GOTO 1860
1800 PRINT
1810 PRINT "IF THE POINTS ARE NOT DEDUCTIBLE IN THE CURRENT PERIOD, THE COST OF"
1820 PRINT "THE EXCESS POINTS ($"P7") ASSOCIATED WITH THE ALTERNATIVE MORTGAGE"
1830 PRINT "WILL BE SMALLER THAN THE TOTAL AFTER-TAX SAVINGS ($"R(N3)")"
1840 PRINT "GENERATED BY THAT MORTGAGE . GIVEN THE INFORMATION SUPPLIED, THE"
1850 PRINT "ALTERNATIVE MORTGAGE WOULD BE BETTER FOR YOU."
1860 PRINT
2020 PRINT
2021 PRINT
2022 PRINT
2030 PRINT "WOULD YOU LIKE TO START AGAIN? (Y OR N)"
2040 INPUT G$
2050 IF G$="N" THEN 2070
2055 ERASE A,B,C,D,E,F,G,H,I,K,L,M,N,P,Q,R
2060 GOTO 82
2070 PRINT
2090 END
```

APPENDIX

23 A Program for Calculating the Price of A Mortgage in the Secondary Mortgage Market—Sample Run

```
THIS PROGRAM WILL CALCULATE THE PRICE OF A MORTGAGE IN THE SECONDARY
MORTGAGE MARKET FOR DIFFERENT YIELDS AND COUPON RATES.

ENTER THE ORIGINAL LOAN AMOUNT
? 100000

ENTER THE ORIGINAL ANNUAL INTEREST RATE IN PERCENT
? 12

ENTER THE ORIGINAL TERM OF THE LOAN IN YEARS
? 30
ENTER THE REMAINING TERM OF THE LOAN IN MONTHS
? 336

ENTER THE ANNUAL REQUIRED YIELD IN PERCENT
? 15
ENTER THE HOLDING PERIOD IN MONTHS
? 84

THE MONTHLY PAYMENT IS $ 1028.613

THE CURRENT BALANCE IS $ 99228.21
```

```
THE BALANCE AFTER 84 MONTHS IS $ 94480.83

THE PRICE OF THE MORTGAGE SHOULD BE $ 86583.21

WOULD YOU LIKE TO CALCULATE THE PRICE FOR A DIFFERENT YIELD?
INPUT Y OR N
? Y

ENTER YOUR REQUIRED YIELD IN PERCENT
? 16

THE MONTHLY PAYMENT IS $ 1028.613

THE CURRENT BALANCE IS $ 99228.21

THE BALANCE AFTER 84 MONTHS IS $ 94480.83

THE PRICE OF THE MORTGAGE SHOULD BE $ 82844

WOULD YOU LIKE TO CALCULATE THE PRICE FOR A DIFFERENT YIELD?
INPUT Y OR N
? N

WOULD YOU LIKE TO START AGAIN?
? N
```

APPENDIX

24 A PROGRAM FOR CALCULATING THE PRICE OF A MORTGAGE IN THE SECONDARY MORTGAGE MARKET

```
68 PRINT
70 PRINT "A PROGRAM FOR CALCULATING THE PRICE OF A MORTGAGE IN THE "
72 PRINT "SECONDARY MORTGAGE MARKET"
74 PRINT
76 PRINT
78 PRINT "THIS PROGRAM WILL CALCULATE THE PRICE OF A MORTGAGE IN"
80 PRINT "THE SECONDARY MORTGAGE MARKET FOR DIFFERENT YIELDS AND COUPON RATES."
100 PRINT
110 PRINT "ENTER THE ORIGINAL LOAN AMOUNT"
120 INPUT L
130 PRINT
140 PRINT "ENTER THE ORIGINAL ANNUAL INTEREST RATE IN PERCENT"
150 INPUT I1
160 I=I1/1200
170 PRINT
180 PRINT "ENTER THE ORIGINAL TERM OF THE LOAN IN YEARS"
190 INPUT N1
200 N=12*N1
210 PRINT "ENTER THE REMAINING TERM OF THE LOAN IN MONTHS"
220 INPUT N2
```

```
230 PRINT
240 PRINT "ENTER THE ANNUAL REQUIRED YIELD IN PERCENT"
250 INPUT R1
260 R=R1/1200
270 PRINT "ENTER THE HOLDING PERIOD IN MONTHS"
280 INPUT N3
290 M=L*I/(1-((1+I)^(-N)))
300 B=(M/I)*(1-((1+I)^(-N2)))
310 N4=N2-N3
320 B1=(M/I)*(1-((1+I)^(-N4)))
330 P1=(M/R)*(1-((1+R)^(-N3)))
340 P2=B1/((1+R)^(N3))
350 P=P1+P2
360 PRINT
370 PRINT "THE MONTHLY PAYMENT IS $"M
380 PRINT
390 PRINT "THE CURRENT BALANCE IS $"B
400 PRINT
410 PRINT "THE BALANCE AFTER "N3" MONTHS IS $"B1
420 PRINT
430 PRINT "THE PRICE OF THE MORTGAGE SHOULD BE $"P
440 PRINT
450 PRINT "WOULD YOU LIKE TO CALCULATE THE PRICE FOR A DIFFERENT YIELD?"
455 PRINT "INPUT Y OR N"
460 INPUT B$
470 IF B$="N" THEN 550
480 PRINT
490 PRINT "ENTER YOUR REQUIRED YIELD IN PERCENT"
500 INPUT R1
510 R=R1/100
520 GOTO 330
550 PRINT
560 PRINT "WOULD YOU LIKE TO START AGAIN?"
570 INPUT C$
580 IF C$="Y" THEN 100
590 PRINT
610 END
```

APPENDIX

25 Real Estate Finance Forms

A. FHLMC/FNMA—Residential Loan Application Form

B. Fannie Mae—Request for Verification of Employment Form

C. Fannie Mae—Request for Verification of Deposit Form

D. Freddie Mac Form 70—Fannie Mae Form 1004-Uniform Residential Appraisal Report

E. FNMA/FHLMC—Multistate Fixed Rate Note

F. FNMA/FHLMC—Mortgage (Illinois)

G. Freddie Mac—Multistate Adjustable Rate Rider

H. HUD Settlement Statement

I. HUD Mortgage Credit Analysis Worksheet

Residential Loan Application

MORTGAGE APPLIED FOR ☐ Conventional ☐ FHA ☐ VA ☐ ______ | Amount $ | Interest Rate ___% | No. of Months | Monthly Payment Principal & Interest $ | Escrow/Impounds (to be collected monthly) ☐ Taxes ☐ Hazard Ins. ☐ Mtg. Ins. ☐ ______

Prepayment Option

Subject Property

Property Street Address | City | County | State | Zip | No. Units

Legal Description (Attach description if necessary) | Year Built

Purpose of Loan: ☐ Purchase ☐ Construction-Permanent ☐ Construction ☐ Refinance ☐ Other (Explain)

Complete this line if Construction-Permanent or Construction Loan | Lot Value Data | Year Acquired | Original Cost $ | Present Value (a) $ | Cost of Imps. (b) $ | Total (a + b) $ | ENTER TOTAL AS PURCHASE PRICE IN DETAILS OF PURCHASE.

Complete this line if a Refinance Loan | Year Acquired | Original Cost $ | Amt. Existing Liens $ | Purpose of Refinance | Describe Improvements [ ] made [ ] to be made | Cost: $

Title Will Be Held In What Name(s) | Manner In Which Title Will Be Held

Source of Down Payment and Settlement Charges

This application is designed to be completed by the borrower(s) with the lender's assistance. The Co-Borrower Section and all other Co-Borrower questions must be completed and the appropriate box(es) checked if ☐ another person will be jointly obligated with the Borrower on the loan, or ☐ the Borrower is relying on income from alimony, child support or separate maintenance or on the income or assets of another person as a basis for repayment of the loan, or ☐ the Borrower is married and resides, or the property is located, in a community property state.

Borrower

Name | Age | School Yrs ___

Present Address | No. Years ___ | ☐ Own | ☐ Rent

Street

City/State/Zip

Former address if less than 2 years at present address

Street

City/State/Zip

Years at former address | ☐ Own | ☐ Rent

Marital Status ☐ Married ☐ Separated ☐ Unmarried (incl. single, divorced, widowed) | Dependents other than listed by Co-Borrower: No. | Ages

Name and Address of Employer | Years employed in this line of work or profession? ___ years | Years on this job ___ | ☐ Self Employed*

Position/Title | Type of Business

Social Security Number *** | Home Phone | Business Phone

Co Borrower

Name | Age | School Yrs ___

Present Address | No. Years ___ | ☐ Own | ☐ Rent

Street

City/State/Zip

Former address if less than 2 years at present address

Street

City/State/Zip

Years at former address | ☐ Own | ☐ Rent

Marital Status ☐ Married ☐ Separated ☐ Unmarried (incl. single, divorced, widowed) | Dependents other than listed by Borrower: No. | Ages

Name and Address of Employer | Years employed in this line of work or profession? ___ years | Years on this job ___ | ☐ Self Employed*

Position/Title | Type of Business

Social Security Number *** | Home Phone | Business Phone

Gross Monthly Income / Monthly Housing Expense** / Details of Purchase

Item	Borrower	Co-Borrower	Total		Present	Proposed	Do Not Complete If Refinance	
Base Empl. Income	$	$	$	Rent	$		a. Purchase Price	$
Overtime				First Mortgage (P&I)		$	b. Total Closing Costs (Est.)	
Bonuses				Other Financing (P&I)			c. Prepaid Escrows (Est.)	
Commissions				Hazard Insurance			d. Total (a + b + c)	$
Dividends/Interest				Real Estate Taxes			e. Amount This Mortgage	( )
Net Rental Income				Mortgage Insurance			f. Other Financing	( )
Other† (Before completing, see notice under Describe Other Income below.)				Homeowner Assn. Dues			g. Other Equity	( )
				Other:			h. Amount of Cash Deposit	( )
				Total Monthly Pmt.	$	$	i. Closing Costs Paid by Seller	( )
				Utilities				
Total	$	$	$	Total	$	$	j. Cash Reqd. For Closing (Est.)	$

Describe Other Income

B—Borrower C—Co-Borrower	NOTICE: † Alimony, child support, or separate maintenance income need not be revealed if the Borrower or Co-Borrower does not choose to have it considered as a basis for repaying this loan.	Monthly Amount
		$

If Employed In Current Position For Less Than Two Years, Complete the Following

B/C	Previous Employer/School	City/State	Type of Business	Position/Title	Dates From/To	Monthly Income
						$

These Questions Apply To Both Borrower and Co-Borrower

If a "yes" answer is given to a question in this column, please explain on an attached sheet | Borrower Yes or No | Co-Borrower Yes or No

Are there any outstanding judgments against you?

Have you been declared bankrupt within the past 7 years?

Have you had property foreclosed upon or given title or deed in lieu thereof in the last 7 years?

Are you a party to a law suit?

Are you obligated to pay alimony, child support, or separate maintenance?

Is any part of the down payment borrowed?

Are you a co maker or endorser on a note?

	Borrower Yes or No	Co-Borrower Yes or No
Are you a U.S. citizen?	___	___
If "no," are you a resident alien?	___	___
If "no," are you a non-resident alien?	___	___

Explain Other Financing or Other Equity (if any). ______________________

*FHLMC FNMA require business credit report, signed Federal Income Tax returns for last two years, and, if available, audited Profit and Loss Statement plus balance sheet for same period.

**All Present Monthly Housing Expenses of Borrower and Co Borrower should be listed on a combined basis

***Optional for FHLMC

FHLMC 65 Rev 10 86

Fannie Mae Form 1003 Rev. 10/86

This Statement and any applicable supporting schedules may be completed jointly by both married and unmarried co-borrowers if their assets and liabilities are sufficiently joined so that the Statement can be meaningfully and fairly presented on a combined basis; otherwise separate Statements and Schedules are required (FHLMC 65A/FNMA 1003A). If the co-borrower section was completed about a spouse, this statement and supporting schedules must be completed about that spouse also.

☐ Completed Jointly ☐ Not Completed Jointly

Statement of Assets and Liabilities

Assets

Description	Cash or Market Value
Cash Deposit Toward Purchase Held By	$
Checking and Savings Accounts (Show Names of Institutions (Account Numbers) Bank, S & L or Credit Union	
Addr.	
City	
Acct. No.	
Bank, S & L or Credit Union	
Addr.	
City	
Acct. No.	
Bank, S & L or Credit Union	
Addr.	
City	
Acct. No.	
Stocks and Bonds (No./Description)	
Life Insurance Net Cash Value Face Amount $	
Subtotal Liquid Assets	
Real Estate Owned (Enter Market Value from Schedule of Real Estate Owned)	
Vested Interest in Retirement Fund	
Net worth of Business Owned (ATTACH FINANCIAL STATEMENT)	
Automobiles Owned (Make and Year)	
Furniture and Personal Property	
Other Assets (Itemize)	
Total Assets	A $

Liabilities and Pledged Assets

Indicate by (*) those liabilities or pledged assets which will be satisfied upon sale of real estate owned or upon refinancing of subject property

Creditors' Name, Address and Account Number		Acct. Name if Not Borrower's	Mo. Pmt. and Mos. Left to Pay	Unpaid Balance
Installment Debts (include "revolving" charge accounts)			$ Pmt/Mos	$
Co.	Acct No			
Addr				
City			/	
Co.	Acct No			
Addr				
City			/	
Co.	Acct No			
Addr.				
City			/	
Co.	Acct No			
Addr				
City			/	
Co.	Acct. No.			
Addr.				
City			/	
Other Debts including Stock Pledges			/	
Real Estate Loans Co.	Acct No		X	
Addr.				
City				
Co.	Acct No		X	
Addr.				
City				
Automobile Loans Co.	Acct No			
Addr.				
City			/	
Co.	Acct. No.			
City			/	
Alimony/Child Support/Separate Maintenance Payments Owed to			/	X
Total Monthly Payments			$	X
Net Worth (A minus B) $			Total Liabilities	B $

SCHEDULE OF REAL ESTATE OWNED (If Additional Properties Owned Attach Separate Schedule)

Address of Property (Indicate S if Sold, PS if Pending Sale or R if Rental being held for income)	▽	Type of Property	Present Market Value	Amount of Mortgages & Liens	Gross Rental Income	Mortgage Payments	Taxes, Ins. Maintenance and Misc.	Net Rental Income
			$	$	$	$	$	$
	TOTALS →		$	$	$	$	$	$

List Previous Credit References

▽ B–Borrower C–Co-Borrower		Creditor's Name and Address	Account Number	Purpose	Highest Balance	Date Paid
					$	

List any additional names under which credit has previously been received ____________________

AGREEMENT. The undersigned applies for the loan indicated in this application to be secured by a first mortgage or deed of trust on the property described herein, and represents that the property will not be used for any illegal or restricted purpose, and that all statements made in this application are true and are made for the purpose of obtaining the loan. Verification may be obtained from any source named in this application. The original or a copy of this application will be retained by the lender, even if the loan is not granted. The undersigned ☐ intend or ☐ do not intend to occupy the property as their primary residence.

I/we fully understand that it is a federal crime punishable by fine or imprisonment, or both, to knowingly make any false statements concerning any of the above facts as applicable under the provisions of Title 18, United States Code, Section 1014.

____________________ Date ________ ____________________ Date ________

Borrower's Signature Co-Borrower's Signature

Information for Government Monitoring Purposes

The following information is requested by the Federal Government for certain types of loans related to a dwelling, in order to monitor the lender's compliance with equal credit opportunity and fair housing laws. You are not required to furnish this information, but are encouraged to do so. The law provides that a lender may neither discriminate on the basis of this information, nor on whether you choose to furnish it. However, if you choose not to furnish it, under Federal regulations this lender is required to note race and sex on the basis of visual observation or surname. If you do not wish to furnish the above information, please check the box below. (Lender must review the above material to assure that the disclosures satisfy all requirements to which the Lender is subject under applicable state law for the particular type of loan applied for.)

Borrower: ☐ I do not wish to furnish this information
Race/National Origin:
American Indian, Alaskan Native Asian, Pacific Islander
Black Hispanic White
Other (specify): ____________
Sex: Female Male

Co-Borrower: ☐ I do not wish to furnish this information
Race/National Origin:
American Indian, Alaskan Native Asian, Pacific Islander
Black Hispanic White
Other (specify): ____________
Sex: Female Male

To Be Completed by Interviewer

This application was taken by:

☐ face to face interview
☐ by mail
☐ by telephone

Interviewer ____________ Name of Interviewer's Employer ____________

Interviewer's Phone Number ____________ Address of Interviewer's Employer ____________

FannieMae

Request for Verification of Employment

Instructions:

Lender — Complete items 1 through 7. Have applicant complete item 8. Forward directly to employer named in item 1.

Employer — Please complete either Part II or Part III as applicable. Sign and return directly to lender named in item 2.

Part I — Request

1. To (Name and address of employer)	2. From (Name and address of lender)

3. Signature of Lender	4. Title	5. Date	6. Lender's Number (Optional)

I have applied for a mortgage loan and stated that I am now or was formerly employed by you. My signature below authorizes verification of this information.

7. Name and Address of Applicant (Include employee or badge number)	8. Signature of Applicant

Part II — Verification of Present Employment

Employment Data	Pay Data				
9. Applicant's Date of Employment	12A. Current Base Pay (Enter Amount and Check Period) ☐ Annual ☐ Hourly ☐ Monthly ☐ Other (Specify) ☐ Weekly $ ________			12C. For Military Personnel Only	
				Pay Grade	
				Type	Monthly Amount
10. Present Position	12B. Earnings			Base Pay	$
11. Probability of Continued Employment	Type	Year To Date	Past Year	Rations	$
13. If Overtime or Bonus is Applicable, Is Its Continuance Likely?	Base Pay	$	$	Flight or Hazard	$
	Overtime	$	$	Clothing	$
Overtime ☐ Yes ☐ No				Quarters	$
Bonus ☐ Yes ☐ No	Commissions	$	$	Pro Pay	$
	Bonus	$	$	Overseas or Combat	$

14. Remarks (If paid hourly, please indicate average hours worked each week during current and past year)

Part III — Verification of Previous Employment

15. Dates of Employment	16. Salary/Wage at Termination Per (Year) (Month) (Week)
	Base ________ Overtime ________ Commissions ________ Bonus ________

17. Reason for Leaving	18. Position Held

19. Signature of Employer	20. Title	21. Date

The confidentiality of the information you have furnished will be preserved except where disclosure of this information is required by applicable law. The form is to be transmitted directly to the lender and is not to be transmitted through the applicant or any other party.

Fannie Mae
Form 1005 Nov. 85

FannieMae

Request for Verification of Deposit

Instructions: Lender—Complete Items 1 through 8. Have applicant(s) complete Item 9. Forward directly to depository named in Item 1.
Depository—Please complete Items 10 through 15 and return DIRECTLY to lender named in Item 2.

Part I—Request

1. To (Name and address of depository)	2. From (Name and address of lender)

3. Signature of Lender	4. Title	5. Date	6. Lender's No. (Optional)

7. Information To Be Verified

Type of Account	Account in Name of	Account Number	Balance
			$
			$
			$
			$

To Depository: I/We have applied for a mortgage loan and stated in my financial statement that the balance on deposit with you is as shown above. You are authorized to verify this information and to supply the lender identified above with the information requested in Items 10 through 12. Your response is solely a matter of courtesy for which no responsibility is attached to your institution or any of your officers.

8. Name and Address of Applicant(s)	9. Signature of Applicant(s)

To Be Completed by Depository

Part II—Verification of Depository

10. Deposit Accounts of Applicant(s)

Type of Account	Account Number	Current Balance	Average Balance For Previous Two Months	Date Opened
		$	$	
		$	$	
		$	$	
		$	$	

11. Loans Outstanding To Applicant(s)

Loan Number	Date of Loan	Original Amount	Current Balance	Installments (Monthly/Quarterly)		Secured By	Number of Late Payments
		$	$	$	per		
		$	$	$	per		
		$	$	$	per		

12. Please include any additional information which may be of assistance in determination of credit worthiness. (Please include information on loans paid-in-full in Item 11 above.)

13. Signature of Depository	14. Title	15. Date

The confidentiality of the information you have furnished will be preserved except where disclosure of this information is required by applicable law. The form is to be transmitted directly to the lender and is not to be transmitted through the applicant(s) or any other party..

Previous edition will be used until stock is exhausted.

Fannie Mae
Form 1006 Nov. 86

Property Description & Analysis **UNIFORM RESIDENTIAL APPRAISAL REPORT** File No.

SUBJECT

Property Address | Census Tract | LENDER DISCRETIONARY USE
City | County | State | Zip Code | Sale Price $
Legal Description | Date
Owner/Occupant | Map Reference | Mortgage Amount $
Sale Price $ | Date of Sale | PROPERTY RIGHTS APPRAISED | Mortgage Type
Loan charges/concessions to be paid by seller $ | ☐ Fee Simple | Discount Points and Other Concessions
R.E. Taxes $ | Tax Year | HOA $/Mo. | ☐ Leasehold | Paid by Seller $
Lender/Client | ☐ Condominium (HUD/VA)
☐ De Minimis PUD | Source

NEIGHBORHOOD

LOCATION	☐ Urban	☐ Suburban	☐ Rural
BUILT UP	☐ Over 75%	☐ 25-75%	☐ Under 25%
GROWTH RATE	☐ Rapid	☐ Stable	☐ Slow
PROPERTY VALUES	☐ Increasing	☐ Stable	☐ Declining
DEMAND/SUPPLY	☐ Shortage	☐ In Balance	☐ Over Supply
MARKETING TIME	☐ Under 3 Mos.	☐ 3-6 Mos.	☐ Over 6 Mos.

PRESENT LAND USE %	LAND USE CHANGE	PREDOMINANT OCCUPANCY	SINGLE FAMILY HOUSING PRICE $ (000) AGE (yrs)
Single Family	Not Likely ☐	Owner ☐	Low
2-4 Family	Likely ☐	Tenant ☐	High
Multi-family	In process ☐	Vacant (0-5%) ☐	Predominant
Commercial	To:	Vacant (over 5%) ☐	
Industrial			
Vacant			

NEIGHBORHOOD ANALYSIS	Good	Avg	Fair	Poor
Employment Stability	☐	☐	☐	☐
Convenience to Employment	☐	☐	☐	☐
Convenience to Shopping	☐	☐	☐	☐
Convenience to Schools	☐	☐	☐	☐
Adequacy of Public Transportation	☐	☐	☐	☐
Recreation Facilities	☐	☐	☐	☐
Adequacy of Utilities	☐	☐	☐	☐
Property Compatibility	☐	☐	☐	☐
Protection from Detrimental Cond	☐	☐	☐	☐
Police & Fire Protection	☐	☐	☐	☐
General Appearance of Properties	☐	☐	☐	☐
Appeal to Market	☐	☐	☐	☐

Note: Race or the racial composition of the neighborhood are not considered reliable appraisal factors

COMMENTS:

SITE

Dimensions | Topography
Site Area | Corner Lot | Size
Zoning Classification | Zoning Compliance | Shape
HIGHEST & BEST USE: Present Use | Other Use | Drainage

UTILITIES	Public	Other	SITE IMPROVEMENTS	Type	Public	Private
Electricity	☐		Street		☐	☐
Gas	☐		Curb/Gutter		☐	☐
Water	☐		Sidewalk		☐	☐
Sanitary Sewer	☐		Street Lights		☐	☐
Storm Sewer	☐		Alley		☐	☐

View
Landscaping
Driveway
Apparent Easements
FEMA Flood Hazard Yes* No
FEMA* Map/Zone

COMMENTS (Apparent adverse easements, encroachments, special assessments, slide areas, etc.):

IMPROVEMENTS

GENERAL DESCRIPTION	EXTERIOR DESCRIPTION	FOUNDATION	BASEMENT	INSULATION
Units	Foundation	Slab	Area Sq. Ft.	Roof ☐
Stories	Exterior Walls	Crawl Space	% Finished	Ceiling ☐
Type (Det./Att.)	Roof Surface	Basement	Ceiling	Walls ☐
Design (Style)	Gutters & Dwnspts.	Sump Pump	Walls	Floor ☐
Existing	Window Type	Dampness	Floor	None ☐
Proposed	Storm Sash	Settlement	Outside Entry	Adequacy ☐
Under Construction	Screens	Infestation		Energy Efficient Items
Age (Yrs.)	Manufactured House			
Effective Age (Yrs.)				

ROOM LIST

ROOMS	Foyer	Living	Dining	Kitchen	Den	Family Rm.	Rec. Rm.	Bedrooms	# Baths	Laundry	Other	Area Sq. Ft.
Basement												
Level 1												
Level 2												

Finished area **above** grade contains: Rooms; Bedroom(s); Bath(s); Square Feet of Gross Living Area

INTERIOR

SURFACES Materials/Condition	HEATING	KITCHEN EQUIP.	ATTIC
Floors	Type	Refrigerator ☐	None ☐
Walls	Fuel	Range/Oven ☐	Stairs ☐
Trim/Finish	Condition	Disposal ☐	Drop Stair ☐
Bath Floor	Adequacy	Dishwasher ☐	Scuttle ☐
Bath Wainscot	COOLING	Fan/Hood ☐	Floor ☐
Doors	Central	Compactor ☐	Heated ☐
	Other	Washer/Dryer ☐	Finished ☐
	Condition	Microwave ☐	
Fireplace(s) #	Adequacy	Intercom ☐	

IMPROVEMENT ANALYSIS	Good	Avg	Fair	Poor
Quality of Construction	☐	☐	☐	☐
Condition of Improvements	☐	☐	☐	☐
Room Sizes/Layout	☐	☐	☐	☐
Closets and Storage	☐	☐	☐	☐
Energy Efficiency	☐	☐	☐	☐
Plumbing-Adequacy & Condition	☐	☐	☐	☐
Electrical-Adequacy & Condition	☐	☐	☐	☐
Kitchen Cabinets-Adequacy & Cond.	☐	☐	☐	☐
Compatibility to Neighborhood	☐	☐	☐	☐
Appeal & Marketability	☐	☐	☐	☐
Estimated Remaining Economic Life	Yrs			
Estimated Remaining Physical Life	Yrs			

AUTOS

CAR STORAGE:	Garage ☐	Attached ☐	Adequate ☐	House Entry ☐
No. Cars	Carport ☐	Detached ☐	Inadequate ☐	Outside Entry ☐
Condition	None ☐	Built-In ☐	Electric Door ☐	Basement Entry ☐

COMMENTS

Additional features:

Depreciation (Physical, functional and external inadequacies, repairs needed, modernization, etc.):

General market conditions and prevalence and impact in subject/market area regarding loan discounts, interest buydowns and concessions:

Valuation Section

UNIFORM RESIDENTIAL APPRAISAL REPORT

File No.

Purpose of Appraisal is to estimate Market Value as defined in the Certification & Statement of Limiting Conditions.

COST APPROACH

BUILDING SKETCH (SHOW GROSS LIVING AREA ABOVE GRADE)

[illegible]

ESTIMATED REPRODUCTION COST - NEW - OF IMPROVEMENTS

Dwelling ____ Sq Ft @ $ ____ = $ ____

____ Sq Ft @ $ ____ = ____

Extras ____ = ____

Special Energy Efficient Items ____ = ____

Porches, Patios, etc. ____ = ____

Garage/Carport ____ Sq Ft @ $ ____ = ____

Total Estimated Cost New = $ ____

Less Depreciation — Physical | Functional | External ____ = $ ____

Depreciated Value of Improvements = $ ____

Site Imp "as is" (driveway, landscaping, etc.) = $ ____

ESTIMATED SITE VALUE = $ ____

(If leasehold, show only leasehold value.)

INDICATED VALUE BY COST APPROACH $ ____

(Not Required by Freddie Mac and Fannie Mae)

Does property conform to applicable HUD/VA property standards? ☐ Yes ☐ No

If No, explain ____

Construction Warranty ☐ Yes ☐ No

Name of Warranty Program ____

Warranty Coverage Expires ____

SALES COMPARISON ANALYSIS

The undersigned has recited three recent sales of properties most similar and proximate to subject and has considered these in the market analysis. The description includes a dollar adjustment reflecting market reaction to those items of significant variation between the subject and comparable properties. If a significant item in the comparable property is superior to or more favorable than the subject property, a minus (–) adjustment is made, thus reducing the indicated value of subject; if a significant item in the comparable is inferior to or less favorable than the subject property, a plus (+) adjustment is made, thus increasing the indicated value of the subject.

ITEM	SUBJECT	COMPARABLE NO 1		COMPARABLE NO 2		COMPARABLE NO 3	
Address							
Proximity to Subject							
Sales Price	$		$		$		$
Price/Gross Liv. Area	$ ☐	$ ☐		$ ☐		$ ☐	
Data Source							
VALUE ADJUSTMENTS	DESCRIPTION	DESCRIPTION	+ (–) $ Adjustment	DESCRIPTION	+ (–) $ Adjustment	DESCRIPTION	+ (–) $ Adjustment
Sales or Financing Concessions							
Date of Sale/Time							
Location							
Site/View							
Design and Appeal							
Quality of Construction							
Age							
Condition							
Above Grade Room Count	Total · Bdrms · Baths	Total · Bdrms · Baths		Total · Bdrms · Baths		Total · Bdrms · Baths	
Gross Living Area	Sq. Ft.	Sq. Ft.		Sq. Ft.		Sq. Ft.	
Basement & Finished Rooms Below Grade							
Functional Utility							
Heating/Cooling							
Garage/Carport							
Porches, Patio, Pools, etc.							
Special Energy Efficient Items							
Fireplace(s)							
Other (e.g. kitchen equip., remodeling)							
Net Adj. (total)		☐ + ☐ –	$	☐ + ☐ –	$	☐ + ☐ –	$
Indicated Value of Subject			$		$		$

Comments on Sales Comparison: ____

INDICATED VALUE BY SALES COMPARISON APPROACH .... $ ____

INDICATED VALUE BY INCOME APPROACH (If Applicable) Estimated Market Rent $ ____ /Mo x Gross Rent Multiplier ____ = $ ____

RECONCILIATION

This appraisal is made ☐ "as is" ☐ subject to the repairs, alterations, inspections or conditions listed below ☐ completion per plans and specifications.

Comments and Conditions of Appraisal: ____

Final Reconciliation: ____

This appraisal is based upon the above requirements, the certification, contingent and limiting conditions, and Market Value definition that are stated in

☐ FmHA, HUD &/or VA instructions.

☐ Freddie Mac Form 439 (Rev. 7/86)/Fannie Mae Form 1004B (Rev. 7/86) filed with client ____ 19 ____ ☐ attached.

I (WE) ESTIMATE THE MARKET VALUE, AS DEFINED, OF THE SUBJECT PROPERTY AS OF ____ **19** ____ **to be $** ____

I (We) certify: that to the best of my (our) knowledge and belief the facts and data used herein are true and correct; that I (we) personally inspected the subject property, both inside and out, and have made an exterior inspection of all comparable sales cited in this report; and that I (we) have no undisclosed interest, present or prospective therein.

Appraiser(s) SIGNATURE ____ NAME ____

Review Appraiser (if applicable) SIGNATURE ____ NAME ____ ☐ Did ☐ Did Not Inspect Property

Freddie Mac Form 70 10/86 Fannie Mae Form 1004 10/86

NOTE

...., 19.........   ...., ...
[City]   [State]

....
[Property Address]

1. BORROWER'S PROMISE TO PAY

In return for a loan that I have received, I promise to pay U.S. $.. (this amount is called "principal"), plus interest, to the order of the Lender. The Lender is .... I understand that the Lender may transfer this Note. The Lender or anyone who takes this Note by transfer and who is entitled to receive payments under this Note is called the "Note Holder."

2. INTEREST

Interest will be charged on unpaid principal until the full amount of principal has been paid. I will pay interest at a yearly rate of ....%.

The interest rate required by this Section 2 is the rate I will pay both before and after any default described in Section 6(B) of this Note.

3. PAYMENTS

(A) Time and Place of Payments

I will pay principal and interest by making payments every month.

I will make my monthly payments on the .... day of each month beginning on ...., 19.......... I will make these payments every month until I have paid all of the principal and interest and any other charges described below that I may owe under this Note. My monthly payments will be applied to interest before principal. If, on ...., ..., I still owe amounts under this Note, I will pay those amounts in full on that date, which is called the "maturity date."

I will make my monthly payments at .... or at a different place if required by the Note Holder.

(B) Amount of Monthly Payments

My monthly payment will be in the amount of U.S. $..

4. BORROWER'S RIGHT TO PREPAY

I have the right to make payments of principal at any time before they are due. A payment of principal only is known as a "prepayment." When I make a prepayment, I will tell the Note Holder in writing that I am doing so.

I may make a full prepayment or partial prepayments without paying any prepayment charge. The Note Holder will use all of my prepayments to reduce the amount of principal that I owe under this Note. If I make a partial prepayment, there will be no changes in the due date or in the amount of my monthly payment unless the Note Holder agrees in writing to those changes.

5. LOAN CHARGES

If a law, which applies to this loan and which sets maximum loan charges, is finally interpreted so that the interest or other loan charges collected or to be collected in connection with this loan exceed the permitted limits, then: (i) any such loan charge shall be reduced by the amount necessary to reduce the charge to the permitted limit; and (ii) any sums already collected from me which exceeded permitted limits will be refunded to me. The Note Holder may choose to make this refund by reducing the principal I owe under this Note or by making a direct payment to me. If a refund reduces principal, the reduction will be treated as a partial prepayment.

6. BORROWER'S FAILURE TO PAY AS REQUIRED

(A) Late Charge for Overdue Payments

If the Note Holder has not received the full amount of any monthly payment by the end of .... calendar days after the date it is due, I will pay a late charge to the Note Holder. The amount of the charge will be ....% of my overdue payment of principal and interest. I will pay this late charge promptly but only once on each late payment.

(B) Default

If I do not pay the full amount of each monthly payment on the date it is due, I will be in default.

(C) Notice of Default

If I am in default, the Note Holder may send me a written notice telling me that if I do not pay the overdue amount by a certain date, the Note Holder may require me to pay immediately the full amount of principal which has not been paid and all the interest that I owe on that amount. That date must be at least 30 days after the date on which the notice is delivered or mailed to me.

(D) No Waiver By Note Holder

Even if, at a time when I am in default, the Note Holder does not require me to pay immediately in full as described above, the Note Holder will still have the right to do so if I am in default at a later time.

(E) Payment of Note Holder's Costs and Expenses

If the Note Holder has required me to pay immediately in full as described above, the Note Holder will have the right to be paid back by me for all of its costs and expenses in enforcing this Note to the extent not prohibited by applicable law. Those expenses include, for example, reasonable attorneys' fees.

7. GIVING OF NOTICES

Unless applicable law requires a different method, any notice that must be given to me under this Note will be given by delivering it or by mailing it by first class mail to me at the Property Address above or at a different address if I give the Note Holder a notice of my different address.

Any notice that must be given to the Note Holder under this Note will be given by mailing it by first class mail to the Note Holder at the address stated in Section 3(A) above or at a different address if I am given a notice of that different address.

8. OBLIGATIONS OF PERSONS UNDER THIS NOTE

If more than one person signs this Note, each person is fully and personally obligated to keep all of the promises made in this Note, including the promise to pay the full amount owed. Any person who is a guarantor, surety or endorser of this Note is also obligated to do these things. Any person who takes over these obligations, including the obligations of a guarantor, surety or endorser of this Note, is also obligated to keep all of the promises made in this Note. The Note Holder may enforce its rights under this Note against each person individually or against all of us together. This means that any one of us may be required to pay all of the amounts owed under this Note.

9. WAIVERS

I and any other person who has obligations under this Note waive the rights of presentment and notice of dishonor. "Presentment" means the right to require the Note Holder to demand payment of amounts due. "Notice of dishonor" means the right to require the Note Holder to give notice to other persons that amounts due have not been paid.

10. UNIFORM SECURED NOTE

This Note is a uniform instrument with limited variations in some jurisdictions. In addition to the protections given to the Note Holder under this Note, a Mortgage, Deed of Trust or Security Deed (the "Security Instrument"), dated the same date as this Note, protects the Note Holder from possible losses which might result if I do not keep the promises which I make in this Note. That Security Instrument describes how and under what conditions I may be required to make immediate payment in full of all amounts I owe under this Note. Some of those conditions are described as follows:

Transfer of the Property or a Beneficial Interest in Borrower. If all or any part of the Property or any interest in it is sold or transferred (or if a beneficial interest in Borrower is sold or transferred and Borrower is not a natural person) without Lender's prior written consent, Lender may, at its option, require immediate payment in full of all sums secured by this Security Instrument. However, this option shall not be exercised by Lender if exercise is prohibited by federal law as of the date of this Security Instrument.

If Lender exercises this option, Lender shall give Borrower notice of acceleration. The notice shall provide a period of not less than 30 days from the date the notice is delivered or mailed within which Borrower must pay all sums secured by this Security Instrument. If Borrower fails to pay these sums prior to the expiration of this period, Lender may invoke any remedies permitted by this Security Instrument without further notice or demand on Borrower.

WITNESS THE HAND(S) AND SEAL(S) OF THE UNDERSIGNED.

....(Seal)
-Borrower

....(Seal)
-Borrower

....(Seal)
-Borrower

[Sign Original Only]

[Space Above This Line For Recording Data]

MORTGAGE

THIS MORTGAGE ("Security Instrument") is given on ....,
19.......... The mortgagor is ....
.... ("Borrower"). This Security Instrument is given to ....
...., which is organized and existing
under the laws of ...., and whose address is ....
.... ("Lender").
Borrower owes Lender the principal sum of ....
.... Dollars (U.S. $.................................). This debt is evidenced by Borrower's note dated the same date as this Security Instrument ("Note"), which provides for monthly payments, with the full debt, if not paid earlier, due and payable on .... This Security Instrument secures to Lender: (a) the repayment of the debt evidenced by the Note, with interest, and all renewals, extensions and modifications; (b) the payment of all other sums, with interest, advanced under paragraph 7 to protect the security of this Security Instrument; and (c) the performance of Borrower's covenants and agreements under this Security Instrument and the Note. For this purpose, Borrower does hereby mortgage, grant and convey to Lender the following described property located in .... County, Illinois:

which has the address of ...., ...,
[Street] [City]

Illinois .... ("Property Address");
[Zip Code]

TOGETHER WITH all the improvements now or hereafter erected on the property, and all easements, rights, appurtenances, rents, royalties, mineral, oil and gas rights and profits, water rights and stock and all fixtures now or hereafter a part of the property. All replacements and additions shall also be covered by this Security Instrument. All of the foregoing is referred to in this Security Instrument as the "Property."

BORROWER COVENANTS that Borrower is lawfully seised of the estate hereby conveyed and has the right to mortgage, grant and convey the Property and that the Property is unencumbered, except for encumbrances of record. Borrower warrants and will defend generally the title to the Property against all claims and demands, subject to any encumbrances of record.

THIS SECURITY INSTRUMENT combines uniform covenants for national use and non-uniform covenants with limited variations by jurisdiction to constitute a uniform security instrument covering real property.

UNIFORM COVENANTS. Borrower and Lender covenant and agree as follows:

1. Payment of Principal and Interest; Prepayment and Late Charges. Borrower shall promptly pay when due the principal of and interest on the debt evidenced by the Note and any prepayment and late charges due under the Note.

2. Funds for Taxes and Insurance. Subject to applicable law or to a written waiver by Lender, Borrower shall pay to Lender on the day monthly payments are due under the Note, until the Note is paid in full, a sum ("Funds") equal to one-twelfth of: (a) yearly taxes and assessments which may attain priority over this Security Instrument; (b) yearly leasehold payments or ground rents on the Property, if any; (c) yearly hazard insurance premiums; and (d) yearly mortgage insurance premiums, if any. These items are called "escrow items." Lender may estimate the Funds due on the basis of current data and reasonable estimates of future escrow items.

The Funds shall be held in an institution the deposits or accounts of which are insured or guaranteed by a federal or state agency (including Lender if Lender is such an institution). Lender shall apply the Funds to pay the escrow items. Lender may not charge for holding and applying the Funds, analyzing the account or verifying the escrow items, unless Lender pays Borrower interest on the Funds and applicable law permits Lender to make such a charge. Borrower and Lender may agree in writing that interest shall be paid on the Funds. Unless an agreement is made or applicable law requires interest to be paid, Lender shall not be required to pay Borrower any interest or earnings on the Funds. Lender shall give to Borrower, without charge, an annual accounting of the Funds showing credits and debits to the Funds and the purpose for which each debit to the Funds was made. The Funds are pledged as additional security for the sums secured by this Security Instrument.

If the amount of the Funds held by Lender, together with the future monthly payments of Funds payable prior to the due dates of the escrow items, shall exceed the amount required to pay the escrow items when due, the excess shall be, at Borrower's option, either promptly repaid to Borrower or credited to Borrower on monthly payments of Funds. If the amount of the Funds held by Lender is not sufficient to pay the escrow items when due, Borrower shall pay to Lender any amount necessary to make up the deficiency in one or more payments as required by Lender.

Upon payment in full of all sums secured by this Security Instrument, Lender shall promptly refund to Borrower any Funds held by Lender. If under paragraph 19 the Property is sold or acquired by Lender, Lender shall apply, no later than immediately prior to the sale of the Property or its acquisition by Lender, any Funds held by Lender at the time of application as a credit against the sums secured by this Security Instrument.

3. Application of Payments. Unless applicable law provides otherwise, all payments received by Lender under paragraphs 1 and 2 shall be applied: first, to late charges due under the Note; second, to prepayment charges due under the Note; third, to amounts payable under paragraph 2; fourth, to interest due; and last, to principal due.

4. Charges; Liens. Borrower shall pay all taxes, assessments, charges, fines and impositions attributable to the Property which may attain priority over this Security Instrument, and leasehold payments or ground rents, if any. Borrower shall pay these obligations in the manner provided in paragraph 2, or if not paid in that manner, Borrower shall pay them on time directly to the person owed payment. Borrower shall promptly furnish to Lender all notices of amounts to be paid under this paragraph. If Borrower makes these payments directly, Borrower shall promptly furnish to Lender receipts evidencing the payments.

Borrower shall promptly discharge any lien which has priority over this Security Instrument unless Borrower: (a) agrees in writing to the payment of the obligation secured by the lien in a manner acceptable to Lender; (b) contests in good faith the lien by, or defends against enforcement of the lien in, legal proceedings which in the Lender's opinion operate to prevent the enforcement of the lien or forfeiture of any part of the Property; or (c) secures from the holder of the lien an agreement satisfactory to Lender subordinating the lien to this Security Instrument. If Lender determines that any part of the Property is subject to a lien which may attain priority over this Security Instrument, Lender may give Borrower a notice identifying the lien. Borrower shall satisfy the lien or take one or more of the actions set forth above within 10 days of the giving of notice.

5. Hazard Insurance. Borrower shall keep the improvements now existing or hereafter erected on the Property insured against loss by fire, hazards included within the term "extended coverage" and any other hazards for which Lender requires insurance. This insurance shall be maintained in the amounts and for the periods that Lender requires. The insurance carrier providing the insurance shall be chosen by Borrower subject to Lender's approval which shall not be unreasonably withheld.

All insurance policies and renewals shall be acceptable to Lender and shall include a standard mortgage clause. Lender shall have the right to hold the policies and renewals. If Lender requires, Borrower shall promptly give to Lender all receipts of paid premiums and renewal notices. In the event of loss, Borrower shall give prompt notice to the insurance carrier and Lender. Lender may make proof of loss if not made promptly by Borrower.

Unless Lender and Borrower otherwise agree in writing, insurance proceeds shall be applied to restoration or repair of the Property damaged, if the restoration or repair is economically feasible and Lender's security is not lessened. If the restoration or repair is not economically feasible or Lender's security would be lessened, the insurance proceeds shall be applied to the sums secured by this Security Instrument, whether or not then due, with any excess paid to Borrower. If Borrower abandons the Property, or does not answer within 30 days a notice from Lender that the insurance carrier has offered to settle a claim, then Lender may collect the insurance proceeds. Lender may use the proceeds to repair or restore the Property or to pay sums secured by this Security Instrument, whether or not then due. The 30-day period will begin when the notice is given.

Unless Lender and Borrower otherwise agree in writing, any application of proceeds to principal shall not extend or postpone the due date of the monthly payments referred to in paragraphs 1 and 2 or change the amount of the payments. If under paragraph 19 the Property is acquired by Lender, Borrower's right to any insurance policies and proceeds resulting from damage to the Property prior to the acquisition shall pass to Lender to the extent of the sums secured by this Security Instrument immediately prior to the acquisition.

6. Preservation and Maintenance of Property; Leaseholds. Borrower shall not destroy, damage or substantially change the Property, allow the Property to deteriorate or commit waste. If this Security Instrument is on a leasehold, Borrower shall comply with the provisions of the lease, and if Borrower acquires fee title to the Property, the leasehold and fee title shall not merge unless Lender agrees to the merger in writing.

7. Protection of Lender's Rights in the Property; Mortgage Insurance. If Borrower fails to perform the covenants and agreements contained in this Security Instrument, or there is a legal proceeding that may significantly affect Lender's rights in the Property (such as a proceeding in bankruptcy, probate, for condemnation or to enforce laws or regulations), then Lender may do and pay for whatever is necessary to protect the value of the Property and Lender's rights in the Property. Lender's actions may include paying any sums secured by a lien which has priority over this Security Instrument, appearing in court, paying reasonable attorneys' fees and entering on the Property to make repairs. Although Lender may take action under this paragraph 7, Lender does not have to do so.

Any amounts disbursed by Lender under this paragraph 7 shall become additional debt of Borrower secured by this Security Instrument. Unless Borrower and Lender agree to other terms of payment, these amounts shall bear interest from the date of disbursement at the Note rate and shall be payable, with interest, upon notice from Lender to Borrower requesting payment.

If Lender required mortgage insurance as a condition of making the loan secured by this Security Instrument, Borrower shall pay the premiums required to maintain the insurance in effect until such time as the requirement for the insurance terminates in accordance with Borrower's and Lender's written agreement or applicable law.

8. Inspection. Lender or its agent may make reasonable entries upon and inspections of the Property. Lender shall give Borrower notice at the time of or prior to an inspection specifying reasonable cause for the inspection.

9. Condemnation. The proceeds of any award or claim for damages, direct or consequential, in connection with any condemnation or other taking of any part of the Property, or for conveyance in lieu of condemnation, are hereby assigned and shall be paid to Lender.

In the event of a total taking of the Property, the proceeds shall be applied to the sums secured by this Security Instrument, whether or not then due, with any excess paid to Borrower. In the event of a partial taking of the Property, unless Borrower and Lender otherwise agree in writing, the sums secured by this Security Instrument shall be reduced by the amount of the proceeds multiplied by the following fraction: (a) the total amount of the sums secured immediately before the taking, divided by (b) the fair market value of the Property immediately before the taking. Any balance shall be paid to Borrower.

If the Property is abandoned by Borrower, or if, after notice by Lender to Borrower that the condemnor offers to make an award or settle a claim for damages, Borrower fails to respond to Lender within 30 days after the date the notice is given, Lender is authorized to collect and apply the proceeds, at its option, either to restoration or repair of the Property or to the sums secured by this Security Instrument, whether or not then due.

Unless Lender and Borrower otherwise agree in writing, any application of proceeds to principal shall not extend or postpone the due date of the monthly payments referred to in paragraphs 1 and 2 or change the amount of such payments.

10. Borrower Not Released; Forbearance By Lender Not a Waiver. Extension of the time for payment or modification of amortization of the sums secured by this Security Instrument granted by Lender to any successor in interest of Borrower shall not operate to release the liability of the original Borrower or Borrower's successors in interest. Lender shall not be required to commence proceedings against any successor in interest or refuse to extend time for payment or otherwise modify amortization of the sums secured by this Security Instrument by reason of any demand made by the original Borrower or Borrower's successors in interest. Any forbearance by Lender in exercising any right or remedy shall not be a waiver of or preclude the exercise of any right or remedy.

11. Successors and Assigns Bound; Joint and Several Liability; Co-signers. The covenants and agreements of this Security Instrument shall bind and benefit the successors and assigns of Lender and Borrower, subject to the provisions of paragraph 17. Borrower's covenants and agreements shall be joint and several. Any Borrower who co-signs this Security Instrument but does not execute the Note: (a) is co-signing this Security Instrument only to mortgage, grant and convey that Borrower's interest in the Property under the terms of this Security Instrument; (b) is not personally obligated to pay the sums secured by this Security Instrument; and (c) agrees that Lender and any other Borrower may agree to extend, modify, forbear or make any accommodations with regard to the terms of this Security Instrument or the Note without that Borrower's consent.

12. Loan Charges. If the loan secured by this Security Instrument is subject to a law which sets maximum loan charges, and that law is finally interpreted so that the interest or other loan charges collected or to be collected in connection with the loan exceed the permitted limits, then: (a) any such loan charge shall be reduced by the amount necessary to reduce the charge to the permitted limit; and (b) any sums already collected from Borrower which exceeded permitted limits will be refunded to Borrower. Lender may choose to make this refund by reducing the principal owed under the Note or by making a direct payment to Borrower. If a refund reduces principal, the reduction will be treated as a partial prepayment without any prepayment charge under the Note.

13. Legislation Affecting Lender's Rights. If enactment or expiration of applicable laws has the effect of rendering any provision of the Note or this Security Instrument unenforceable according to its terms, Lender, at its option, may require immediate payment in full of all sums secured by this Security Instrument and may invoke any remedies permitted by paragraph 19. If Lender exercises this option, Lender shall take the steps specified in the second paragraph of paragraph 17.

14. Notices. Any notice to Borrower provided for in this Security Instrument shall be given by delivering it or by mailing it by first class mail unless applicable law requires use of another method. The notice shall be directed to the Property Address or any other address Borrower designates by notice to Lender. Any notice to Lender shall be given by first class mail to Lender's address stated herein or any other address Lender designates by notice to Borrower. Any notice provided for in this Security Instrument shall be deemed to have been given to Borrower or Lender when given as provided in this paragraph.

15. Governing Law; Severability. This Security Instrument shall be governed by federal law and the law of the jurisdiction in which the Property is located. In the event that any provision or clause of this Security Instrument or the Note conflicts with applicable law, such conflict shall not affect other provisions of this Security Instrument or the Note which can be given effect without the conflicting provision. To this end the provisions of this Security Instrument and the Note are declared to be severable.

16. Borrower's Copy. Borrower shall be given one conformed copy of the Note and of this Security Instrument.

17. Transfer of the Property or a Beneficial Interest in Borrower. If all or any part of the Property or any interest in it is sold or transferred (or if a beneficial interest in Borrower is sold or transferred and Borrower is not a natural person) without Lender's prior written consent, Lender may, at its option, require immediate payment in full of all sums secured by this Security Instrument. However, this option shall not be exercised by Lender if exercise is prohibited by federal law as of the date of this Security Instrument.

If Lender exercises this option, Lender shall give Borrower notice of acceleration. The notice shall provide a period of not less than 30 days from the date the notice is delivered or mailed within which Borrower must pay all sums secured by this Security Instrument. If Borrower fails to pay these sums prior to the expiration of this period, Lender may invoke any remedies permitted by this Security Instrument without further notice or demand on Borrower.

18. Borrower's Right to Reinstate. If Borrower meets certain conditions, Borrower shall have the right to have enforcement of this Security Instrument discontinued at any time prior to the earlier of: (a) 5 days (or such other period as applicable law may specify for reinstatement) before sale of the Property pursuant to any power of sale contained in this Security Instrument; or (b) entry of a judgment enforcing this Security Instrument. Those conditions are that Borrower: (a) pays Lender all sums which then would be due under this Security Instrument and the Note had no acceleration occurred; (b) cures any default of any other covenants or agreements; (c) pays all expenses incurred in enforcing this Security Instrument, including, but not limited to, reasonable attorneys' fees; and (d) takes such action as Lender may reasonably require to assure that the lien of this Security Instrument, Lender's rights in the Property and Borrower's obligation to pay the sums secured by this Security Instrument shall continue unchanged. Upon reinstatement by Borrower, this Security Instrument and the obligations secured hereby shall remain fully effective as if no acceleration had occurred. However, this right to reinstate shall not apply in the case of acceleration under paragraphs 13 or 17.

NON-UNIFORM COVENANTS. Borrower and Lender further covenant and agree as follows:

19. Acceleration; Remedies. Lender shall give notice to Borrower prior to acceleration following Borrower's breach of any covenant or agreement in this Security Instrument (but not prior to acceleration under paragraphs 13 and 17 unless applicable law provides otherwise). The notice shall specify: (a) the default; (b) the action required to cure the default; (c) a date, not less than 30 days from the date the notice is given to Borrower, by which the default must be cured; and (d) that failure to cure the default on or before the date specified in the notice may result in acceleration of the sums secured by this Security Instrument, foreclosure by judicial proceeding and sale of the Property. The notice shall further inform Borrower of the right to reinstate after acceleration and the right to assert in the foreclosure proceeding the non-existence of a default or any other defense of Borrower to acceleration and foreclosure. If the default is not cured on or before the date specified in the notice, Lender at its option may require immediate payment in full of all sums secured by this Security Instrument without further demand and may foreclose this Security Instrument by judicial proceeding. Lender shall be entitled to collect all expenses incurred in pursuing the remedies provided in this paragraph 19, including, but not limited to, reasonable attorneys' fees and costs of title evidence.

20. Lender in Possession. Upon acceleration under paragraph 19 or abandonment of the Property and at any time prior to the expiration of any period of redemption following judicial sale, Lender (in person, by agent or by judicially appointed receiver) shall be entitled to enter upon, take possession of and manage the Property and to collect the rents of the Property including those past due. Any rents collected by Lender or the receiver shall be applied first to payment of the costs of management of the Property and collection of rents, including, but not limited to, receiver's fees, premiums on receiver's bonds and reasonable attorneys' fees, and then to the sums secured by this Security Instrument.

21. Release. Upon payment of all sums secured by this Security Instrument, Lender shall release this Security Instrument without charge to Borrower. Borrower shall pay any recordation costs.

22. Waiver of Homestead. Borrower waives all right of homestead exemption in the Property.

23. Riders to this Security Instrument. If one or more riders are executed by Borrower and recorded together with this Security Instrument, the covenants and agreements of each such rider shall be incorporated into and shall amend and supplement the covenants and agreements of this Security Instrument as if the rider(s) were a part of this Security Instrument. [Check applicable box(es)]

☐ Adjustable Rate Rider ☐ Condominium Rider ☐ 2–4 Family Rider

☐ Graduated Payment Rider ☐ Planned Unit Development Rider

☐ Other(s) [specify]

BY SIGNING BELOW, Borrower accepts and agrees to the terms and covenants contained in this Security Instrument and in any rider(s) executed by Borrower and recorded with it.

....(Seal)
—Borrower

....(Seal)
—Borrower

[Space Below This Line For Acknowledgment]

ADJUSTABLE RATE RIDER

(Cost of Funds Index—Payment and Rate Caps)

THIS ADJUSTABLE RATE RIDER is made this .... day of ...., 19........., and is incorporated into and shall be deemed to amend and supplement the Mortgage, Deed of Trust or Security Deed (the "Security Instrument") of the same date given by the undersigned (the "Borrower") to secure Borrower's Adjustable Rate Note (the "Note") to .... (the "Lender") of the same date and covering the property described in the Security Instrument and located at:

....

[Property Address]

THE NOTE CONTAINS PROVISIONS ALLOWING FOR CHANGES IN THE INTEREST RATE AND THE MONTHLY PAYMENT. THE BORROWER'S MONTHLY PAYMENT INCREASES MAY BE LIMITED AND THE INTEREST RATE INCREASES ARE LIMITED.

ADDITIONAL COVENANTS. In addition to the covenants and agreements made in the Security Instrument, Borrower and Lender further covenant and agree as follows:

A. INTEREST RATE AND MONTHLY PAYMENT CHANGES

The Note provides for changes in the interest rate and the monthly payments, as follows:

2. INTEREST

(A) Interest Rate

Interest will be charged on unpaid principal until the full amount of principal has been paid. I will pay interest at a yearly rate of ....%. The interest rate I will pay may change.

The interest rate required by this Section 2 is the rate I will pay both before and after any default described in Section 7(B) of this Note.

(B) Interest Change Dates

The interest rate I will pay may change on the first day of ...., 19 .... and on that day every month thereafter. Each date on which my interest rate could change is called an "Interest Change Date." The new rate of interest will become effective on each Interest Change Date.

(C) Interest Rate Limit

My interest rate will never be greater than ....%.

(D) The Index

Beginning with the first Interest Change Date, my interest rate will be based on an Index. The "Index" is the monthly weighted average cost of savings, borrowings and advances of members of the Federal Home Loan Bank of San Francisco (the "Bank"), as made available by the Bank. The most recent Index figure available as of the date 15 days before each Interest Change Date is called the "Current Index."

If the Index is no longer available, the Note Holder will choose a new index which is based upon comparable information. The Note Holder will give me notice of this choice.

(E) Calculation of Interest Rate Changes

Before each Interest Change Date, the Note Holder will calculate my new interest rate by adding .... percentage points (.................%) to the Current Index. The Note Holder will then round the result of this addition to the nearest one-eighth of one percentage point (0.125%). Subject to the limit stated in Section 2(C) above, the rounded amount will be my new interest rate until the next Interest Change Date.

3. PAYMENTS

(A) Time and Place of Payments

I will pay principal and interest by making payments every month.

I will make my monthly payments on the first day of each month beginning on ...., 19 .... I will make these payments every month until I have paid all of the principal and interest and any other charges described below that I may owe under this Note. My monthly payments will be applied to interest before principal. If, on ...., 20 ...., I still owe amounts under this Note, I will pay those amounts in full on that date, which is called the "maturity date."

I will make my monthly payments at .... or at a different place if required by the Note Holder.

(B) Amount of My Initial Monthly Payments

Each of my initial monthly payments will be in the amount of U.S. $ .... This amount may change.

(C) Payment Change Dates

My monthly payment may change as required by Section 3(D) below beginning on the .... day of .... , 19........, and on that day every 12th month thereafter. Each of these dates is called a "Payment Change Date." My monthly payment will also change at any time Section 3(F) or 3(G) below requires me to pay the Full Payment.

I will pay the amount of my new monthly payment each month beginning on each Payment Change Date or as provided in Section 3(F) or 3(G) below.

(D) Calculation of Monthly Payment Changes

At least 30 days before each Payment Change Date, the Note Holder will calculate the amount of the monthly payment that would be sufficient to repay the unpaid principal that I am expected to owe at the Payment Change Date in full on the maturity date in substantially equal installments at the interest rate effective during the month preceding the Payment Change Date. The result of this calculation is called the "Full Payment." The Note Holder will then calculate the amount of my monthly payment due the month preceding the Payment Change Date multiplied by the number 1.075. The result of this calculation is called the "Limited Payment." Unless Section 3(F) or 3(G) below requires me to pay a different amount, I may choose to pay the Limited Payment. **If I choose the Limited Payment as my monthly payment, I must give the Note Holder notice that I am doing so at least 15 days before my first new monthly payment is due.**

(E) Additions to My Unpaid Principal

My monthly payment could be less than the amount of the interest portion of the monthly payment that would be sufficient to repay the unpaid principal I owe at the monthly payment date in full on the maturity date in substantially equal payments. If so, each month that my monthly payment is less than the interest portion, the Note Holder will subtract the amount of my monthly payment from the amount of the interest portion and will add the difference to my unpaid principal. The Note Holder will also add interest on the amount of this difference to my unpaid principal each month. The interest rate on the interest added to principal will be the rate required by Section 2 above.

(F) Limit on My Unpaid Principal; Increased Monthly Payment

My unpaid principal can never exceed a maximum amount equal to one hundred twenty-five percent (125%) of the principal amount I originally borrowed. My unpaid principal could exceed that maximum amount due to the Limited Payments and interest rate increases. If so, on the date that my paying my monthly payment would cause me to exceed that limit, I will instead pay a new monthly payment. The new monthly payment will be in an amount which would be sufficient to repay my then unpaid principal in full on the maturity date at my current interest rate in substantially equal payments.

(G) Required Full Payment

On the 5th Payment Change Date and on each succeeding 5th Payment Change Date thereafter, I will begin paying the Full Payment as my monthly payment until my monthly payment changes again. I will also begin paying the Full Payment as my monthly payment on the final Payment Change Date.

4. NOTICE OF CHANGES

The Note Holder will deliver or mail to me a notice of any changes in the amount of my monthly payment before the effective date of any change. The notice will contain the interest rate or rates applicable to my loan for each month since the prior notice or, for the first notice, since the date of this Note. The notice will also include information required by law to be given me and also the title and telephone number of a person who will answer any question I may have regarding the notice.

B. TRANSFER OF THE PROPERTY OR A BENEFICIAL INTEREST IN BORROWER

Uniform Covenant 17 of the Security Instrument is amended to read as follows:

Transfer of the Property or a Beneficial Interest in Borrower. If all or any part of the Property or any interest in it is sold or transferred (or if a beneficial interest in Borrower is sold or transferred and Borrower is not a natural person) without Lender's prior written consent, Lender may, at its option, require immediate payment in full of all sums secured by this Security Instrument. However, this option shall not be exercised by Lender if exercise is prohibited by federal law as of the date of this Security Instrument. Lender also shall not exercise this option if: (a) Borrower causes to be submitted to Lender information required by Lender to evaluate the intended transferee as if a new loan were being made to the transferee; and (b) Lender reasonably determines that Lender's security will not be impaired by the loan assumption and that the risk of a breach of any covenant or agreement in this Security Instrument is acceptable to Lender.

To the extent permitted by applicable law, Lender may charge a reasonable fee as a condition to Lender's consent to the loan assumption. Lender may also require the transferee to sign an assumption agreement that is acceptable to Lender and that obligates the transferee to keep all the promises and agreements made in the Note and in this Security Instrument. Borrower will continue to be obligated under the Note and this Security Instrument unless Lender releases Borrower in writing.

If Lender exercises the option to require immediate payment in full, Lender shall give Borrower notice of acceleration. The notice shall provide a period of not less than 30 days from the date the notice is delivered or mailed within which Borrower must pay all sums secured by this Security Instrument. If Borrower fails to pay these sums prior to the expiration of this period, Lender may invoke any remedies permitted by this Security Instrument without further notice or demand on Borrower.

BY SIGNING BELOW, Borrower accepts and agrees to the terms and covenants contained in this Adjustable Rate Rider.

.... (Seal)
Borrower

.... (Seal)
Borrower

34087

To Reorder Call
Great Lakes Business Forms, Inc.
Nationally 1-800-253-0208 • In Michigan 1-800-358-8843

OMB No. 2502-0265 (Exp. 12-31-86)

A. U.S. DEPARTMENT OF HOUSING AND URBAN DEVELOPMENT
SETTLEMENT STATEMENT

B. TYPE OF LOAN

1. ☐ FHA 2. ☐ FMHA 3. ☐ CONV. UNINS.
4. ☐ VA 5. ☐ CONV. INS.
6. FILE NUMBER 7. LOAN NUMBER:
8. MORTGAGE INS. CASE NO.

C. NOTE: *This form is furnished to give you a statement of actual settlement costs. Amounts paid to and by the settlement agent are shown. Items marked "(p.o.c.)" were paid outside the closing; they are shown here for informational purposes and are not included in the totals.*

D. NAME OF BORROWER:
ADDRESS OF BORROWER:

E. NAME OF SELLER:
ADDRESS OF SELLER:

F. NAME OF LENDER:
ADDRESS OF LENDER:

G. PROPERTY LOCATION:

H. SETTLEMENT AGENT:
PLACE OF SETTLEMENT:

I. SETTLEMENT DATE:

J. SUMMARY OF BORROWER'S TRANSACTION		K. SUMMARY OF SELLER'S TRANSACTION	
100. GROSS AMOUNT DUE FROM BORROWER:		**400. GROSS AMOUNT DUE TO SELLER:**	
101. Contract sales price		401. Contract sales price	
102. Personal property		402. Personal property	
103. Settlement charges to borrower: *(from line 1400)*		403.	
104.		404.	
105.		405.	
ADJUSTMENTS FOR ITEMS PAID BY SELLER IN ADVANCE:		**ADJUSTMENTS FOR ITEMS PAID BY SELLER IN ADVANCE:**	
106. City/town taxes to		406. City/town taxes to	
107. County taxes to		407. County taxes to	
108. Assessments to		408. Assessments to	
109.		409.	
110.		410.	
111.		411.	
112.		412.	
120. GROSS AMOUNT DUE FROM BORROWER: ▶		**420. GROSS AMOUNT DUE TO SELLER:** ▶	
200. AMOUNTS PAID BY OR IN BEHALF OF BORROWER:		**500. REDUCTIONS IN AMOUNT DUE TO SELLER:**	
201. Deposit or earnest money		501. Excess deposit *(see instructions)*	
202. Principal amount of new loan(s)		502. Settlement charges to seller *(line 1400)*	
203. Existing loan(s) taken subject to		503. Existing loan(s) taken subject to	
204.		504. Payoff of first mortgage loan	
205.		505. Payoff of second mortgage loan	
206.		506.	
207.		507.	
208.		508.	
209.		509.	
ADJUSTMENTS FOR ITEMS UNPAID BY SELLER:		**ADJUSTMENTS FOR ITEMS UNPAID BY SELLER:**	
210. City/town taxes to		510. City/town taxes to	
211. County taxes to		511. County taxes to	
212. Assessments to		512. Assessments to	
213.		513.	
214.		514.	
215.		515.	
216.		516.	
217.		517.	
218.		518.	
219.		519.	
220. TOTAL PAID BY/FOR BORROWER: ▶		**520. TOTAL REDUCTIONS IN AMOUNT DUE SELLER:** ▶	
300. CASH AT SETTLEMENT FROM/TO BORROWER		**600. CASH AT SETTLEMENT TO/FROM SELLER**	
301. Gross amount due from borrower *(line 120)*		601. Gross amount due to seller *(line 420)*	
302. Less amount paid by/for borrower *(line 220)*	( )	602. Less total reductions in amount due seller *(line 520)*	( )
303. CASH (☐ *FROM*) (☐ *TO*) **BORROWER:** ▶		**603. CASH** (☐ *TO*) (☐ *FROM*) **SELLER:** ▶	

Previous Edition Is Obsolete
Form No. 1581
3/86

SB 4 3538 000 1
HUD-1 (3-86)
RESPA HB 4305.2

[illegible] Great Lakes Business Forms, Inc.
Nationally 1-800-253-0208 Michigan 1-800-358-8843

LENDER'S COPY

L. SETTLEMENT CHARGES

	PAID FROM BORROWER'S FUNDS AT SETTLEMENT	PAID FROM SELLER'S FUNDS AT SETTLEMENT
700. TOTAL SALES BROKER'S COMMISSION: BASED ON PRICE $ @ %		
DIVISION OF COMMISSION (LINE 700) AS FOLLOWS:		
701. $ to		
702. $ to		
703. Commission paid at settlement		
704.		
800. ITEMS PAYABLE IN CONNECTION WITH LOAN:		
801. Loan Origination fee %		
802. Loan Discount %		
803. Appraisal Fee to:		
804. Credit Report to:		
805. Lender's Inspection fee		
806. Mortgage Insurance application fee to		
807. Assumption fee		
808.		
809.		
810.		
811.		
900. ITEMS REQUIRED BY LENDER TO BE PAID IN ADVANCE:		
901. Interest from to @ $ /day		
902. Mortgage insurance premium for mo. to		
903. Hazard insurance premium for yrs. to		
904. *Flood Insurance Premium for* yrs. to		
905.		
1000. RESERVES DEPOSITED WITH LENDER:		
1001. Hazard insurance months @ $ per month		[redacted]
1002. Mortgage insurance months @ $ per month		
1003. City property taxes months @ $ per month		
1004. County property taxes months @ $ per month		
1005. Annual assessments months @ $ per month		
1006. *Flood Insurance* months @ $ per month		
1007. months @ $ per month		
1008. months @ $ per month		
1100. TITLE CHARGES:		
1101. Settlement or closing fee to		
1102. Abstract or title search to		
1103. Title examination to		
1104. Title insurance binder to		
1105. Document preparation to		
1106. Notary fees to		
1107. Attorney's fees to		
(includes above items Numbers:)	[redacted]	[redacted]
1108. Title insurance to		
(includes above items Numbers:)	[redacted]	[redacted]
1109. Lender's coverage $	[redacted]	[redacted]
1110. Owner's coverage $	[redacted]	[redacted]
1111.		
1112.		
1113.		
1200. GOVERNMENT RECORDING AND TRANSFER CHARGES:		
1201. Recording fees: Deed $; Mortgage $; Releases $		
1202. City/county tax/stamps: Deed $; Mortgage $		
1203. State tax/stamps: Deed $; Mortgage $		
1204.		
1205.		
1300. ADDITIONAL SETTLEMENT CHARGES:		
1301. Survey to		
1302. Pest inspection to		
1303.		
1304.		
1305.		
1306.		
1307.		
1400. TOTAL SETTLEMENT CHARGES *(Enter on line 103, Section J – and – line 502, Section K)* ▶		

I have carefully reviewed the HUD-1 Settlement Statement and to the best of my knowledge and belief, it is a true and accurate statement of all receipts and disbursements made on my account or by me in this transaction. I further certify that I have recieved a copy of HUD-1 Settlement Statement.

Borrowers ______________________ Sellers ______________________

The HUD-1 Settlement Statement which I have prepared is a true and accurate account of this transaction. I have caused or will cause the funds to be disbursed in accordance with this statement.

Settlement Agent ______________________ Date ______________

WARNING: It is a crime to knowingly make false statements to the United States on this or any other similar form. Penalties upon conviction can include a fine or imprisonment. For details see Title 18 U.S. Code Section 1001 and Section 1010.

Mortgage Credit Analysis Worksheet

U.S. Department of Housing and Urban Development
Office of Housing
Federal Housing Commissioner

Case Number

1. Name a. Borrower	2. Social Security Number a.	3. Age ▲ a.	4. Dependents a. Age	b. No.
b. Co-Borrower	b.	b.		

5. Mortgage Without MIP ▲	6. Total MIP▲	7. Mortgage With MIP ▲
$	$	$

8. Current Housing Expense ▲	9. Term of Loan	10. Interest Rate	11. First Time Home Buyer ▲	12. Adj. Buy Down Interest Rate
$		%	☐ Yes ☐ No	%

13. Settlement Requirements

- a. Existing Debt (Refinance) ▲ $ ______
- b. Contract Price $ ______
  C.C. Pd. by Seller (Subtract) $ ______ ▲ $ ______
- c. Repairs and Improvements $ ______
- d. Closing Costs (Inc.C.C. Pd. by Seller, Disc. if Ref.) ▲ $ ______
- e. Total Acquisition Cost ▲ $ ______
- f. Mortgage (Without MIP) $ ______
- g. Required Investment $ ______
- h. Discounts ▲ $ ______
- i. Prepayable Expenses ▲ $ ______
- j. MIP-Paid in Cash ▲ $ ______
- k. Non-Realty and Other Items $ ______
- l. Total Requirements ▲ $ ______
- m. Paid ☐ Cash ☐ Other (Explain) $ ______
- n. To Be Paid ☐ Cash ☐ Other ▲ $ ______
- o. Assets Available ▲ $ ______
- p. 2nd Mortgage Proceeds (If Applicable) $ ______

14. Monthly Effective Income

- a. Borrower's Base Pay ▲ $ ______
- b. Other Earnings (Explain) $ ______
- c. Co-Borrower's Base Pay ▲ $ ______
- d. Other Earnings (Explain) $ ______
- e. Income, Real Estate (Net) $ ______
- f. Total Monthly Income (Gross) ▲ $ ______
- g. Less Federal Tax $ ______
- h. Net Effective Income ▲ $ ______

16. Debts and Obligations

	Mo. Pmt.	Unpd. Bal.
a. State and Local Tax	$ ______	
b. Social Security/Ret.	$ ______	
c. Total Installment Debt	$ ______	$ ______
d. Child Support, Etc.	$ ______	
e. Other	$ ______	$ ______
f. Total Monthly Pmts.	$ ______	

15. Future Monthly Payments

- a. Principal and Interest - 1st $ ______
- b. ☐ MIP ☐ Ground Rent $ ______
- c. Principal and Interest - 2nd $ ______
- d. Total Debt Service ▲ $ ______
- e. Hazard Insurance $ ______
- f. Taxes, Special Assessments ▲ $ ______
- g. Total Mortgage Payment ▲ $ ______
- h. Maintenance and Common Expenses $ ______
- i. Heat and Utilities $ ______
- j. Total Housing Expense ▲ $ ______
- k. Other Monthly Payments (From 16f) $ ______
- l. Total Fixed Payment ▲ $ ______

17. Borrower Rating

- a. Credit Characteristics ______
- b. Adequacy of Effective Income ______
- c. Stability of Effective Income ______
- d. Adequacy of Available Assets ______

18. Ratios, Etc.

- a. Loan/Value (Exclude MIP) ▲ ______ %
- b. Net Effective Income
  1. Total Housing Expense ▲ ______ %
  2. Total Fixed Payment ▲ ______ %
- c. Residual Income ______

19. Remarks

20. Final Application Decision ☐ Approve ☐ Reject	21. Signature of Examiner	22. Date
23. Signature of Reviewer		24. Date

Retain Original in Case Binder, Forward Copy to Housing Information and Statistics Division with HUD-92900-7
Previous Editions Obsolete

HUD-92900-WS (1-88)
HB-4155.1

About The Author

Arefaine G-Yohannes is Associate Professor of Finance at the University of Michigan, Dearborn. He holds a Ph.D. in Economics from Northwestern University and has published a number of books and many articles for various professional journals. He currently is Managing Director of Columbia Financial Services, a consulting firm specializing in providing financial advisory services to the real estate industry.